Values That Pay

Values That Pay

*Complicity, Sincerity, and Hip Hop
in Contemporary Moroccan Life*

———

Kendra Salois

UNIVERSITY OF CALIFORNIA PRESS

University of California Press
Oakland, California

Suggested citation: Salois, K. *Values That Pay: Complicity, Sincerity, and Hip Hop in Contemporary Moroccan Life*. Oakland: University of California Press, 2025. DOI: https://doi.org/10.1525/luminos.230

Library of Congress Cataloging-in-Publication Data

Names: Salois, Kendra, author.
Title: Values that pay: complicity, sincerity, and hip hop in contemporary
   Moroccan life / Kendra Salois.
Other titles: California series in hip hop studies; 5.
Description: Oakland: University of California Press, [2025] |
   Series: Hip Hop Studies; 5 | Includes bibliographical references
   and index.
Identifiers: LCCN 2024041083 (print) | LCCN 2024041084 (ebook) |
   ISBN 9780520379763 (paperback) | ISBN 9780520976917 (ebook)
Subjects: LCSH: Rap (Music)—Morocco—History and criticism. |
   Rap (Music)—Social aspects—Morocco. | Hip-hop—Morocco. |
   Neoliberalism—Morocco. | Morocco—Social life and customs.
Classification: LCC ML3531 .S24 2025 (print) | LCC ML3531 (ebook) |
   DDC 782.4216490964—dc23/eng/20241008

LC record available at https://lccn.loc.gov/2024041083
LC ebook record available at https://lccn.loc.gov/2024041084

GPSR Authorized Representative: Easy Access System Europe,
Mustamäe tee 50, 10621 Tallinn, Estonia, gpsr.requests@easproject.com

34   33   32   31   30   29   28   27   26   25
10   9   8   7   6   5   4   3   2   1

CONTENTS

ILLUSTRATIONS

NOTE ON TRANSLITERATION AND TRANSLATION

This text follows the *International Journal of Middle East Studies* (IJMES) system of transliteration in most cases. Exceptions include proper nouns (such as place names) that are already well known in a different spelling. I retain individuals' preferred spellings of their names. When I quote from individuals' written texts, I retain their preferred transliterations as well as other grammatical and orthographic choices. In some cases, I have re-transliterated lyrics whose romanization I cannot verify as original (e.g., lyrics from Genius.com, which are typically uploaded anonymously).

All translations from French and Moroccan Arabic in this text are mine unless otherwise noted. Many people generously checked and corrected my translations over the course of preparing this manuscript, and they have my fervent gratitude and best wishes. Any remaining mistakes and misinterpretations are my own.

ACKNOWLEDGMENTS

In a perfect world, this book would not bear the name of a single author but of an enormous network stretching across time and space. Honoring the people I can fit in these acknowledgments is the greatest pleasure this manuscript has afforded.

First, my deepest thanks continue to go to all of the artists and participants whose time and energy made this book possible. While the voices of DJ Casa-Flayva, Fouzia Chemaoui, Dr. Mourad el-Fahli, DJ Gee-Bayss, H-Name, Younes Lazrak, Mol Mic, DJ Nina, Nores, Talos Ostad, DJ Redshirt, DJ Sekhfa, and others do not appear in the text, I am grateful for their insights and their generous, often hilarious, conversation. Special thanks, as well, to artists who also took the time to correct my translations or discuss my interpretations over the years, including but not limited to Don Bigg, Would Chaab, Masta Flow, Soultana, and Amine Snoop aka al-Kayssar. Any mistakes in this text are mine. I am delighted to thank Yassine "Yoriyas" Alaoui Ismaili and Morocco's finalist in the 2024 women's Olympic breaking competition, b-girl Fatima Zahra Elmamouny, for the phenomenal cover photo.

Many professional and natural teachers were vital to my research. These included DJ Sim-H and DJ Key, who exhibited patience during my lessons at Funky Noise School; my Moroccan academic mentors, including Dr. Taieb Belghazi and Dr. Said Graiouid; my teachers and administrators at the Center for Cross-Cultural Learning, Qalam wa Lawh, and the Arabic Language Institute in Fes, each of whom modeled rigor and good humor; and my darbukka instructor at Subul As-Salam Center. Though I conversed with them for only moments, the wisdom of elders such as 'Omar Es-Sayed and Ahmed Aydoun was apparent in person and foundational in scholarship.

It is both humbling and joyful to think back on the many forms of support I've received before and during the development of this book. My work has been indelibly shaped by my academic advisors Jocelyne Guilbault, Benjamin Brinner, Charles Hirschkind, Gabriel Solis, and Bonnie Wade. Informal advising and feedback from many other inspiring scholars, including Hisham Aidi, H. Samy Alim, Aomar Boum, Dominique Caubet, Alessandra Ciucci, Tim Fuson, Jane Goodman, Emily Benichou Gottreich, Adam Haupt, Heike Raphael-Hernandez, Deborah Kapchan, Catherine Miller, James Miller, Karin van Nieuwkerk, T. Carlis Roberts, Griff Rollefson, Zakia Salime, and Martin Stokes, have been enormously influential on my scholarship. I have benefited profoundly from the work and the welcome of scholars in too many conferences, symposia, and workshops to name. I acknowledge and thank the scholars who proposed and organized these, as well as the grantmaking agencies who funded them and, often, provided transportation support for graduate students.

The brilliant colleagues who read drafts and/or wrestled with ideas in this work—sometimes over years—including Cristina Moreno Almeida, Catherine Appert, Vanessa Paloma Elbaz, Alma Heckman, Miki Kaneda, Nina Ter Laan, Larisa Mann, Melanie Magidow, Meredith Schweig, Shayna Silverstein, Aleysia Whitmore, and Chris Witulski, are a dream team of support and insight. My present and former colleagues at UC Berkeley, University of Maryland College Park, and American University listened (oh-so-patiently) to the many stages of this project's development. The kind, constructive feedback offered by the scholars who reviewed this manuscript made a huge difference to the final version.

Between 2008–18, my research was supported by UC Berkeley, the Foreign Languages Area Studies program, the Fulbright US Student Program, the West African Research Association, the American Institute for Maghrebi Studies, and American University. Dissertation fieldwork was made more manageable by the staff at the Moroccan-American Center for Education and Cultural Exchange. Several employees of the US embassies and consulate in Morocco and Senegal agreed to interviews over the years, and I appreciate their time and perspectives. During language study and fieldwork in Morocco, friends and colleagues including but not limited to Sam Anderson, Nicola Dach, Abdelkader Fares, Aisha Fukushima, Kim Junmookda, Moulay Driss al-Maarouf, Caitlyn Olson, Yuval Orr, Rod Solaimani, Matt Streib, and Catherine Thompson were there for travel, coffee, and more.

At UC Press, my unflappable editors LeKeisha Hughes and Raina Polivka, editorial assistants Nora Becker and Sam Warren, senior production editor Stephanie Summerhays, copyeditor Leah Caldwell, and the art direction and production staff are tireless professionals who navigated the upheavals of COVID-era publishing with aplomb. The George Gund Foundation Imprint made possible open-access publication, and the FirstGen Program for first-generation scholars offered behind-the-scenes information, a supportive cohort, and an unrestricted grant for use in preparing the manuscript for publication. I am profoundly grateful for comments from the Hip Hop Studies series' editorial board as well as the breadth of UC Press's support.

While I conceptualized and drafted this manuscript, the planet suffered a pandemic of still-unknown proportions, governments contended with or oversaw growing authoritarianism and unimaginable destruction, and I gave birth to two astonishing daughters. I remain convinced that ethnography, the immense privilege of receiving others' gifts of time and energy, can lead us to the best versions of ourselves. Gratitude and love beyond words goes to my family; my parents; my husband, Mike; and our children, Vivian and Jayna. I hope I bring the best version of myself to you, every day.

Introduction

The Wave

In 2010, Morocco's biggest state-sponsored musical event gave hip hop artists a central place in its programming. During the weeklong Mawazine festival, pioneering Casablanca emcee Don Bigg performed tracks from his most recent album, *Byad Ou K7al* (White and Black), in new arrangements written and performed with Cuban jazz pianist Omar Sosa and his band.[1] Facing several hundred screaming fans on a massive outdoor stage, Bigg not only performed international connection and debuted a hip hop performance practice innovative among his fellow Moroccans. As one of Morocco's best-known and most controversial solo emcees, he also represented the nation in a collaboration designed to express the festival's advertised commitment to cosmopolitan tolerance.

The same week that Bigg and Sosa's prime-time concert was broadcast live by state-owned television and radio station 2M, the Mawazine festival held a youth showcase called L'Mouja (*al-mouja*, "the wave"). The first edition of L'Mouja celebrated the state's embrace of youth musical cultures on all the platforms at the government's disposal. "18 groups in 12 hours," said the billboards at major intersections in Rabat, the capital city. "Under the high patronage of His Majesty Mohamed VI, see groups from *la nouvelle scène*," announced a cheery woman in bilingual ads played on 2M. "Don't miss this call," winked the banners advertising the national phone company's sponsorship of L'Mouja. Blazing with Maroc Telecom's bright logo, the banners hung in front of Parliament and protectorate-era landmarks along Avenue Mohammed V, and from the thick crenellated wall of Bab al-Ḥad, the southern entrance to Rabat's seventeenth-century medina.

L'Mouja was a finale to the weeklong, multistage festival, but separate from it, too. To get there, one had to cross the Bouregreg River to the neighboring town of Salé, then walk down to the edge of the beach where the Bouregreg meets the Atlantic. Starting at 2 p.m., ten hip hop groups dominated the roster, interspersed with a handful of musicians from other genres. Whether the performer was an old-school emcee known only to the most devoted hip hop fans, or a fresh new trio getting lots of attention on Facebook, everyone got twenty minutes. Nearly all of the performers had won a nationwide musical contest in the past three years.

By late afternoon, the sun still high over the ocean, perhaps two hundred teenagers and young adults were scattered within earshot of the stage's massive speakers. Between sets, I recognized a circle of young men standing a few yards away. Eventually, we realized how we knew each other: they had worked on a video shoot I had attended months before, several hours away in Fes.

The three friends, born and raised in Salé, visibly enjoyed testing my knowledge of their city's contribution to Moroccan hip hop history. Did I know that the first Moroccan hip hop album was made here in Salé? Yes, I did—by a duo named Double A. They were the first group to record raps in Derija (Moroccan Arabic). I interviewed an emcee from the early Salé group 19-Contre-Attack who told me a lot about local hip hop history, I added. My comment was greeted with a roar of surprise and approval as the students assured me of their pride in that group, especially its best-regarded emcee, Majesticon. "He is still my favorite rapper," said Mehdi, unbuttoning his flannel shirt to show off his handmade critique of contemporary hip hop: in iron-on letters, his T-shirt read "Where are you and where is rap? Where is respect for Majisticon?" The beginning of the next set cut off our conversation, but not before the three playfully showed off their amateur raps in front of a gathering cypher of friends and strangers.

Looking back, this festival and others like it throughout the summer of 2010 represent a peak of visible state involvement in hip hop culture. On one hand, major concerts like Don Bigg's collaboration with Omar Sosa leveraged the country's best-known hip hop toward the state's public relations goals, successfully provoking statements on Morocco's cultural wealth and modernity in international media. Young Moroccans, tourists, and journalists were simultaneously targeted by the festival's explicit messages of racial and religious tolerance. At the same time, practitioners took advantage of Mawazine's multiple smaller performance spaces to continue to cultivate the culture. On Salé's beach at the edge of Rabat, where few international journalists ventured, young people met, honed their skills, and celebrated local histories through hip hop.

Many of today's most fervent fans have never heard of Majesticon. Without archives of the tapes and burned CDs on which early hip hop circulated, they couldn't hear him if they wanted to. But long before the state decided to embrace "the wave" that had washed over Morocco's Atlantic coast, pioneers like Majesticon sought—and built—a genre that could sound out the future, a music as expansive and poignant as their critiques.

Over the first two decades of Moroccan hip hop history, roughly from 1990 to 2011, hip hop music and dance moved from makeshift rehearsal spaces, bedroom

FIGURE 1. Mehdi Lyoubi, aka Mehdi Black Wind, shows the author his T-shirt, 2010. Photo by author.

studios, and empty youth centers to ad campaigns, royal commendations, and the nation's biggest festivals. When Moroccan hip hop practitioners first gained national attention in the early 2000s, unsympathetic commentators had used the term "wave" differently: something that had rolled in from outside and would soon recede from the nation's shores. As late as 2007, London-based daily *Asharq al-Awsat* found that a professional musician judging a Moroccan musical competition thought of hip hop as a foreign fad. "What are the opinions of musicians on this new musical wave?" asked the Rabat correspondent in an article sensationally headlined "'Revolutionary' Songs and Their Effects on the Youth: Sports Jerseys, Baggy Jeans, Chains and Earrings." Belaid al-ʿAkkaf, a decorated Amazigh composer best known to the public from his 1970s fusion band Ousmane, noted that "this kind of song is heard a lot . . . in Black neighborhoods in the US and on the edges of French cities, where . . . it has a great effect on social and political life, and its authors are [politically] aware." By contrast, al-ʿAkkaf felt "songs by Moroccan rap groups are empty, full of insults and pessimism." However, he stressed that the answer to this aesthetic and cultural problem did not lay with the youths themselves, but with the ministry of culture, which had failed up to that point to "direct the youth through specialized cultural centers" in order to advance "the country's artistic sector" (al-ʿArousi 2007).

Al-ʿAkkaf's response was not simply that of a curmudgeonly classical musician. He voiced widespread assumptions about hip hop that are still commonplace, and still contested, in Morocco today. First, he assumed that "rap music" is a style, rather than one facet of a generationally significant and thoroughly indigenized multimedia culture encompassing emceeing, beatmaking and production, graffiti and visual art, dance, photography, and fashion. Instead of defining that style through its aesthetic characteristics, he defined it as a tool for making social and political change. He also expressed an ingrained Moroccan exceptionalism, implying that while engaged artists in France and the United States may have legitimate grievances, Moroccan youths are merely enjoying the opportunity to flout authority. Finally, al-ʿAkkaf expected the Moroccan state to respond to the changing needs of youths—not to support their interests, but to reach its own goals for shaping the citizenry. Mawazine's L'Mouja, which ran from 2010 to 2012, met all of al-ʿAkkaf's goals: the event promoted the state's competitions by showcasing the winners—offering artists fleeting exposure to international journalists and fans—and allowed the state to claim it was building the infrastructure for a robust popular music market.[2]

This book argues that the wave has, in fact, saturated the center: hip hop artists were at the leading edge of Morocco's neoliberal transition, and today—despite their continuing struggles to be better heard—are vital to the neoliberalized nation-state. Moroccan neoliberalization included embracing the top-down economic policies imposed on many developing nations during the 1980s and '90s. But the effects of these policies, and the rhetorics that accompanied them, also encouraged young Moroccans to think of themselves as a different kind of person than their parents. Through their investments in hip hop culture, practitioners imagine, rehearse, and embody new forms of citizenship during a new political-economic conjuncture for the nation.[3] At the same time, the varied ways practitioners have institutionalized their musical culture align with, if not support, many goals of the state.

For many state and state-sponsored agencies, hip hop has been a useful tool. For its practitioners, it is a way of life, with daily implications for ethics, aesthetics, and relationships, as well as politics. For over thirty years, the first generation of Moroccan hip hop artists has advanced a theory of citizenship that posits that Moroccans do have the power to change things about their country—specific things, in specific ways. For over twenty years, their success on state-sponsored stages has helped neutralize the radical potential of that theory. Like a wave, Moroccan hip hop cannot be separated from the broader circulatory context of the transnational hip hop tradition, yet its emergence at the end of the 1980s rearranged the world it engulfed in particular ways.

VALUES THAT PAY

Part of the story of this genre—and of this book in turn—is the history of practitioners' struggles to benefit from state instrumentalization rather than to be controlled by it. North Africanists frequently analyze Moroccan life in terms of the state's authoritarianism, a tendency heightened by the need to grapple with unfinished reforms prompted by the February 20 movement in 2011–12, during the so-called Arab Spring.[4] Yet musicians' struggles over aesthetics and ideals are not solely a repudiation or embrace of the state's vision of its subjects. Like anywhere else, practitioners also debate musical beauty, poetic virtuosity, proper conduct, and many other issues well beyond their resonances at the national level. At the same time, the control and legitimacy accorded the Moroccan monarchy, the four-hundred-year-old ʿAlaoui dynasty, and the powerful circle known as the Makhzen does affect every horizon of possibility.[5] Throughout this book, I demonstrate that individuals' experiences of state power are diverse and fragmented, differentiated by many factors including their class position, religion, ethnic background, education, gender, and sexuality. Yet across these different experiences, the state can and does shape not only what musicians can compose, where they can play it, whether they are compensated, and how their music is heard, but what they desire to create. Nor is this state of affairs incompatible with practitioners' own experiences as market actors: today's state is deeply invested in producing a transnational market for Moroccan popular musics that reaches north across the Mediterranean and south into West and Central Africa.

How, then, to write about the political, economic, and symbolic control exercised by the monarchy and the state without writing as if, as Barry Shank puts it, "the music has simply served as a vehicle, conveying already shared political sentiments back and forth among singers and listeners" (2014: 2)? How to keep not only aesthetic but also political and ethical ambiguity in play in this text as it is in everyday life?[6] I have responded to these questions by focusing on the multiple registers of "value." The title of this book comes from a 2007 interview given by Don Bigg to Magharebia.com, a trilingual news outlet sponsored by the US Department of State from 2004 to 2015. Don Bigg answered a question about his success by asserting that "authenticity and sincerity are values that pay."[7]

"Value" simultaneously designates those attributes of anything worth exchanging and personal beliefs that may be recognized in others, but cannot be traded. Yet for the neoliberal subject disadvantaged in the global market economy, both kinds of value collapse into each other precisely because one is forced to imagine oneself—including one's beliefs and intentions—as a collection of attributes in order to extract value from them (Foucault 2008; Muehlebach 2012; Rudnyckyj 2010).[8] Some of hip hop's most trenchant critiques, in the United States and elsewhere, start from the recognition of this reality, while simultaneously celebrating what Wendy Brown characterizes as a "sacrificial" relation to capital (2015: 210–12; Rose 1994). Across very different places, relations within communities and to oneself are profoundly reshaped by the feedback loop of increasing precarity and individuals' self-cultivation as both market actors and marketable assets.

Values That Pay makes visible two threads of what Loïc Wacquant calls "actually existing neoliberalism" (2012). One focuses on technologies of governance that reinforce state power even as they shift expectations and material support from public to private. The other locates subjects' understandings of themselves within the emergent marketization, or "economization," of formerly nonmarket domains of life (Brown 2016; Ganti 2014; Hilgers 2011). My interlocutors create unexpected meanings at the intersection of these threads. Following Marc D. Perry (2016), Eithne Quinn (2005), Lester Spence (2011), and others, I track hip hop as both an expression of neoliberalization as well as a tool for intervening in it. Framing Moroccan hip hop in this way intervenes in a third dimension of neoliberalism research, one in which ordinary people are not only subject to neoliberal discourses and rationalities but agents of their local spread, expression, and acceptance (Elyachar 2005).

Morocco's history offers a distinctive vantage point on economic and cultural neoliberalization. Wacquant insists that *"what is 'neo' about neoliberalism . . . [is] the remaking and redeployment of the state . . . [to fabricate]* the subjectivities, social relations and collective representations suited to making the fiction of markets real and consequential" (2012: 68, italics in original). However, the Moroccan monarchy and Makhzen's control over and profit from both publicly and privately owned corporations and agencies is only the most modern instantiation of the dynasty's historic imbrication of state and economy. Like his father King Hassan II, King Mohamed VI embodies a continuity between precapitalist and neoliberal forms in which different sources of power are united in a single individual. The contemporary state's efforts to make markets "real and consequential" rely on the monarchy's traditional strategies of patronage, distribution, and coercion.[9] In the following chapters, I show that while neoliberalization's economic benefits were largely captured by existing elites (Catusse 2009; Zemni and Bogaert 2011), the cultural neoliberalization that accompanied this transition found visible and audible leadership in hip hop artists.

Morocco received its first loans from the International Monetary Fund in the first years of the 1980s (Cohen and Jaidi 2006). As in other postcolonial states at that time, the IMF required a number of macroeconomic reforms in exchange for funding. These included opening capital and consumer markets, increasing foreign direct investment, privatizing state-owned industries, deregulating industries, lowering taxes on enterprise, shedding public-sector jobs, and cutting domestic subsidies (Maghraoui 2001 and 2002; Pfeifer 1999). While the political rationalities (Brown 2003) that undergirded neoliberalization in Europe and the Americas during the 1980s and '90s grafted conservative ideologies onto an economic model, arguing that shifting states' provisions for its citizens onto markets was freeing, North African economic neoliberalization has helped maintain or even enhance the powers of the regions' authoritarian governments (Cavatorta 2007; Kabel 2021; Kohstall 2015).

Moroccan neoliberalization is less a transformation of political and economic power than a shift in elite economic tactics whose effects reverberate throughout society. At the same time, continuing social, moral, and ethical regimes are deeply integrated into Morocco's newly created or formalized markets (Kapchan 1996). Though the state has carried out sweeping economic reforms that reduced its roles in health, education, employment, and other domains since the 1980s, this has not lessened the government's power nor citizens' perception of its power.

Government-supported rhetoric about who was a valued Moroccan, and whose visibility and audibility was boosted by state efforts, changed starting in the late 1990s. While the ascension of King Mohamed VI in 1999 raised expectations of increased cultural and press freedoms, the new monarch also called repeatedly for his subjects to embrace their roles in market reform. Young artists observed and responded to socioeconomic change throughout the 1990s and 2000s, modeling the ways a neoliberal citizen might simultaneously challenge the harms of new policies and come to see their interpersonal, cultural, and social capital in economic terms. Throughout the first decades of the twenty-first century, as the faces, images, and sounds of hip hop began to be incorporated into state-sponsored and private advertising, the cultural edge of Morocco's socioeconomic upheaval came to index young, leisured consumers as the ideal citizen who would carry the country into the future.

Well before select artists gained national recognition in the early 2000s, amateur hip hop artists and their fans developed ways of interacting with each other and state institutions that responded to new state-market forms. On the one hand, practitioners followed an ideology circulated both through international neoliberal norms and mainstream US hip hop's representations of a neoliberal self—locating the solutions to social problems in individual choices, celebrating wealth, and investing in themselves to produce social and cultural capital. At the same time, artists and listeners also used hip hop's tradition of synthetic argumentation to insist on a holistic conception of citizenship, in which social, economic, and political rights are seen as inseparable from one another, to critique and make claims on the state.

For hip hop practitioners with whom I worked, being a citizen ideally means sharing the wealth created by the nation-state's global market participation and the eventual telos that participation implies—accession to the "developed" world. Throughout this book, I show how my interlocutors understood market participation, whether as consumers, advertisers, or creators, as an act of identification with the nation. In this way, citizenship becomes associated with economic progress as much as, if not more than, with ideas about national identity or fealty to the state and its rulers. Paradoxically, this has occurred over the same time and in relationship to the ways that the state has ceased to take responsibility for economic security. In subsequent chapters, I break out how hip hop practitioners responded to, and in some cases anticipated, the reduction and transformation of public and social institutions to private capital by building the market-oriented institutions encouraged by both King Mohamed VI and neoliberal guardians like the World Bank (Chauffour 2018: vi–xv). Practitioners' vision of citizenship is then, willingly or unwillingly, participating in the state's unavoidable need to bet on the nation's future in the global market economy.

In creating thriving local expressions of transnational hip hop culture, first-generation practitioners taught each other and the next generation their own citizenship praxis, seeking to influence their political and economic futures simultaneously.[10] In this way, practitioners fill what Anita Chari calls "a debilitating lacuna" in the study of neoliberal societies: "the inability to grasp the relationship between a sensate micropolitics of subjectivation and a critique of political economy" (2020: 2). Precisely because hip hop practitioners pursued their vision of a more engaged, more empowered citizenry within the norms of neoliberal entrepreneurship, they found themselves no longer considered "surplus" but valuable to the state (Gilmore 1998; Wacquant 2008: 266).

Yet, as micropolitical moments emerge in performance through each chapter of this book, I show that focusing solely on the state's strategies of incorporation obscures practitioners' investments in their own visions of citizenship.[11] These investments include participating in historic forms of patronage but do not preclude artists' and audiences' agency to align with some authority figures or issues and not others. Starting from the premise that artists genuinely believe in what they imagine the state can be, I show how some actively sought to integrate both the potential conflicts and alignments of hip hop culture's aesthetics and ethics with their devotion to their preferred Moroccan future.

I conceptualize hip hop artists' and fans' citizenship practices, whether in one-on-one interactions or shouted from a massive stage, as expressive of necessities in tension with each other. These tensions serve as themes that weave throughout the book. First, the institutionalization of Moroccan hip hop embodies the productive frictions between historicism and innovation in hip hop's genre conventions and between the collective and the individual in its values (Tsing 2005). Here, institutionalization includes not only the ways that hip hop practitioners and practices emerge within state-sponsored agencies, but what practitioners have built among themselves. Second, my interlocutors' citizenship practices require, and produce, tensions between complicity and sincerity, competition and solidarity. I argue that these practices and values encompass individuals' desire for both mobility and secure community and thus hinge on a productive ambiguity. And most importantly, each of these tensions is simultaneously central to transnational hip hop aesthetics and to everyday life under neoliberalism.

REDEFINING COMPLICITY

What does obligation mean to a neoliberal citizen? What might new ties and senses of obligation sound like?

Concerns about ethnographers' complicity, developed among feminist anthropologists and subsequently incorporated into the reflexive turn of the 1990s, are vital to contemporary anthropology and ethnomusicology (Abu-Lughod 1990; Behar and Gordon 1995; Marcus 1997; Visweswaran 1997).[12] Less often do we address the ways our research subjects are simultaneously agents and victims of structural harm. Despite the fact that many of my interlocutors broadly agreed with the state's goals for its citizens, no term evokes the queasy mix of celebration and containment, tactics and traps, carrots and sticks they negotiated under Morocco's authoritarian neoliberalism better than complicity.

Since the 1990s, when music scholars began to grapple with the production and circulation of "world music" as a manifestation of neocolonial economic structures (e.g., Feld 2000; Frith 2000; Guilbault 1993; Taylor 1997), scholars have continued to focus on the ways relatively disenfranchised musicians attempt to gain advantage from international circulation despite—or through—processes of exoticization vital to that circulation (e.g., Kapchan 2007; Kheshti 2015; Meintjes 2004 and 2017; Whitmore 2013 and 2016). On these and other topics, we strive to depict our research subjects as critical actors who weigh many considerations as they select tactics from a circumscribed set of options. We pay close attention to factors that impinge upon those options, and we describe a wide variety of responses to inequity beyond traditional political mobilization or overt protest. We generally avoid judging approaches to working within inequity as successes or failures, even if they have no or negative effects.[13] We value what we can learn from others as they navigate overlapping, locally specific discourses on politics, ethics, and aesthetics, and we seek to understand their reasoning rather than assuming the universality of our own.

I suggest that in acknowledging the diverse orientations, politics, and unintended consequences of our interlocutors' agency, we acknowledge power relations that are best understood through a renewed definition of complicity. Used in its everyday sense, complicity is an accusation or judgment on a person or group of individual actors. Discussions of complicity in literature, legal studies, and philosophy focus, typically, on how to assess individual culpability in singular acts as a witting or unwitting bystander, beneficiary, or supporter (Zola 1996 [1898]; Sanders 2002; Ziemer 2017; Mellema 2016).[14] Complicity frequently connotes an action or lack of action that reveals misplaced loyalties, a breach of obligations to one group in favor of benefits from another.

Such formulations imply that whether we are doing or not doing something, saying or not saying something, complicit individuals are those who have the power to align themselves with greater powers. Traditional accusations of complicity hold people higher in intersecting hierarchies responsible for having more freedom—more choices, more agency, greater ability to impact unequal structures. On the other hand, Thomas Docherty argues that "complicity" should instead imply unfreedom: "If a bond is entered into by someone who is so constrained by circumstance that *the bond itself is simply an articulation of power*, then cooperation has become complicity" (2016: 69, italics mine). In this perspective, economic and social elites can benefit from unequal advantages and access and still be unable to successfully challenge the source of their power. This framing resonates with the Moroccan monarchy's historic strategies of elite capture, as well as with recent reform efforts by relatively affluent actors (Schroeter 1998; Bennani-Chraïbi 2011; Heckman 2021).

At the same time, considering those with less capital, power, or freedom complicit with a dominant regime recognizes both their entrapment and their survival tactics. It simultaneously accepts the reach of disciplinary forms of power and the agency of the dominated, without requiring a position on their beliefs (e.g., Stein 1998).[15] Just as citizens can oppose their nation-state's policies and benefit from them at the same time, other citizens can support policies that diminish everyone's rights in favor of an idea, a value, or the belief that their group is diminished the least. Both positions appear internally contradictory; both could make sense for people across social classes; both involve complicity with dominant power in different ways.

The idea of complicity captures the simultaneous economic participation and (partial, varied, contextual) ideological rejection characteristic of neoliberal life across socioeconomic classes—precisely because its historic usage presumes the agency and awareness of the complicit subject. Confusion between agents' choices, or lack thereof, and the structures in which they are implicated is part of what makes traditional accusations of complicity so devastating. If, as Fred Moten suggests, "appeals . . . are always already embedded in the structure they would escape," then assessing complicity may involve untangling agents' felt acceptance or rejection of structures from their possible moves within those structures (Moten 2003: 2).[16]

For Mark Sanders, responsibility begins with a recognition of all humanity's "foldedness," our complicity with the worst and best parts of ourselves. In *Complicities: The Intellectual and Apartheid*, he argues that we have essential responsibilities to each other by virtue of our shared humanness. To deny those, as in South African apartheid, is to deny humanity to others. Yet in order to make radical arguments for love and respect based on shared humanity, we must affirm our complicity with humans who fundamentally disagree with the notion of shared humanity itself and who align themselves with the dehumanizing state (Sanders 2002: 8). Moreover, even militant forms of resistance are complicit in this broad sense. Like Moten using Judith Butler to note our inescapable connections to and responsibility for the structures that constrain us, Sanders invokes Derridean deconstructionism to argue that "opposition takes its first steps from a footing of complicity" (Sanders 2002: 8).

For these and other thinkers, the bedrock idea unifying concepts of complicity is an unavoidable commitment to other people, whether individuals, a group, or the idea of humanity.[17] We might gloss complicity, most simply, as the inability to avoid participation in something, but this misses the connotations that give complicity its important role. Without the dimensions of judgment and responsibility, the concept of complicity makes little sense, because the need for it seems to disappear. Instead, if we describe it more fully as the recognition that one bears responsibility for one's inability to avoid participating in something that harms others, then these inalienable dimensions illuminate how the complicity concept challenges ideas of the individual subject (Butler 2020). Yet complicity also continues to insist on the agent, however compromised, in what is a collective (because somehow coerced) event. In this way, feeling and acting responsible for another individual for the length of a specific interaction or relationship, and feeling and acting responsible for humanity in general over one's lifetime, are fundamentally envisioned as similar.

From this perspective, complicity is not only possible in many different kinds of relationships; it is a shared, constitutive, constantly renegotiated part of the human condition. Thus, despite their important differences, both scholarly and popular understandings of complicity engage in a systemic way of thinking about human collectivity that neoliberalization fundamentally seeks to negate. Complicity requires and reveals collectivity, a belonging through collective responsibility, that continues even in the face of increased cultivation and celebration of the individual. In exploring this dynamic, I seek a theoretically and ethnographically sound response to neoliberalism's naturalization of *Homo economicus* that renders alignments with its political, economic, and cultural hegemony more visible—regardless of how individuals in this book feel about the effects of neoliberalization.[18] Grappling with relations of complicity as a theoretical framework and a lived necessity helps me to see similarities and differences during and after neoliberal transition.

Throughout this book, I reframe complicity as a diagnosis of shifting topologies of power, using it to describe relationships between agents instead of a critique of those agents. By tracking both the limits and possibilities my interlocutors face at different scales, I seek to foreground the paradoxical relationship between individual and community in concepts of complicity. As an analytic, complicity allows me to refocus on chosen and unchosen collectivities, link structural effects and individual actions, and place anticipated and unanticipated outcomes in conjunction with other agents and forces.[19] Framing my interlocutors as complicit—just like their co-citizens—enables me to recognize various kinds of agency and constantly changing relational identities without losing sight of practitioners' very real constraints.

Before, during, and after the Arab Spring, Moroccan police and judicial forces capriciously leveled fines, jail, and physical harm in response to sufficiently explicit expressions of resistance, in ways that recalled for many the postindependence period of political repression known as the Years of Lead (Fr. *les années de plomb*, Ar. *al-zaman al-rusas*). In such a context, Moroccan artists of all genres may reasonably understand themselves as unfree. In cases throughout this book, political and economic inequality constrain and perpetuate the partnership some hip hop artists appear to enter into with the state, making analyses of complicity an entry point into analysis of the co-construction of Moroccan power.

As I use it here, complicity continues a commitment to illustrating my interlocutors' agency while capturing the limits of peoples' choices, including in situations where critical or resistant actions still support normative ethics, politics, or sociality. In examples throughout this book, emcees have perfected the invocation of the state's ostensible goals, its simultaneous statements of universality and Moroccan exceptionalism, in order to critique the state's failures by its own supposed standards. With their fellow musicians, emcees make audible the "state of exception" that must exist for neoliberalization to exist (Ong 2006). Crucially, they can do this and be personally committed to the version of governmentality for which the state ostensibly strives at the same time. In this way, before and alongside Moroccan practitioners' inability to avoid state and municipal sponsorship of most live performances, they cannot avoid complicity with the state's goals and rationalities.

Finally, in thinking through relations of and as complicity, I am not claiming the lived experience to appropriately apply the multiple logics of moral responsibility that Moroccans might use. Instead, I am attempting to present my interlocutors as complex, contradictory actors and thinkers. In interrogating my representations of them in relation to common narratives in hip hop or North African studies, I have sought to take seriously their self-understanding as moral, rather than merely political, subjects.

During the period of my research, Moroccan hip hop artists were committed to their art forms, the social world their art makes possible, and, frequently, to each other in the short-term collaborative sense emphasized in legal definitions of criminal complicity (Ziemer 2017). At the same time, their commitment to each other and themselves was often aligned with the state's expressed goals. Their complicit relations were neither entirely involuntary nor entirely unwitting, precisely because my interlocutors make experience-based calculations about the short- and long-term benefits of their actions to themselves and their communities. But they were also not understood as a "choice" in the traditional sense of the term, whether because hip hop practitioners felt compelled to make art or because they were compelled to accept and support some—if not all—state policies and effects. As the emcee Masta Flow once told me, echoing many and perhaps riffing on Jay-Z's "December 4th," "I didn't choose rhymes. Rhymes, they chose me."[20]

My analysis thus redefines complicity as the double-edged impulse that allows us to see all humankind as related, while also suspending that vision to tacitly accept unjust things that benefit us. From this perspective, complicity reveals a constant dynamic of community formation and reformation. Likewise, strategizing among the options provided by the powerful, or "making a way out of no way," reappears as an unavoidable way to maintain one's safety and security by embracing the realities of complicitous relations.

This is another way of stating the obvious: people struggling to flourish within the spaces they are allowed do not always have the luxury of rejectionist politics. Reflecting on the US Department of State's Next Level program, hip hop theater artist Will Power suggested that "the real question . . . is not if one is complicit, but whether one can do good in the world despite the inescapable complicity of modern life" (Katz 2020: 137). Mark Katz concludes that State Department–affiliated artists "*know* that to live with these ambiguities without seeking to resolve them is . . . the mark of a good citizen" (Katz 2020: 137, my italics). Like the artists Katz worked with as Next Level's director, Moroccan hip hop artists cannot avoid the unresolvable tensions that accompany the state's valorization (or "marking") of specific expressions of citizenship. Suspending attempts to resolve them is an action, or lack of action, both hip hop practitioners and Moroccans in general must take at least some of the time to navigate authoritarianism. Throughout this book, I argue that when artists follow their vision of the good through their complicity with Morocco's intertwined state and markets, their actions reverberate, reshaping Moroccan ideals of contemporary citizenship.

SINCERITY

Months before the first L'Mouja event at the 2010 Mawazine festival, Tangerois emcee Muslim released "A.K.A. Moutamarred (A.K.A. Rebel)." "My rap is a revolution, not just a wave," he declared in his signature growl in the second verse. "Rap's not my life, it's rap or my death."[21] Widely celebrated as Morocco's leading underground stylist because of his "hard" beats, persona, vocal timbre, and laser-like focus on inequality, Muslim had carefully guarded a reputation as an uncompromising critic since his solo debut in 2005. While he and others who shared his topics often performed at state-sponsored festivals, until 2018 fans rarely saw Muslim's performance venues as contradicting his critiques.

In spring 2018, the simmering discontent annually provoked by the Mawazine festival's lavish budget and high ticket prices overlapped with a related movement against Moroccan- and European-owned conglomerates. The French dairy company Danone and the Moroccan Afriquia gas and Sidi Ali bottled water, each of whom lead their markets in the country, were accused of price gouging. Facebook posts and profile pictures with the phrase ‏#مقاطعون‎ (#*muqatʿaoun*, or "boycotter") spread from April throughout the summer, leading to an actual boycott designed to force lower prices. Widespread participation resulted in significant drops in sales, protests, and counterprotests by Moroccan Danone employees.[22] The boycott of everyday items revived calls for a boycott of the Mawazine festival—the biggest, most expensive, and most obviously elite of Morocco's state-sponsored festivals, a centerpiece of the state's international tourism strategy.[23]

In this heated moment, when complaints about the Moroccan business elite's abuses of power and ties to the government were suddenly public, Muslim was allegedly caught negotiating to publicly support Mawazine. A viral video uploaded by "Saddam Darwish" purported to have recorded Muslim taking a phone call from a Canadian PR firm. According to the caller, the firm was working to counter negative sentiments about Mawazine among Moroccans at home and abroad. The speaker, "James," who mixed Canadian-accented English with fluent Modern Standard Arabic, proposed that Muslim promote VIP packages to the festival on his social media accounts for a fee of $20,000. After some discussion—and encouragement from James to name his price—a muffled voice responded, "Can we make it double? (Fin nʿamel double?)"[24] While many assumed the video was a hoax, several people I spoke to and followed the comments of insisted that Muslim had been successfully exposed. Reactions ranged from indifference to disgust to disbelief.

Later that day, I was told afterward, Muslim prompted a fresh round of discussion when he posted a Facebook note. Without confirming or denying his participation, he took issue with what he saw as commentators' insufficient support for artists' labor: "Whether I am paid four thousand or forty thousand, it's my business," my friends reported him writing.[25]

Experienced performers saw the entire viral event as a reflection of the state of Moroccan hip hop culture. "If you look at all of my [Facebook page], two comments are about *le Mondial* [the World Cup], and 99 percent are about Muslim," exclaimed Casablancan emcee Soultana the night the video was released. She compared Muslim to the equally famous rap group Fnaire, generally regarded as his stylistic and ideological opposite. "I used to clash with them all the time in my interviews," she recalled. "But they are not like Muslim. We know what they wanted from hip hop."

"You mean, to be pop stars?" I clarified.

"Yes! We knew this."[26]

For the many fans who left irate, mocking, or heartbroken comments on Muslim's Facebook and Instagram pages, the disjuncture between Muslim's artistic persona and his behavior—the appearance of hypocrisy—was upsetting. However, the accusations of hypocrisy did not center on the exposure of the businessman, and therefore the business, of hip hop. The problem was not in Muslim asking to be paid more; it lay in allegedly accepting to leverage his reputation to push expensive tickets to the most affluent concertgoers. Instead of being paid for his artistry, he would earn money helping the Moroccan state do what he consistently critiqued in his songs: circulate capital and access between elites to the exclusion of others.

Muslim's reported defense—essentially, that he should get whatever the market for his services would bear—sidestepped the issue of whether his values matched those of his songs by invoking a tenet of neoliberal doctrine: maximizing one's opportunity is self-evidently good and appropriate.[27] At issue, in the end, were competing definitions of sincerity. That this was his only public response suggested that Muslim saw his forthright expression of desire for greater capital as a sufficient rationale. Some fans, on the other hand, understood his alleged choice to partner with Mawazine as calling into question his self-representation as unmediated and sincere. For some of the disgruntled fans who believed what they heard in that viral video, when Muslim asked for "double" the proposed fee, he was speculating on the value of his previous, trenchant critiques of Moroccan inequality.

Sincerity is a core value in the transnational hip hop tradition, expressed through both live performance and everyday interaction.[28] Yet it is difficult to define. Paradoxically, as a performance practice, it is often expressed through intensity, through bending or breaking norms and thus revealing local, intersectional standards of "the real." John L. Jackson theorizes sincerity as an alternative framework to authenticity that privileges "each subject's individual ability to determine the contours of the real" (2004: 192). While authenticity requires constant reauthorization, he argues, analytically "'sincerity' provides a mechanism for asking how the deconstructed identity continues to powerfully/unfairly structure people's lives and life chances" (2010: S285). Yet precisely because it is internal, sincerity is difficult or impossible to locate as a quality, rather than as moves that serve to reinvent and subsequently reinforce authentications (2004: 175).

My emphasis on sincerity stems from its value for Moroccan hip hop practitioners. Like Muslim's recorded repertoire, many emcees both depend on and play with listeners' expectations that their professional personae and their lyrics are accurate depictions of, if not their own "real" lives, someone's lived experience. As many artists have explained to me over the years, they were initially drawn to hip hop because it offered a way to discuss "real" subjects: to transform popular musicking into a site where injustice and inequality could be debated and denounced, rather than a site exclusively for what they saw as repetitive, love song-based escapism. When Bigg told his interviewer, in 2007, that "authenticity and sincerity are values that pay," he referred to his then-shocking choice to critique both state power and apathetic Moroccans in equal measure, in a way both fans and detractors recognized as honest and reflective of their opinions. While ironic and sarcastic expressions pepper Moroccan hip hop lyrics as they do in other places, overall, artists' sincere affect makes a counterpublic possible (Salois 2014).

Don Bigg's statement not only crystallized the neoliberal contradiction within the transnational hip hop tradition for me, but recalled the interdependence of authenticity and sincerity within hip hop cultures. Some early hip hop scholarship focused on authenticity in response to a widespread discourse, invoked by some and critiqued by others, in which successful commodification was opposed to authentic expression (Holt 2020). Assumptions, or less often explicit invocations, of sincerity appear in US hip hop studies to bridge this presumed contradiction (Harrison 2006; Zanfanga 2017).

Similar assumptions appear in Moroccan artists' statements. In an interview published in the earliest years of Moroccan media interest in hip hop, pioneering emcee and ragga artist Barry claimed that "nearly all the kids of the rich who pretend to be underground are not," but he also sought to transcend background by defining "underground" as a quality of sincerity: "If it's not money that makes the difference, it's the spirit. I can't explain it to you, the underground is a lot of things. A true underground artist is [underground] in the soul. An underground [artist] who plays sentimental [music] or writes insipid words leaves the underground" (Amale 2004). Being underground, in Barry's sense, was to be both politically and musically committed, regardless of how popular one's music became.

Writing from a much different perspective, the beatmaker and producer West posted a Facebook manifesto he titled "Hitologie" in 2010:

> [To] make a hit is to have made your heart vibrate at the same time as the kick [drum], the hand at the same time as the snare . . . the hit is an art that only he

who loves music can appreciate. . . . It's an essence that is drawn from the most profound of our sensibilities. . . . I did not create my music, I gave birth to it. It is beautiful and I admire it in all sincerity and simplicity because it is born of my love (March 13, 2010).

In his passionate defense of the musical and sensorial value of "hits," West invoked the same devotion Barry suggests is central to the underground sensibility. Today, with his beats sought after by leading Moroccan and French trap artists, West continues unapologetically to reach mass markets.

Debates over authenticity and sincerity entangle with the commodification of race and difference—and the equally commodified combat of destructive racial stereotypes—throughout the transnational hip hop tradition. If sincerity is considered to belong exclusively to "moderns," then both Black and Muslim subjects are categorized as nonmodern, to the extent that observers have refused to grant them sincerity's associated qualities of spontaneity, interiority, and individualism.[29]

In the logic deployed by American courts, in which amateur emcees' lyrics are routinely taken as confessional evidence of their crimes, Black Americans are assumed to be inalienably "real." As Erik Nielsen and Travis Gosa explain, "Reading . . . violent lyrics as *a type of autobiography* ignores rap's artistic conventions, thereby negating it as an art form, and perpetuates enduring stereotypes about the inherent criminality of young men of color" (Nielsen et al. 2015: 6, italics mine; Nielsen and Dennis 2019).[30] When artists are not allowed the possibility that their rhymes voice a character, they are not allowed the possibility of a distinctive personhood separate from that character. Choosing to understand some people's expressions as authentic, and others as sincere, can be a form of racecraft (Fields and Fields 2012). Further, artists must find a way to succeed by creating products that conform, for those who hear them this way, to a demand for transparent Black subjectivities. Both hip hop and SWANA-region scholars have described artists' felt knowledge of this requirement by building on Sarah Thornton's concept of "subcultural capital" (Thornton 1995; Quinn 2005; Nooshin 2005; Spence 2011; Nickell 2020).

In a similar fashion, in Mediterranean and Middle Eastern anthropology of the mid-twentieth century, ethnographers theorized societies built around honor and shame instead of guilt, obligation instead of spontaneity, collectivity instead of interiority (e.g., Péristiany 1966). This framework intersected with that of religious scholars, who continue to grapple with the lack of interiority granted to Muslim subjects by earlier disciplinary assumptions. As Paul Powers notes, early non-Muslim scholars of Islam denigrated Muslims as "mere formalists" (Tisdale 1910, as quoted in Powers 2004). He argues that contemporary scholars still fail to recognize their own belief that "embodied praxis has less value than inward, silent, private, meditative, 'spiritual' activity" (Powers 2004: 452).[31] Ingrained assumptions define what is seen as properly religious and properly individual in terms of each other: both depend on a model of the individual in which the self, and its emotions, exist before the action. In this way, ethnographers and religious scholars positioned emphases on social ties, interdependence, and embodied worship practices in opposition to liberal selfhood, a tradition of reasoning that Saba Mahmood effectively turned inside out (2005).[32]

In these logics, who gets to be the liberal, fully human self is policed from the outside (Skeggs 2014: 8). As an analytic, sincerity's opacity is perhaps its greatest strength, precisely because it forces recognition of practitioners' interiority. Understanding hip hop artists' performances and choices as sincere not only embraces the conventions of the form, but can also be an antiracist way of listening to music heard as synonymous with Blackness and its history of assumed transparency and forced doubleness.

As a quality of everyday interaction, sincerity—demonstrated through openness, inclusivity, and trust—has often characterized relationships I have witnessed and participated in during my research. Whether interviewing American artists about their international collaborations or watching the ways Moroccan elders share knowledge with aspiring younger artists, I have heard sincerity underpinning conversations, enabling people to vehemently disagree while conveying respect for the other's knowledge and experience. But it is not just a social good. Sincerity makes possible aesthetic critique and therefore continuing competency (Schloss 2009: 3). Asked to recollect their memories of hip hop fandom from the early 1990s, pioneering Moroccan artists described nascent collectives where sincerity enabled both artistic achievement and lifelong friendships. Close bonds emerged from trying (and failing) to improve one's awkward footwork or clunky rhymes with one's peers and across neighborhood and socioeconomic boundaries.

In the examples above, I am equating sincerity with trust, earnestness, vulnerability, and care. These qualities describe both practitioners' relationships to their art and an idealized way of relating to others. Throughout my research, hip hop artists and fans characterized their devotion to the genre as, in part, a desire for a different way of speaking, listening, and interacting with their peers, unbound from previously stifling expectations about what to voice aloud and with whom. By growing and maintaining an expectation of sincerity within the culture, Moroccan practitioners offer each other "a subjunctive," a space where an alternative order could grow, which copes with the contradictions imposed by what they see as the hypocrisy of everyday life (Seligman et al. 2008: 20). In a very different context than the United States, emergent hip hop practitioners felt—and feel—that the constraints of their upbringings suppress certain kinds of thoughts and feelings, that they encourage a single kind of relationship between public and private selves. Practitioners, then, invoke the multiplicity of the self that sincerity implies through the aesthetics, sociality, and comportment of hip hop, in part because the genre arrived with few fixed associations in the 1980s and '90s.

In subsequent chapters, I show how sincerity is expressed in part through practitioners' labors for and with each other. The kinds of work that practitioners do for each other, for their imagined publics, and for themselves can be read simultaneously as care for each other and as investments in, or speculations on, a potentially productive future. At times, they also cross socioeconomic and gendered boundaries that my interlocutors are accustomed to in other parts of their lives.

Grappling with Intention

One might note, at this point, that my theoretical framework joins a concept I observe at work (complicity) with one my interlocutors openly value (sincerity). On the one hand, I am arguing that the former can be read through the intended and unintended effects of individual actions. On the other, my interlocutors and I can only analyze how well expressions of sincerity match avowed ideas of what it means to be sincere. In both cases, my use of the terms turns their typical relations to intention and intentionality upside down. In addition, my interlocutors demonstrate a widespread belief in intentionality as a critical category of analysis in social life.

Moroccan practitioners incorporate an understanding of intention, or *niyya*, into everyday judgments and conversations. In a familiar hadith, the Prophet Muhammad is recorded as saying: "Actions are defined by intentions, and to every person what he intends (Innama al-a'mal bi-l-niyyat wa-innama li-kull imri'in ma nawa)" (Powers 2004: 427). In Islamic jurisprudence's technical definition, one formulates niyya to provide the proper mental preparation and frame for ritual acts like prayer and ablutions. Accordingly, Sufis in Morocco's several brotherhoods use the invocation of niyya during *dhikr*, the Sufi practice of "remembrance," to "[set] the self's affections toward God, removing the believer from the profane world and placing the believer in a spiritual space" (Waugh 2005: 24).

My interlocutors frequently understood one's niyya to inform everyday actions. As the hadith implies, niyya is generally understood to lie behind any behavior in any context and to be "stable and subject to the will" (Powers 2004: 454).[33] In turn, niyya informs an understanding of the individual as properly in control of her own internally transparent desires and emotional state, as well as able to correctly judge how her actions will affect others.[34] Discussions of the intentions behind others' actions reveal that intention is an important category of practice, considered a reasonable standard by which to understand others.

Moroccan musicians' use of niyya can evoke religious or moral force or, alternatively, describe one's internal struggles without reference to faith. Lyrics from patriotic first-generation hip hop groups like Fnaire and H-Kayne demonstrate how the phrase *bi niyya*, "with intention," connotes moral clarity and the desire to benefit others. In these examples, describing actions and positions encouraged by the state as performed with intention identifies them as properly Muslim and reinforces the role of the monarch as the head of Morocco's Muslim community.[35] Other lyrics from rock and hip hop ensembles frequently contrast intentions with outcomes or use the term to compare interior and exterior presentations of the self.[36] In each of these examples, recognizing intention is one way of recognizing sincerity.[37]

In the following chapters, sincerity has moral force not just in a traditional liberal sense, but in our contemporary relationships to ourselves as both a resource and a product characteristic of neoliberal subjectivity. As Jackson puts it, sincerity exceeds the boundaries of authenticity imposed by the transnational hip hop tradition. At the same time, Moroccan practitioners' sincerity repairs the inevitable breaks—with one's peers and oneself—that accompany forced and unforced complicity with state discourses and goals.

COMPETITION AND SOLIDARITY

Competition and solidarity figure throughout this book as concrete ways that my other pair-in-tension, complicity and sincerity, are lived. Years ago, on a sticky August night, I found myself gossiping with Soultana about the strengths and weaknesses of various emcees. For her, she explained, the comparisons weren't made out of jealousy. Recalling her teenage love of basketball, she said both it and emceeing gave her a chance to fulfill her competitive drive. "I don't compete with people to make them feel bad. I do it to get better. When we compete we all get better," I remember her saying. "And if I cannot compete with them because I am already better, I will compete with myself. I will be better than myself" (August 2010).

Competition always risks failure. For Soultana, that risk was at once an entrepreneurial and an ethical imperative. As one of a handful of successful female Moroccan emcees to date, Soultana fervently believed in hip hop culture as a place where women were not yet presumed to be inferior, where she could engage with her peers through her talent. Competition was a pragmatic response to insecure conditions for professional musicians, a form of self-care that enabled a valued state of continual improvement, and, perhaps, a way to open up possibilities for other women.

For her and many other practitioners I worked with, competition and risk are moral and practical investments in oneself, expressions of confidence in the future. As theorists frequently note, risk and its accompanying self-management techniques help people both embrace and cope with neoliberalism's pervasively antisystemic perspective, with its expectation that they alone are responsible for their successes and failures (e.g., Gershon 2011).

As Soultana demonstrates, risk and competition are also deeply ingrained in hip hop aesthetics and culture. Artists and fans have embraced the rhetoric and practice of market-based competition since the birth of hip hop, producing an aesthetics that celebrated innovation and entrepreneurship. When New York artist and entrepreneur Fab 5 Freddy argued that the hip hop artist's goal is to constantly push the boundaries of accepted practice, to achieve "a style nobody can deal with" (quoted in Rose 1994: 80–81), his explanation at once fit modernist teleologies of artistic evolution, capitalist drives to proliferate consumable difference, and a commitment to resisting external evaluations of Black creativity. At the same time, living that goal requires solidarity: peers maintaining bonds across and despite scarcity and competition, striving for the pleasure and necessity of making better art separately and together.

If for Soultana every performance is a competition, she and other artists of her generation have also invested much in others: judging literal competitions, mentoring younger musicians, giving countless unpaid interviews. Just as sincerity sustains people and their relationships in the face of the contradictions provoked by complicity, solidarity promotes mutual respect within individual competitions and in the lifelong, large-scale competition for socioeconomic mobility in which Moroccans participate.

Each chapter that follows unpacks how these paired tensions work together. Many of the interactions depicted throughout this book take place in Casablanca, Morocco's economic center and the hub of hip hop practitioners' social and musical networks since hip hop's emergence at the end of the 1980s. While my research encompasses artists identified with and events in diverse Moroccan cities, including Meknes, Fes, Salé, Rabat, Tangier, and Kenitra, aspiring and established artists frequently visit Casablanca to pursue performance, recording, collaboration, or other goals.

The emphasis on Casablanca in the following chapters reveals the city's relative abundance of events and opportunities. However, in each chapter, vignettes and close readings locate the reader in a distinct time, place, and social setting, offering a counterpoint to more general observations. In this way I depict continuities from the late 2000s to my most recent in-person research in 2018.

POSITIONING EXTRACTION

The best—or the best-intended—way to think through complicity-sincerity and competition-solidarity tensions is to apply them to myself. I am an American, a non-Muslim, and a past recipient of US federal research funds. The unearned, unavoidable currency attached to me as a young, single white woman during my dissertation research has been replaced, over time, with modest cultural capital as a familiar face, a professor, and a reasonably good speaker of Moroccan Arabic. Like any ethnographer, my positioning has allowed me access to some information while preventing access to other people, events, and knowledges. Learning about how I was perceived, and the advantages and disadvantages those perceptions conferred during my research, took time. Yet I am nonetheless responsible for acting respectfully within them.

This book fits into postcolonial patterns of underdevelopment in which I obtain data from the "raw material" of my interlocutors' lives and create a monograph whose "value added" is directed toward my peers in Europe and North America. This remains true regardless of whether this book succeeds in destabilizing larger narratives about North African or Muslim difference, or whether you as a reader find that my approach sufficiently interrogates its own culpability. As voices from within and without the discipline have recently observed, such patterns have underpinned American ethnomusicology since its earliest endeavors, rendering the discipline strikingly similar in logic to the "world music" industry we often critique and to the neo- and postcolonialism we often study (Brown 2020; Kheshti 2015; Kim and Veal 2016; Taylor 2014).

This structure obtains through, not despite, the "friendship model" of ethnography upon which I have relied. In a controversial essay, Benjamin Teitelbaum cites mostly ethnomusicologists to describe the friendship model as "both forming sympathetic and affectionate relationships with research participants and using friendship as a metaphor for a more harmonious type of interaction in the field" (2019: 417). Yet in arguing that "solidarity with abandon" leads to more insightful research, he also refers to anthropologists who "justify [friendship] as a tool for increasing knowledge," a win-win approach that nevertheless conveys that the value of one's research to one's scholarly peers is the bottom line (Teitelbaum 2019: 418). In parallel with other forms of neoliberal reasoning, the promise of a connection that the ethnographer can feel good about—what is described in various periods as rapport, solidarity, or friendship—not only reinscribes a white, cisgendered, male subject as the universalized figure of the researcher (Appert 2017), but is valued simultaneously for its personal and professional benefits.

Moroccanists have often sought and theorized from more mutual forms of connection, producing reflexive analyses of scholars' and research subjects' inevitably unequal co-construction of a shared reality (e.g., Rabinow 1977; Crapanzano 1980; Dwyer and Muhammad 1982; Crawford and Newcomb 2013). Their insights shape this book in part because of those professional benefits—the authors' conceptual innovations brought them high disciplinary recognition, leading to later scholars' careful consideration of their work. Like other white ethnographers read as female, my attempts to follow canonical standards of relationship-building and "access" acquisition often ran up against local standards of propriety. At the least, this limited my own publicly judged belonging to certain networks of people and, at worst, imposed on my interlocutors my own tiresome insistence on reading gendered cross-cultural interactions as "neutral."

In overlapping situations and time periods, I have been complicit with various projects at multiple scales. My interlocutors' generous gifts of time, energy, and expertise were colored by the specter of potential benefits from my whiteness, Americanness, and mobility. My inability to confer the opportunities practitioners imagined were accessible to me have caused pain and disappointment for them and for me, yet I continue to return to Morocco for research. I have also been complicit in my interlocutors' desires to represent themselves well toward potential connections at home or abroad. And as a Fulbright recipient, I participated in a broad post-9/11 enterprise in which the United States awarded funding to produce knowledge about targeted populations. None of these projects were undertaken in bad faith by me, or, to my knowledge, by those who made them possible. In fact, our good faith was necessary to their functioning. I not only perform a sincere interest in my interlocutors and their life chances, but believe in my own sincerity.

To accept this state of affairs, especially as I understood it better over time, is itself a kind of complicity with the powers of whiteness as sculpted by the United States' postwar hegemony. These powers were and are observable and concrete, historic and historicized, yet require continuous analysis before and during fieldwork in order for them to feel less than natural in the moment.[38] Complicity must be the word for my relationship with advantages that have been attached to my body, that I have lived with and relied on before I could identify them. It must be the word for advantages that I cannot fully remove myself from, but that I can choose to critique or to overlook as I prefer. At the same time, I argue throughout this book for a capacious understanding of complicity that enables analysis of how those on the flip side of social hierarchies—those who cannot fully remove themselves from their *dis*advantages—enact assumptions and ideals they share with the powerful even as they work to dismantle dominant structures.

Recent decolonial and antiracist scholarship, as well as histories of anthropology's ties to colonial ethnology, demonstrate that ethnography's ancestors maximized the privilege of knowing and imagining knowability—the privilege of declaring other people and worlds transparent to knowledge-making—claimed by whiteness itself. At the ends of most chapters I turn onto myself the same lens through which our writing asks us to view our interlocutors: as both unique individuals and representatives of groups, whether defined by themselves or by scholarly tradition. Following probing calls for reflection from Danielle Brown (2020), Denise Gill (2020), Dylan Robinson (2020), Deonte Harris (2022), Trevor Reed et al. (2023), and others, I offer my unresolved tensions in the hope that other ethnographers see themselves in my concerns.[39] Yet in one of the cul de sacs of complicity, efforts to avoid a heroic narrative where the fieldworker redistributes her "expert" knowledge, wisdom, and empathy to her students could be read as merely substituting different tropes of white self-discovery (wa Ngũgĩ 2021). My theoretical framework and argumentative moves in these passages resonate with perhaps futile attempts to "contain the unbearable searchlight of complicity, of having harmed others just by being one's self" (Tuck and Yang 2012: 9).

Asking, then, if other practices of listening, acting, representing, or writing can render ethnography less extractive is also asking whether we can escape complicity. Within this question are several further considerations, including: Can (or should) ethnographic research by institutionally employed scholars be other than transactional in nature?[40] If not, what amount of "giving back" compensates for rendering Moroccans' culture as a source of professional capital, as an object valued for its ability to produce value elsewhere or, more pointedly, its ability to act as a reflection of my own intellectual value? Or, to put it in Casablancan emcee Amine Snoop's words, "How can you help us?" (personal conversation, May 9, 2018).

If this book adequately addresses any of these questions, it is unfortunately through, rather than despite, the structures of knowledge-making discussed above. The following chapters center urban youths and young adults rather than the traditionally favored subjects of Moroccanist ethnography in order to underscore that self-described "Westernized" Moroccan subjects are equally worthy of study on their own terms. In this, I follow H. Samy Alim's vital insistence that hip hop artists are "critical interpreters of their own culture" who theorize through and about their craft (2006: 11). Yet each time I happily support a Moroccan artist by purchasing music, circulating their work, or connecting them to opportunities to perform, speak, or network, it becomes more clear that singular actions at the margins of an unequal market merely cement that market and its imbalances.

My information and authorial voice depend on typical ethnographic practice, forms of witnessing in the field, and on postethnographic consumption. In the latter, my research and relationships fruitfully inform the way I hear new music and interact with newer artists. Yet my persistent unease with social media and commercial releases as sources of information shows me how fully I have accepted an insistence on ontological difference between the knower and the known, a difference traditionally expressed in reports based on the knower's continuous physical presence (Fabian [1983] 2014: 151, 177; Hammoudi and Borneman 2009: 260). As a partial response to this, throughout this book, the complicity-sincerity dyad focuses attention on the ways both I and my interlocutors are incentivized to perform in our respective contexts. I hope this undermines the separation I introduce by identifying as a researcher, as well as highlighting the continuing temptation to write in the image of my own concerns.

In developing this book's framework, I act in what I believe to be solidarity with my interlocutors by taking seriously all of their impacts, big or small, intended or otherwise.[41] My goal is to undermine unexamined assumptions that certain subjects are legible only when they undertake certain actions, or are represented in certain ways (El Zein 2016: 98). However, succeeding at this goal would do little to upset the extractive nature of contemporary ethnography. Solidarity does not afford me the right to claim effects that do not occur or to project a future that may not come to exist; it "neither reconciles present grievances nor forecloses future conflict" (Tuck and Yang 2012: 3). It is, instead, a powerful imaginative force that, like the bedrock assumptions of complicity discourse, insists on excavating what we owe to each other and searching for ways to act within that debt.

CHAPTER OUTLINES

Each chapter that follows unpacks how the twin tensions of complicity-sincerity and competition-solidary work together. Many of the interactions depicted throughout this book take place in Casablanca, Morocco's economic center and the hub of hip hop practitioners' social and musical networks since hip hop's emergence at the end of the 1980s.

It is important to this book's argument, my interlocutors, and me to avoid "allochronic" representations of Moroccan hip hop, in which music or people are depicted as static (Fabian [1983] 2014). I do this by refusing the use of the ethnographic present and by considering changes over short periods of time as part of recent history. Since the 1990s, hip hop studies has often legitimated itself within academia as a way to study racial, economic, and political inequalities that affect "youth." While music scholars have crafted nuanced histories of US hip hop, Anglophone research into non-US hip hop communities' musical or social histories *as* history is still limited. Many practical problems, including a lack of archival material or even agreement on what belongs in a community's archive, can stand in the way of a more substantial historical focus. However, in terms of our work's collective impact on readers, prioritizing the recent over the historic in global hip hop scholarship may inadvertently mimic representations of nonwhite subjects as "people without history" (Wolf 1982). In the worst case, "non-Western" hip hop artists' work might serve to illustrate arguments that center US themes, issues, or readers. With this in mind, this book asserts the value of my interlocutors' recollections and my own, building a partial, contestable picture of Moroccan hip hop's history primarily through the experiences of its first generation.

In chapter 1, I describe a poetics of ambiguity that has accompanied Moroccan popular musics since the Years of Lead, the postindependence decades in which King Hassan II governed through fear, surveillance, and political violence. Today's hip hop artists and fans inherit not only the lyrical tactics that protected the musicians of the 1960s and '70s, but a tradition of ambiguous listening, in which one interprets opacity or omission in tune with one's political affiliations. By listening for and with sincerity, practitioners adopt a holistic approach, in which a critique of everyday socioeconomic injustice can be heard as a critique of larger structures, policies, and policymakers. Yet by necessity, the same rhetorical and listening strategies also enable acquiescence, or political quietism.[42]

Chapter 2 introduces ways that, in striving to educate and empower their fans, the first generation of Moroccan hip hop artists advanced a theory of citizenship that accepts complicity with the state and its neoliberalizing goals. Artists simultaneously critiqued themselves, listeners' selves, and widespread inequalities, linking "individual mentalities" (Fr. *mentalité*, Ar. *'aqliyya*) to national policies. The preferred person one infers from these critiques no longer suffers under the internalized oppression of the previous generation, but instead embraces personal responsibility as a mode of freedom. In turn, this focus locates social change in the individual, deemphasizing collective political action and working with, not against, the reduced role of the state.

Chapter 3 explores how musicians built supportive institutions that took the form of competitions and how these helped to produce their understandings of the state/market nexus and of themselves as market actors. In the late 2000s, a boom in state-funded tournaments like L'Mouja encouraged the national adoption of specific styles and reinforced the state's control of popular culture and pathways into international markets. At the same time, practitioners continue to build solidarity through their own forms of competition for audiences, recognition, and physical and economic mobility.

In chapter 4, I explore another dimension of artists' sincere investment in social change: their practice of speaking about and for marginalized Moroccans. Through music videos, live performance, volunteerism, and youth workshops, artists from varied socioeconomic locations imagine rural, low-income, or politically disenfranchised youths as targets of concern and objects of governance. The success of Morocco's first emceeing workshop served to further institutionalize the hip hop arts and shift the discourse on poverty away from an emphasis on poor urban youths' religiosity. At the same time, nonprofits and individual musicians took up some of the goals and practices previously monopolized by state agencies.

Chapter 5 twists the angle of this argument to look at how hip hop artists and fans themselves are imagined, by the state and in global north settings, as a specific category of Moroccan: harbingers of Arabs' and Muslims' deferred modernity. To do this, I focus on how Casablancan emcee Soultana's career formed within an international market for representations of female Muslim resistance. The market analyzed here both expresses and stimulates demand for the visibility of women who appear to contradict orientalist conflations of Arabness, Muslimness, and patriarchy. Navigating multiple representational puzzles, Soultana, her female colleagues, and I all struggle with enforced and self-reinforcing complicity.

Finally, the epilogue returns to the argument that under neoliberalism, complicit and sincere relations reinforce each other, as sincerity becomes both necessary and insufficient to leading an ethical life. I discuss how some younger practitioners have circulated beyond the nation in ways earlier artists could only imagine in the 2000s, provoking a subtle but important shift from discourses of cultivation to those of speculation. By considering the debates Moroccan trap artists provoked among pioneering first-generation artists, I throw into relief the ways both waves are naturalized as neoliberal citizens, including the different ways both conflate one's self with one's present and future capital.

As a form born from and expressive of those left behind in postindustrial New York, transnational hip hop's embrace of the tensions I have outlined here—complicity and sincerity, competition and solidarity—serves to critique neoliberalism from the inside. As in Paul Gilroy's formulation of Black Atlantic modernity, hip hop contests anti-Blackness through its mastery of techniques and aesthetics vital to neoliberal subjectivity itself (1993: 73). While Moroccan hip hop's history differs markedly from that of 1970s South Bronx and Queens, its practitioners know that as people constantly reinscribed within "global" narratives as different and as constitutive of difference, their mastery is never apolitical.

1

Critical Traditions

The Poetics and Politics of Ambiguity

In August 2010, I was sitting in Park Yasmina in downtown Casablanca, talking with the emcee Amine Snoop. Amine, who also goes by the name al-Kayssar (Caesar), was old-school. He began his career as a b-boy in a team of friends, dancing at La Cage, the nightclub that the city's hip hop fans went to in the 1990s. His peers believed he was one of the first to rap in Derija in the city, if not the entire country. In later years, he would tell me more about late nights on the corner near his home in Bernoussi, a working-class neighborhood in Casablanca, reciting rhymes to himself while listening to the boomboxes of the dancers practicing on the sidewalk in front of Café Safir. But at this point, we were talking about his first recordings.

"I used to rap the lyrics of Nass el-Ghiwane," he remarked, describing how he and his friends went from imitating their favorite American emcees to attempting their own lyrics. "Al-qaran al-ʿashreen."

"Al-qaran al-ʿashreen (the twentieth century)," the phrase Amine remembers the song by, is the turning point in the opening poem in one of Nass el-Ghiwane's most iconic songs, "Lebtana (The Sheepskin)."[1] As a kid working on his Arabic rhymes in 1994 and 1995, this poem made part of his repertoire along with his own texts. Like others near his age, Amine hadn't thought much about preserving his music at that time. His recordings of those first songs were made to cassette tape, and his copies were lost long ago. But he could remember how he had performed it.

In the original song, a member of Nass el-Ghiwane recites the poem freely before the instruments enter. When Amine rapped his version for me on a park bench, he left out certain lines and edited others, sometimes eliding words so he could maintain the right number of syllables in a line. He timed his flow so that stressed syllables nearly always landed on the 2 and 4 of the four-beat measure in

28

his head. The end-rhymes from the original poem landed on the beginning of the 4th beat of each measure.

"Al-qaran al-ʿashreen" became line 5 out of 8, and Amine built the verse to revolve around it: he took a surprise unmetered breath at the beginning of measure 8, then uttered the phrase explosively, twice as fast as the rest of the text. Then, when the next line resumed the rhythmic pattern squarely on beat 1 of the next measure, it had renewed energy, commensurate with the weight his listeners placed on the line "we're living the life of the flea in the sheepskin (ʿaisheen al-ʿaish al-dbana fil bṭana)."

Line by line and moment by moment, Amine's small changes adapted "Lebtana" to the boom-bap percussion, rhythmic intensity, and punchy pronunciation of the East Coast emcees he fell in love with as a kid. Most didn't appreciably change the meaning of the original text. However, his edit to the penultimate line stood out. Instead of saying "you know there's a great difference between the apple and the pomegranate," Amine said, "*They make* a great difference (Darou farq ʿathim bin al-tufaḥ wa al-romana)." The final line—"what's the difference between you, and you, and you and me?"—lands differently as a result.

Was teenage Amine unsatisfied with the impact of Nass el-Ghiwane's genteel observation about fruit? Or had he always remembered the line beginning with "darou," with what most people believed the band really wanted to say? Either way, Amine made explicit the consensus interpretation of the song without identifying "they." The target of critique is still obscured, but this version sounds like a bullhorn to the previous generation's ears.

This chapter considers how artists have fused Moroccan histories and ideologies of critique with hip hop's aesthetics of resistance since the early 1990s. Often described as "the Ghiwanien generation" after the germinal band, the popular folk-rock musicians of the 1960s and '70s anchor today's nostalgia for the perceived promise, cohesion, and solidarity of the postindependence years. Hip hop emcees and beatmakers who draw from techniques pioneered by these musicians not only invoke listeners' profound associations with the Ghiwanien generation, but continue a tradition of ambiguous positioning in the face of state violence, in which audiences appreciate critiques pursued through oblique gestures and strategic omissions.

In the first section, I describe how, despite living under nominally different economic paradigms, both Ghiwanien and contemporary hip hop musicians' work have been enabled by increasing inequality and its accompanying anxieties about Moroccan identity. In the second section, I detail the tactics that both '60s and '70s leftists and popular musicians and contemporary hip hop artists used to avoid state scrutiny. In the third section, I argue that the politicized narrative that developed around Nass el-Ghiwane between 1970 and today conditions how today's hip hop practitioners perform and hear sincerity in their music. Artists use a Moroccan tradition of listening in and for ambiguity, in which a critique in one domain is often read as indicating a critique in another, to promote a holistic understanding of citizens' rights and privileges as simultaneously political, economic, and social. At the same time, ambiguity that protects musicians and listeners can also protect the powerful.

HIP HOP GENERATIONS

Young people today have one foot down and don't know where to put the other foot. They want to study but they know if they have a diploma they might work in a call center or not work at all. They want to work but they can't make enough money to get married and leave the house. They want to leave but they can't afford it and they might die on the boat.
(PERSONAL CONVERSATION [P.C.] WITH SOULTANA, AUGUST 27, 2010)

[In the 1990s,] things were changing . . . families were completely changing. The change happened on all levels . . . music included. People said, "This kind of music is quite new, it's a danger to Moroccan culture."
(P.C. WITH ISMAIL RAQI, JANUARY 19, 2024)

Moroccan hip hop history has only begun to take shape as a single, continuous narrative with shared reference points. During the earliest years of my research, practitioners from different cities told their own stories of the move from scattered teenage amateurs to national recognition between the early 1990s and the early 2000s. While the people and places involved were different, the kinds of events that merited retelling were often the same. The adoption of Facebook and YouTube; the establishment of influential websites; national press; and nationally televised performances helped to consolidate the story for Moroccans, as recordings and events circulated through various platforms as key points in an emergent timeline.

In what follows, I trace this history in an open-ended fashion by threading events my interlocutors found significant with their political and economic context. My sketch here is inevitably partial and leans heavily on what my oldest, most experienced interlocutors remember about the emergence of Moroccan hip hop. It privileges Casablancan events and people because that is where most of my knowledge came from, but also because Casablancan institutions and musicians came to be understood as central to the genre. I also elaborate on a periodization of Moroccan hip hop that follows practitioners' usage. The goal is not to create a universally accepted, authoritative history, but to illustrate that the youths who first adopted hip hop in the late 1980s and 1990s lived through intense socioeconomic change. At the same time, while they faced less overt political violence, they coped with sensations of loss, lack, disorientation, and inequity similar to what their parents felt in the 1960s and 1970s.

Moroccan hip hop practitioners speak of three generations of artists, loosely defined. The first is generally understood to include the earliest adopters, who began imitating and creating hip hop in the late 1980s and early 1990s. Those who began in the mid 2000s, after national and municipal government agencies made substantial investments into urban popular cultures, are considered part of the second generation (Salois 2013: 88). Today, the boundaries between generations are blurry, with some performers from the late 2000s and early 2010s heard as stylistically closer to the first generation in comparison to later practitioners.

Khalid Hoummas, a multimodal artist who has run an open mic night for aspiring emcees since 2011, describes three generations in the context of that event. Khalid named H-Kayne and Fez City Clan, two groups from the late 1990s, as his examples of the first generation. Khalid, who is best known for performing with the progressive hip hop band LooNope in 2010–12 and under his solo moniker Boummask today, locates himself in the middle "second generation" (interview, July 1, 2018; Saadi 2012). Shayfeen, a duo from the small Atlantic town of Asfi that introduced trap to the broader Moroccan public, was founded in 2006. They also defined themselves as part of the second generation, telling an interviewer that they formed a "buffer" between the historicist styles of the pioneers and the latest, trap-oriented wave, which they dated to 2016 (Simonian 2018).

The new generation, as my interlocutors still refer to it, is usually dated to the mid-2010s and is situated in relation to trap and other new styles as well as new social media and streaming platforms, marketing strategies, and performance opportunities. In part because of the successful move into platforms like Instagram, Spotify, Deezer, and Genius, as well as the high levels of internet adoption among the Moroccan youths who listen to them, this new generation sustains much greater stylistic diversity than its predecessors.[2] Throughout this text, I use the terms "generation" and "wave" interchangeably. However, my interlocutors use "generation" almost exclusively, evoking metaphors of lineage and family.

Before the Wave: The Ghiwanien Generation

Born and raised in the nation's major cities, the first generation of Moroccan hip hop artists grew up with narratives of their parents' and grandparents' rebellious pursuit of cultural and political independence from France. As these young people grew along with their craft, the same narratives reappeared again and again, heard in stark contrast to the inequity and immobility of the 1980 and 1990s.

For commentators then and now, cultural change and experimentation could not be separated from political ferment in the late 1960s and '70s. Leftist journals, including *Souffles, Anfas,* and *Lamalif,* mutually opposed Islamist and Marxist-Leninist students' movements, and labor unions' agitation were all responses to the increasing economic inequality and autocracy of King Hassan II's regime (Sefrioui 2014; El Guabli 2020). Violent responses to protests and riots in the 1970s and early

'80s, and the constant fear provoked by the state's repressive practices, character-ized Morocco's Years of Lead (Slyomovics 2005: 110; Bouaziz 1999: 74).[3] This long period of surveillance, forced disappearance, and censorship, roughly from 1975 to the 1990s, coincided with Morocco's preparation for and adoption of the standard practices of economic neoliberalism. The state was encouraged, and in some cases forced, to grant more freedoms to national and international corporations in the 1980s and 1990s as it opened to global markets.[4] Yet, at the same time, its citizens experienced a generation-defining lack of freedoms.

In this emerging climate of socioeconomic upheaval, cultural experimenta-tion, and political repression, the band Nass el-Ghiwane and its counterparts appeared at the end of the 1960s. In Morocco's urban centers of the 1950s and '60s, the most popular recording artists represented local traditions, partici-pated in pan-Arab song forms, or both. Artists who spoke to the nation's recent independence, whether through satire or expressions of unity, were widely beloved (Bargach 1999; Karl 2014; Silver 2020). In the meantime, young musi-cians were experimenting with "Western" genres, leading to remarkable if short-lived careers for soul and rock acts like Vigon or Les Golden Hands (Samie 2004; Bensalmia 2004).

Nass el-Ghiwane and bands like it, such as Jil Jilala and Lem Chaheb, crafted distinct sounds despite sharing cultural backgrounds, musical aspirations, and occasionally band members. Despite—or perhaps because of—the fact that Nass el-Ghiwane's music drew heavily from genres traditionally heard as marginal, it quickly set a standard, inspiring a wave of similar groups and producing a popular music that was at once nationally representative and responsive to trans-Atlantic trends. The band was made possible by postindependence migration to Casa-blanca, as each of its members' families came from a different region of the coun-try.[5] Band members were also shaped by the creative and political ferment of Hay Mohammedi, a working-class Casablanca neighborhood that was already famous for its resistance during the nation's independence movement (Slyomovics 2005: 108). Living near first- or second-generation migrants from all over the country provided Nass el-Ghiwane with firsthand opportunities to study other Moroccan musics and folkways.

The original band members honed their creative sensibility in Masraḥ an-Nass (The People's Theater), a troupe led by the playwright, dramaturg, and director Tayeb Saddiki. There, they and fellow musicians acted and sang in *Diwan Sīdī Abdelrahmān al-Majdūb* (1965), an adaptation of Moroccan street performances (*ḥalqat*, sing. *ḥalqa*) that drew on the traditions of the sixteenth-century Sufi poet al-Majdub (Miller 2017: 94; Amine 2001: 61). Nass el-Ghiwane would become famous for their references to al-Majdub, as well as their invocations of *malḥun*, a form of Derija-language song from the sixteenth century that al-Saddiki fre-quently used in his theater pieces (Amine 2001: 60; Magidow 2016: 32).

Already well-known in Casablanca, Nass el-Ghiwane performed in 1970 and 1971 on Moroccan television for the first time, revealing to a delighted national public their effortless Moroccanization of trans-Atlantic popular styles (Es-Sayed et al. 2011: 391). They combined the American banjo with the sub-Saharan guimbri, the classical ʿoud, and an array of traditional Moroccan percussion, each of which indexed different regions and genres.[6] Their songs sounded the band members' familiarity with a wide range of genres, including the ʿaita of the central plains, the ritual music of the Gnawa, and Sufi traditions of Meknes and Fes. By bringing these gestures together, they presented something radical and neotraditional at the same time—something that recuperated marginalized groups' musics for a broad public while also working in the folkloric paradigm established by colonial curators and affirmed by postcolonial elites. At the same time, the band unmistakably embraced trans-Atlantic fashion, musical form, and performance practice (Schuyler 1993).

By contemporary accounts, the appearance of Nass el-Ghiwane was transformational. Moroccan scholars and commentators continue to celebrate the band's impact, often through the lens of their own formative years (Simour 2016). Speaking in 2010, cultural studies professor Said Graiouid recalled the band's debut as changing youth culture overnight: "Literally overnight, we woke up in the morning, we [all] found ourselves on the streets humming the lyrics to this piece that we had heard the night before on Moroccan television. That was the beginning of a ... subcultural movement. And that was actually the beginning of Nass el-Ghiwane" (Graiouid 2010). Abdelhaï Sadiq argues that the band offered listeners a powerful new way to understand themselves: "Nothing distinguished them from their audience. ... In a way, the Ghiwane was the voice of an expression that belonged to all of us. It was only bringing to the stage and singing by 'proxy' the protest of a youth which, otherwise, was singularly prepared to take the path of violence" (2014: 33).

In the years after independence, artists and writers concerned about the loss of popular traditions under the French took stock of how music, storytelling, poetry, and other arts had maintained oral transmission (e.g., Bouanani 1966). Nass el-Ghiwane and bands that became popular following its innovations—Lem Chaheb, Essiham, Mesnaoua, Jil Jilala, Izenzaren, and others—offered a recuperation of Moroccan musical heritage at a time when many, across socioeconomic locations, were still wrestling with their sense of French cultural superiority. For some whose traditions were incorporated, here was a wholesale re-valuation: an opportunity for young people to see their practices wrapped into a trans-Atlantic rock frame, played for thousands in concerts across North Africa and France. For some of the elite, educated to hold the colonizer's culture in higher regard than their own, it awakened a sense of the creative potential in their Moroccan heritage (van der Peer 2017: 168). This alone afforded this musical moment enormous cultural import. But today, most Moroccans still remember Nass el-Ghiwane best for their lyrics—and the perception that their lyrics spoke truth to power in an era of swift, brutal repression.

The First Wave

As with their predecessors, who drew on pop and rock currents from the Black Atlantic world in the 1960s to 1980s, the teens who encountered and adapted the hip hop arts in the 1980s and 1990s experienced them as both exciting aesthetic practices that seemed to offer new possibilities for translocal connection, and a reaffirmation of Morocco's marginal position in global north circuits of culture (Salois 2016). Like other locations across the world at this time, Moroccan hip hop lovers were introduced to the genre through transnational media rather than directly from its New York originators. However, the ways media reached Morocco were shaped by postcolonial patterns of access and of migration.

The oldest practitioners I worked with described learning about hip hop culture soon after it was made available to audiences in Europe through informal exchanges with relatives and friends who studied or worked in France, the Netherlands, and less often Spain, Italy, or Belgium. These sojourners would bring home cassettes, LPs, dance moves, magazines, fashions, and knowledge. Satellite television became widely available in the early 1990s, allowing people to find American and Francophone hip hop in European music programs (DJ Key 2004: 12). Two early adopters mentioned watching Viva, a music-video program they remember to be Russian, for information about hip hop in the early and mid-1990s (DJ Key 2004; p.c. Soultana, July 2015). Khalid Douache, a.k.a. DJ Key, Morocco's finest hip hop turntablist and a sought-after director of music videos, noted how difficult it was to find the materials needed to study and perform hip hop in these early years. "[T]he hip hop movement appeared at the end of the 1980s, but it did not take. . . . The lack of the means employed [to make hip hop] kept us from reaching our objective" (2004: 12).

In the 1980s and '90s, the heyday of neoliberal economic doctrine, commentators regarded Morocco and other North African countries as "success stories" for their zealous adoption of prescribed reforms (Pfeifer 1999). As it had done with the Moroccanization law of 1973, the monarchy used early-1990s privatization to reinforce its patronage network, further concentrating business interests in the hands of the existing economic elite (Gilson-Miller 2013: 208). Through its two holding companies, the royal family acquired some of the largest assets made available, literally transferring state assets to the king's and his family's personal accounts. In other cases, the former European owners of Moroccan companies, who sold them under the 1973 law, bought back the same assets (Catusse 2009: 194–95).[7] In addition, the government shed large numbers of public sector jobs just as a generation of college graduates educated to expect a place in the country's bureaucracy was coming to the workforce. This led, starting in 1991, to the formation of several highly organized groups demanding a return to pre-neoliberalization levels of public employment (Emperador 2007: 298).

By the early 1990s, teens not yet finished with high school were coming of age in an environment where old expectations about attainable education, employment, and income were diminishing and detaching from the nation-state (Cohen 2017: 48–50). New narratives were forming around them about the recent past and the present. Nores, a beatmaker and emcee from Salé, bitterly recalled how King Hassan II had given speeches encouraging students to seek degrees in STEM fields in the early 1980s. According to what he was told—he was a small child at the time—engineers and scientists then graduated into a nation with little industry to support them (p.c., June 2010).

In most of Morocco's major cities, small groups of these same teens were picking up information about hip hop music and culture wherever they could find it. The paucity of hip hop media available at the time enabled connections across neighborhoods and social classes that would not otherwise exist. Teens dressed in hip hop signifiers would spot each other in public spaces and strike up conversations. The inherited magazines, copied tapes, and knowledge acquired from friends and family sojourning in Europe were shared with new acquaintances without such connections.

As in elsewhere on the continent, the first generation of musicians often began their acculturation into the hip hop arts as dancers before moving into emceeing or deejaying (Appert 2017: 17; Shipley 2013: 60). Artists from Fes, Salé, and Casablanca explained in interviews that their earliest experiences were imitating dances they had seen with their friends. Several spent multiple years dancing with friends before moving into other art forms. Amine Snoop, who opens this chapter, encountered "the Smurf" as early as 1985 (p.c., August 2, 2010). The men of the Fez group Syndi-K recalled beginning to dance in 1993 or 1994 (p.c., October 2009). Soultana, who started out by practicing dancing with a crew of young men and one other young woman between 1997 and 2000, remembered "waiting until after midnight so we could go and practice" in front of Café Safir (p.c., July 2015, August 2022). Others recall seeking out the smooth floors at the Autohall and elsewhere in Casablanca. The emcee Masta Flow, who was already an experienced group performer by the time his quartet Casa Crew was founded in 1998, echoed others' memories of attempting Michael Jackson choreography before beginning to imitate b-boys. An injury ended his dance career and led him to start writing rhymes (interview, June 8, 2010).

While students of hip hop learned from newly imported media and each other, the music and fashions were acceptable in few public places in the 1990s. To my knowledge, only Casablanca had any commercial infrastructure that supported hip hop at this time. Morocco's free-trade agreement with the EU dates to 1996 (Gilson-Miller 2013: 208) and may have impacted deejays' ability to purchase the music they played at La Cage and Club 84, two sites frequently mentioned as central for hip hop fans in the 1990s. By 1996, La Cage held all-ages sessions from 3 to 8 p.m., when no alcohol was served and two Moroccan deejays played American hip hop. Writing in 2004, DJ Key can still recall the first names of the emcees who impressed the youths at both clubs: "MC Youss . . . Abdelghani and Naïm . . . were the leaders of that era, with their *Beat Street* and their Adidas sneakers . . . they showed up every weekend . . . rapping on instrumentals like 'Feel Me Flow' by Naughty by Nature or 'Ain't New to This' by Ice T" (2004: 12).

Casablancans in their thirties and forties remember La Cage as home to a golden age of youthful experimentation. "It was like a *madrasa*, like an *école*," recalled Hisham Sajir, a professional dance teacher who frequented La Cage starting in 1997. "For everyone who came there, it was the place to meet and raise your level and listen to the hip hop you loved. . . . It was the only place where the deejay could play a whole set of hip hop" (interview, Casablanca–DC, August 9, 2022). Barry, an emcee and singer, called it "my best school," where he learned hip hop arts and some English (p.c., October 21, 2009).[8]

Pioneers from Casablanca formed relationships at La Cage that influence their work to this day. Dancers competed in battles there before the first municipally funded cyphers opened in a *dar al-chabab* (youth house) in downtown Casablanca in 1999 (interview, Hicham Abkari, June 24, 2010; Cestor 2008; interview, Hisham Sajir, August 19, 2022). Young people who would go on to become members of leading groups, or skilled in deejaying, videography, recording, and other capacities, built a network they would draw upon into the 2010s. When the club closed in 2002 to make way for redevelopment of the Casa Port train station and marina, practitioners lost their earliest hip hop institution, as well as the site of some cherished memories.[9] The building itself was demolished in 2006, two years before work began on the new train station (*LaVieÉco* 2008). Both the train station and the marina "mega-project" were made possible by policy changes required by Morocco's structural adjustment program, in which the state sought out foreign direct investment, often through agencies created especially for the purpose (*LaVieÉco* 2008, Barthel and Planel 2010).

While Casablanca's public and commercial infrastructure allowed some emerging artists to move between neighborhoods to find each other, youths in Morocco's other major cities were also experimenting with hip hop culture. Often, the earliest practitioners in each city did not know much about their fellow hip hop fans in other cities or even other neighborhoods.[10] Aspiring emcees began by reciting American and French rhymes from their favorite artists, then attempting their own in those languages. Today, the duo Double A from Salé is generally accepted to have released the first album in Derija, in 1996. However, youths in many cities began to record rhymes in Derija in the same years. By the late 1990s, most emcees were working in Derija, while some of the best-known first-generation groups from multiple cities—including H-Kayne from Meknes (established in 1996); Fez City Clan (established in 2000); and Casablanca's Bizz2Risk—included emcees of diverse backgrounds who specialized in French.

By the end of King Hassan II's reign in 1999, Moroccans had lived with decades of surveillance, silencing, and self-censorship. Direct involvement in electoral politics was understood as pointless at best. Rahma Bourquia and her colleagues write of the university students they surveyed in the 1990s: "Political action inspires among our youths . . . fear; it is synonymous with a lack of interest and a discredited political class who meets with derision. In this sense, the Moroccan youths of the 1990s are very different from the youths of the 1960s and '70s" (Bourquia et al. 2000: 16). Fadoua Loudiy explains, "The past has been a 'foreign land' for most Moroccans for a long time, because of both fear and a blackout on information. Prior to the creation of the IER [Equity and Reconciliation Commission, in 2003], to speak of the past was to be political and to be political was synonymous with subversion, making one a potential victim of state violence" (2014: 7).

When Hassan II's son King Mohamed VI ascended the throne, he made a series of gestures toward further change. Among the most important was the firing of Minister of the Interior Driss Basri, who was understood as the "symbol of state secrecy and oppression under Hassan II" as well as its chief perpetrator (Gilson-Miller 2013: 222). Basri's removal led many to hope for a decisive break with the former surveillance state. Taken together with other moves, such as the return of political exiles, the appearance of enhanced press freedoms, and the creation of a royal consultative council on human rights, Mohamed VI's leadership seemed to signal a new commitment to Moroccans' economic and political freedom in the 2000s (Zerhouni 2004: 68). This climate influenced the creation of new institutions for hip hop and popular musics starting in 1999.

In the early 2000s, as a result of events and choices that I detail more thoroughly in chapters 3 and 4, state and private sponsorship provided sudden new levels of support for hip hop performance. This occurred over the same period that highly visible forms of foreign direct investment and public-private partnerships began to reshape Moroccan cities according to whether they were envisioned as centers of commerce or of tourism (Barthel and Planel 2010; Bogaert 2012; Strava 2018). Artists' sounds and bodies frequently accompanied the public introduction of what Koen Bogaert, following Neil Brenner, calls "new state spaces," locations "seen to exemplify Morocco's openness to global capital," marking what kinds of citizens were understood as the proper beneficiaries of those spaces (2012: 256).

Competitions and festivals of all sizes, in which hip hop practitioners could perform and perfect their craft, emerged in the early 2000s. In part because of these events, which suddenly made small, dedicated networks of people seem highly visible to outsiders, Morocco's press produced a flurry of pieces on the new hip hop and popular music scenes.

Their authors, often members of those scenes, immediately pointed to the suppression of the public sphere under Hassan II. "One only has to listen to understand that after thirty years' absence, a generation of artists is born. Finally!" exclaimed Chadwane Bensalmia and Ahmed Benchemsi in the liberal weekly *TelQuel*, of which Benchemsi would later serve as editor (Benchemsi 2006). They quote Awdellil ("night horse"), an early, celebrated emcee who continues to be anonymous, on the role of hip hop: "Our society has a great need to express itself and has not really had this in the artistic productions currently circulating in our country" (Benchemsi 2006). A roundtable published in the daily *Libération* declared that "these young people are the reflection of a youth who . . . reclaims its right to speak and to freedom of expression" (Alaoui et al. 2007).[11]

However, the intense media attention to hip hop did not indicate a wide acceptance of the music. I vividly recall sitting in a friend's home in Fez, trying to convince a musician near my own age that hip hop was worth studying. "Some people study biology, geology, physics . . . but hip hop music?" he asked, his barely visible smile conveying skepticism rather than humor (June 5, 2010). Reda Allali, a journalist and member of the rock band Hoba Hoba Spirit, cited a then-recent television program where Abdelkrim Berchid, a former official of the ministry of culture, declared, "'Rap is a stolen music, it doesn't belong to us. It's like the contraband products that enter [the country] via Ceuta: they are dangerous for the consumer. What is the government doing to fight against this?'" Allali notes, wryly, that "he spoke in the name of one of the two principal Moroccan artists' unions" (2006).

In this climate, when journalists counter-framed hip hop musicians as inheritors of Nass el-Ghiwane, they not only argued for the authenticity of their music, but they counteracted the anti-Black stereotypes that underpinned reactionary responses to hip hop. As one writer insisted, "Thirty years after the appearance of Nass el-Ghiwane, the Moroccan music scene is witnessing a revolution. Young people think hip hop is about ideas and aspirations as much as it is about art. Most rap and hip hop artists assert that their message condemns violence and calls for peace, optimism, love of life and the bold expression of youth issues" (Belhaj 2008).

As first-generation artists described in statements and songs, teenagers wearing hip hop fashions or practicing in the street with their friends were subject to suspicion from the police throughout the 1990s.[12] Relating artists and their music to Nass el-Ghiwane offered a form of protection from rhetorical and material violence. The ultimate support for this framing came from Nass el-Ghiwane's singer and spokesperson, ʿOmar Es-Sayed, who told his interviewers in the documentary *Casanayda!* that hip hop and other Western-identified musicians "are our children" (Belyazid and Mettour 2007). In mobilizing the memory and meaning of Nass el-Ghiwane, journalists and commentators positioned the hip hop arts in an ongoing debate about changes to youth culture and the social fabric wrought by economic neoliberalization.

LISTENING FOR AMBIGUITY: THE USES OF NASS EL-GHIWANE

The widely held belief that Nass el-Ghiwane's lyrics were consistently critical of the repressive government of the 1970s is sustained by their vagueness. The lyrics' proverbs, allusions, outdated vocabulary, and elaborate imagery celebrated the power of Moroccan traditions, allowed them to avoid censorship, and promoted speculation about their political meanings all at the same time. In the early to mid-1970s, when adult literacy was low, oral transmission was not simply an elaboration of or alternative to the state-owned TV and radio stations; it was a crucial source of information. In this context, Nass el-Ghiwane's lyrics were interpreted as an alternative form of media, one that took positions state news would not allow (Zoulef and Dernouny 1980: 14).

The early hit "Es-Ṣiniyya (The Tea Tray)" is frequently cited as evidence that the band buried oppositional intent well below the surface of their work. In lines that recall the melodic contours of ʿaita and the responsorial singing of the ʿAissawa Sufi brotherhood, the lead singer personifies his empty tea glass (Zoulef and Dernouny 1980: 17). Over the course of the opening verses, the glass might be understood as the nation-state ("Where are the people of good intentions who [once] gathered around you?") or the singer himself ("Where is my neighborhood and my people? . . . Why is my glass still alone?").[13]

Asserting a unified interpretation, Philip Schuyler explains that "when the singer demanded to know why his glass had not been filled, listeners understood that he was accusing the king of monopolizing rights and material goods in the country" (1993: 292n5).[14] Others recall that the band encouraged resistant readings of their songs through performance practice (Muhanna 2003: 146). In films, concert recordings, and my own concertgoing experiences, audiences frequently chant or sing along with the lyrics heard as most significant, sometimes overriding the vocalists with joyous sarcasm and chaotic force.

However, one can just as easily focus on the way "Es-Ṣiniyya" evokes the disorientation and isolation of the migrant experience. Without his friends and family, the singer's sense of self and place, his lived experiences of his roots, are also lost to him.[15] ʿOmar Es Sayed, the oldest performing member of the group and the band's de facto spokesperson, consistently refuses narrow interpretations of their repertoire. "Despite what you say, I don't think the average listener thought of us as a political group," he told Elias Muhanna in 2003. "They were songs of protest, sure, but they were more than merely political" (Muhanna 2003: 144–46). Instead, he emphasizes that "Es-Ṣiniyya" and other songs seek to transcend their political moment, asking listeners to consider what has been lost over generations of forced migration to cities (Muhanna 2003: 146).

Audience interpretations demonstrate how important it is, for many Moroccans, to remember that era's political repression and forms of critique in certain ways. When listeners who were born after Nass el-Ghiwane's debut—or its first three decades—sing their belief in the band's lyrical subversion back to the stage during concerts, it is the audience who carries narratives of past resistance into the present. They perform what Brahim El Guabli calls "other-archives," "cultural production that . . . encompass[es] all forms of sources that provide access to uncomfortable histories, which lie outside the purview of classical official archives" (2022: 209).[16]

The multiple meanings in Nass el-Ghiwane's repertoire stem from skillful use of Derija. At every opportunity, Es-Sayed stresses the beauty and potential of Derija, its potential latent in practices and places understood as belonging to Morocco's past. In one interview with the linguist Dominique Caubet, he focused on the idea that Derija was more elevated than many believed: "The Derija that we had was powerful and had 'imagery' in it . . . not some superficial Derija . . . and this Derija I find in *melḥun* and I find it in the *zawaya* and I find it in the south" (Caubet 1999: 122).[17]

For Es-Sayed, this power comes from Moroccans' rural ancestors and must be preserved: "Our parents spoke in a . . . vernacular that was very poetic. It was creative and complicated, and they had learned it from their parents. That language is almost seductive in its descriptiveness" (Muhanna 2003: 143). For language full of "imagery" to have an effect, listeners must be well versed in its interpretation. Nass el-Ghiwane's practice of sustaining deliberate ambiguity, a context-based skill that many perceived as resisting state repression, was framed by Es-Sayed as a piece of Derija-speaking Moroccans' culture under threat of disappearance along with the proverbs and references themselves.

To this day, musicians and practitioners speak admiringly of the ways that Moroccan Derija can contain multiple meanings at once. The lead singer of the punk band Haoussa emphasized its orality, telling his interviewers that "[the Derija] dialect is good . . . the same sentence, you hear it from two different people, and you'll get two different understandings" (quoted in Kiwan 2014: 985). Hicham Bahou, cofounder and current head of the Boulevard Festival, grew up speaking Tamazight as his first language. He recalled that Nass el-Ghiwane, who performed in Derija, "meant nothing to me" until he matured as a Derija speaker. For his parents' generation, however, the band's use of archaic vocabulary and allusions was meaningful precisely because of its multiplicity. "Their parents—our parents—to them it was perfectly clear. There was a layer and another layer and they were clear" (p.c., July 2, 2018).

Artists' reflections on the creativity and possibility that Derija affords mirror the value placed on ambiguity in everyday social interactions. Generations of Moroccanist ethnographers have been fascinated by the productive roles that ambiguous statements and actions play in ordinary Moroccans' public and private lives, as well as in its most powerful institutions (e.g., Hammoudi 1997; Rosen 1984; Kapchan 1996; Carey 2012). From the 1960s to the '90s, independent journals were forced to calculate how much critique and how many subscriptions would lead to censorship (Bennani 2006). Today, media scholars consider the relationship between the public and private sectors, where the state has wide authority over content, competes with privately owned TV and radio, and uses legal and social tactics to intimidate journalists, to be "ambivalent," "conflicted," "incoherent," or "contradictory" (Zaid 2017; El-Issawi 2016).

"Listening," here, indicates a literal description of an activity, a metaphor for analyzing information from a variety of sources, and, in a broad sense, a technique for deciding what constitutes the interesting and the knowable. Attitudes toward listening are shaped by hearing and reciting religious texts, but also historic and current forms of news media. The vast majority of Moroccans' media consumption comes via TV, radio, and internet video. Sound and speech, in place of or supplemented by text, continue to be the predominant ways that most Moroccans get their news coverage (Sonay 2017: 419).

In historic and current contexts, maintaining ambiguity is both a vital skill and a source of pleasure. Many different forms of expression, from music to newspaper editorials, proverbs to Facebook comments, promote listening for potential meanings in multiple registers. Hip hop artists, like other musicians, exploit this practice for a variety of reasons. In her video for "B.W.B. (Brani Wst Bladi) [Outsider in My Country]" (2020), the Casablancan emcee Tendresse the One alternates between two characters rapping the same text. One presents as wealthy and successful, the other as impoverished and suffering. Her rhymes on the lack of honesty and integrity in society could be aimed at individuals, an entire citizenry, or both. Performing hip hop conventions through one character and visualizing a mainstream Moroccan morality through the other, Tendresse not only asserts cross-class solidarity but invites the viewer to consider how their interpretations change as the scene flips (Almeida 2023: 452).

Katharina Schmoll argues that women in the Islamist Justice and Development Party conceptualize "listening" to a wide variety of audio and visual news sources—from party-identified newspapers to Facebook comments—as simultaneously an obligation, a right, and a source of pride. "Where listening as a right is restricted, assembling valuable civic knowledge, for instance, through media reception, becomes a major task" concludes Schmoll (2020: 5–6). Schmoll's interlocutors stressed the time and skill it takes to arrive at one's own point of view informed by listening to others. They also framed their listening as labor on behalf of and with others, explaining that "listening served as an invitation for fellow citizens to enter into dialogue and thus become empowered active citizens" (Schmoll 2020: 13).

The women Schmoll interviewed were generally unlike my interlocutors in their commitment to Islamist forms of governance. However, their belief in the power and agency of the listening subject, as well as their techniques for overcoming disinformation, resonate with the ways hip hop artists and fans of my acquaintance practiced listening to each other and to broader public debates. Adept at reading and listening through the lines of musical performances or recordings, news, and social media, my interlocutors frequently listened for more information than I realized was available in everyday situations. For example, when an emcee I knew was passed over for a teaching gig, he took it as both a referendum on his popularity and as assurance that the person hiring would simply book a friend for the position. When I declined social invitations, my stated reasons were almost never accepted at face value. My interlocutors were more likely to work from locally relevant assumptions, speculating about what I was doing instead and with whom, and to proceed from their conclusions rather than from my words (e.g., Carey 2012).[18] Whether the context was song lyrics, a newscast, or a friend's narrative, listening required critical reasoning.

CRAFTING AND CHALLENGING AMBIGUITY: HIP HOP ARTISTS' INHERITANCE

Hip hop artists' work has both reflected and heightened characteristic forms of ambiguity. As the pioneers of Moroccan hip hop refined their local and national norms over the 1990s and 2000s, audiences experienced their speech as unprecedentedly direct. In 2004, the prominent journalist Driss Ksikes proclaimed of hip hop artists, "Cultural globalization . . . combined with the need to approach more concretely their tangible, raw, Moroccan reality, has given birth to the pioneers of 'truth-speaking' in Morocco" (Ksikes et al. 2004). Ksikes compared the emcees he cited directly to Nass el-Ghiwane, noting that they were "no longer detoured through metaphor in order to speak taboos, but no longer the will to revolt, either" (Ksikes et al. 2004).

Emcees continue to use time-honored strategies of deflection and inference in their work. In many hip hop songs, as in the most celebrated of Nass el-Ghiwane's lyrics, emcees critique without naming their targets. They reference allusions, proverbs, and other oral tradition to authenticate their arguments; develop metaphors, imagery, and wordplay to illustrate their critiques; and represent dissent through the figure of the other. In this section and the next chapter, I show that practitioners combine values from both their Moroccan predecessors and their adopted musical culture. Even as practitioners enjoy playing with aesthetic and rhetorical ambiguity in their music and lyrics, they nonetheless strive for overarching narrative and moral clarity. As in Amine Snoop's recollections at the beginning of this chapter, artists often cite or allude to Nass el-Ghiwane itself as they use these tactics (Salois 2014).

Drawing as much from local models of testimony as from influential first-person hip hop narratives, Muslim's "Machi Ana Li Khtart (I Didn't Choose This)" (2010) uses sonic and lyrical contrasts and ambiguities to create a sympathetic portrait of an outcast. Like other examples in which hip hop artists portray people on the margins of Moroccan society, Muslim asks listeners to imagine these figures in new ways while retaining a firm moral viewpoint.

To contextualize the close reading of "Machi Ana" that follows, I begin here with the first time I saw Muslim live. In November 2009, I attended a benefit concert he headlined at Dar al-Kabira, an orphanage on the outskirts of the small city of Kenitra. I was already well aware of Muslim's reputation as an underground artist. He had announced his departure from popular music in 2008, citing concerns that it was inconsistent with his religious beliefs. His reversal led to feverish anticipation of his 2010 comeback album, on which he toured in late 2009.

Before and after his much-discussed break, Muslim's fidelity to his aesthetic, political, and moral positions rendered legible his use of musical and vocal indices from US gangsta rap. First-generation hip hop artists with whom I worked often mentioned stereotypical attributes of gangsta rap, dismissing them as unconnected to Moroccan realities and inappropriate for Moroccan sensibilities. But with his repertoire of songs that rejected poverty, powerlessness, and inequality as morally wrong, Muslim's musical and onstage persona projected fierce commitment to his fans' concerns. Where other people might be mocked for splicing their own verses into Tupac's "All Eyez on Me" (retitled "All Eyez on Me feat. Tupac" [2005]), Muslim was understood by his fans as paying homage and professing genuine convictions.

Knowing this reputation helped me interpret my experience at Dar al-Kabira that evening. The orphanage cared for children of all ages, some of whom had experienced homelessness before arriving. The long, whitewashed building surrounded by an empty yard and a low wall sat at the edge of an industrial section of Kenitra, sandwiched between factories and facing newly built villas across the street. Though even the youngest residents attended the show, most of the crowd filling the courtyard in front of the temporary stage were boys and young men from Kenitra itself. Each had paid forty dirhams to enter—at that time an unusual requirement for live hip hop. Dar al-Kabira's main costs for the event appeared to be renting the stage, lights, and sound equipment, and paying the numerous private security guards who surrounded the stage.

Muslim's set that night was preceded by two local acts and a third from Kachela Records, his independent label in Tangier. During the first performance, I noticed groups in the crowd sending scouts to catch glimpses of the artists. Two or three boys would run back and forth from the back door of Dar al-Kabira to their friends in the courtyard, relaying anything they had seen. When an emcee passed by inside the building, a tight semicircle would materialize around the door or window as young men jostled for a better view. A ripple of excitement spread through the whole audience when Muslim and his colleagues finally emerged from the building, turning almost everyone's gaze away from the local rapper mid-song. The third act, who also functioned as hype men once Muslim took the stage, wore T-shirts with the logo for Muslim's new album, *al-Tamarroud Vol. 1: al-Rissala* (The Rebellion Vol. 1: The Message). Though I was a head taller than much of the audience, I struggled to get a good look as the artists carved a path through the courtyard, since they were surrounded by private security with raised batons. One guard guided a German Shepherd on a short leash.

Rows of young children from Dar al-Kabira, wearing matching neon yellow vests with the orphanage's logo, stood just in front of the stage. The Dar's director introduced me to those nearby as she ushered me into the VIP section. Behind me, the young men closest to the metal fence separating us from the rest of the audience knew every word of Muslim's set. When the power went out two songs in, the crowd made a game out of the wait, chanting titles of songs. Some minutes later, a light came back on in the Dar, and the cheering behind me was so gleeful that I wondered whether the moment was planned to hype up the crowd.

Near the end of his set, Muslim launched into the lead single "A.K.A. Moutamarred (A.K.A. Rebel)" from his forthcoming album. The song begins with a fiercely staccato chorus, delivered twice in Muslim's gravelly voice:

> Muslim is one of the people
> My rap is a revolution, not just a game
> North, south, east, west
> 'Bring the glory or get out of the way' always in [my] heart[19]

The introduction to "A.K.A. Moutamarred" is built for mass participation: a two-measure minor arpeggio in straight eighth notes forms the key building block of the eight-measure cycle under both the verses and chorus. The rapped chorus is rhythmically simple and repetitive, with clear stresses on the 1 and 3 of each measure balanced by the backbeat. Many in the audience that night knew the chorus and launched into the song as energetically as Muslim himself. Some rapped along with the verses, though the song had been released less than two months prior.

From the first lines, Muslim reassured his fans about his return to hip hop and his steadfast principles, invoking "the people" and the role hip hop artists occupied, or should occupy, toward them. As he raps in the first verse, "When I started I knew rap wasn't a game / I brought myself to look out for the people / I brought myself to be responsible for the generation."[20] These sentiments were echoed throughout his album as he delved into related topics, such as on "Hob al-Watan (Love of the Homeland [or Patriotism])," which opens with the declaration, "My country gave me nothing, yet it wants my love / And one-sided love leads only to rejection" (Almeida 2017: 96). Throughout his work and his concert, Muslim returned to his message—that as citizens have responsibilities to each other, so does the state to them; that as Muslims should look out for each other, so should the state.

As the crowd filed out at the end of the evening, I got into a conversation with a young man who had been standing behind me. *Muslim is your favorite rapper?* I asked. *Yes!* He shouted over the chatter. *He is the best rapper in Morocco*, he asserted. *He speaks the truth about our problems.*

But other rappers talk about politics, too, I countered. He seemed to know where I was headed. *Yes, others talk*, he said, *but they don't always tell the truth. Or they talk about real problems, but they also want money. Muslim is an underground rapper—he doesn't want money*, said the young man, waving his arm toward the Dar.[21]

In 2009, Muslim's stylistic and lyrical trademarks were still understood as underground despite his wide popularity. Events like this benefit concert drew a dedicated fan base, and he earned capital he could spend on situations like that described in the introduction of this book. Muslim's frequent insistence that rap music was more than entertainment—more than "a game"—and his direct claim of responsibility to the community were heard as both morally upright and as a rebuke of the state that had withdrawn from or delegated its obligations to citizens. In this framework, young people must have a leader who is "responsible for the generation." They are as much in need of moral guidance as they are material support, and, indeed, these are sometimes two sides of the same coin. In the context of the monarchy's patriarchal relationship to the nation, in which the king is simultaneously the political head and the leader of the nation's Muslims, claiming one is responsible indicates a powerful but safely veiled critique.

With this experience and others in mind, I hear many continuities in "Machi Ana li Khtart," which appeared on the same 2010 album as "A.K.A. Moutamarred." On the surface a bleak first-person rant from a gangster, it uses some of the tactics inherited from the previous generation of musicians and activists to very different ends. The first sound we hear in "Machi Ana" is a minor arpeggio, breathlessly unfolding itself into empty space, outlining the same harmonies again and again. Voiced by what sounds like a tinny electric piano, the pattern immediately groups the measure into two sets of sixteenth notes. Each arpeggio peaks on the second and fourth beats of the measure, foreshadowing the snare that will sound at those moments and creating a wave-like action that raises one's heart rate and speeds one's breathing. Four measures into this foreboding environment, Muslim intones the title of the song as a pickup to the fifth measure, dropping *khtart* ("choose") on beat 1 and underscoring it with the deep buzz of the song's bass. The phrase's echoes fade behind the arpeggio, and we are suspended for a few measures, anticipating the percussion's entry, listening to the distance between the highest ranges of the piano and the lowest of the increasingly active bass line.

From the moment Muslim speaks, his voice is double-tracked; the gruff timbre and micro-discrepancies in his delivery create a thick spoken texture. The opening verse shifts the rhythm of the phrase *machi ana li khtart* so that the *chi* of *machi* lands on the first beat of the first measure and *khtart* lands on the second, with the snare drum behind it.[22] Then, he leaves a full beat of silence in the middle of the measure before spitting with rising intensity, cresting on the one of the next bar and placing the third line—"It just happened to me"—in the same place as the first. His short phrases imitate at an offset the pace and shape of the arpeggio underneath his voice, giving the impression of someone blurting out his feelings after a long silence. Throughout the song, Muslim uses these overlapping densities of sound, syllable, and meaning to illustrate an unrelenting, confessional urgency.

Like an opera character whose aria portrays her most despairing moment, Muslim plunges the listener into his character's thoughts without explanation, relying on the backing track and his flow to convey a frenzied emotional state. Only a few lines in the first verse refer to how the character became a homeless criminal. "Brother I am not convinced / that I am human, I was created for life on the streets," he cries. "You don't know why I left for this path, my sister, and why it was necessary / They were my reasons, parents and poverty and everyone." This phrase only hints at the trauma the character may have endured before leaving (or being forced to leave) home. Most Moroccan listeners have some awareness— some more intimately than others—of the depth of poverty in major cities, as well as the incidence of untreated physical and mental illness across incomes (Hajer 2015).[23] While the "sister" in this line needs a few words of explanation, implicitly we listeners, by contrast, can picture the character's profound alienation.

The next two verses heighten both the character's unstable psychology and his artistry. The second verse increases rhythmic interest, running poetic lines over measure lines and creating a sense of unbalance with dense interior rhymes. Because many Arabic words that serve the same function have the same vowel patterns, emcees often ensure end-rhymes by structuring each line in parallel ways. Muslim uses this device in the first portion of his second verse:

> The streets are crazy (*majnouna*)
> They taught me how to survive through a prison mentality (*mesjouna*)
> And how to make people fear me so they respect us (*yhtirmouna*)
> They taught me to reject the world and I couldn't reject us (*nakhouna*)
> The streets are cursed (*mela ʿouna*)[24]

"The streets are cursed" then serves as both the ending of one thought and the beginning of another in the next four-bar section of the verse. Throughout the second verse, interior rhymes connect one idea to the next, as in the pair "I wish I was locked up (*mahbous*), but even if I give Satan (*Iblis*) my hand he would kiss it (*ghaybous*) / and the police (*bouliss*) are always at your service (*sirfis*)." "Locked up" (*mahbous*) and "kiss it" (*ghaybous*) land on the first beats of their measures; in between, *Iblis* rhymes with the next measure's interior word, *bouliss*. The measure is neatly concluded with a sardonic end-rhyme on "service." These are some of the few loan words in the song, heightening the mocking effect of Muslim's delivery.

The final lines of the third verse return our attention to the conceit of the song—that Muslim is sympathetically narrating a character while retaining a clear moral position on the story—through an extended metaphor.

> I see bullets coming at my chest and my heart is pierced
> Even death is determined
> And I knew that a book has been written
> And it was me who chose the style

Muslim uses the word *qasida* (قاصدة) before "my chest," conveying that the bullets are destined for him. (The root of this word can also give "purpose" or "goal.") Pronounced in nearly the same way, *qasida* (قصيدة) is an ancient poetic form that closes every line with the same rhyme, just as these four lines do. In the next line, one would typically say that death is "written," but Muslim finds another rhyme here in "determined" (*meḥsoub*) to give the same sense of inevitability. Finally, we arrive at the metaphor prepared by the related meanings shading the previous lines. Muslim's character alludes to the widely shared idea that one's life is *mektoub*, "written," in the sense that it is preordained by God. In a twist we are not that surprised to hear, his character stops defending or self-aggrandizing at the moment of his death; it was, in fact, he who made his choices, despite the hand he was dealt.

The three verses of "Machi Ana li Khtart" depict a character's mental and emotional responses to the trauma of being surplus to society. The sonic and poetic contrast of the chorus, however, adds a new layer to this character study. The chorus moves just as quickly as the rest of the text, but it is sung rather than rapped. It uses easily intelligible terms shared with Modern Standard Arabic, elevating the text and ensuring non-Moroccan Arabic speakers will understand some part of the song. And instead of continuing the first-person narrative, it places the character in a reflective moment:

> What value has a rose when it withers?
> What value has the ground without a mountain?
> What value has the Sahara without sand?
> What value has the bee without honey?
> . . .
> Even if the rose grew up in the garden
> You will die cold among the thorns

The first six lines of the chorus ask "what value" or "what worth" (*shnou qimt?*) each object could have without a purpose or a context to which it belongs.[25] Muslim's character asks himself, and Muslim asks us, what is the point of life as an outcast from human society? The end of the chorus returns to the character's perspective on that society, serving as a transition back to the verses and a moral to the story.

The first-person narrator in "Machi Ana" is an antihero in the tradition of iconic US tracks like Mobb Deep's "Shook Ones Pt II" (1995) or Geto Boys' "Mind Playin' Tricks on Me" (1991). He never loses sight of the pain and injury he has caused, and his regret makes him long for death, even as he describes the cruelty of others. Muslim's ordering of the story, his musical semiotics of panic and dread, and his public persona contribute to the song's reception as an unmistakable morality tale. At the same time, listeners are well prepared to hear descriptions of poverty and resentment as indictments of society's and the state's neglect. When the character finally admits that "it was me who chose the style" of his life and death, he takes more responsibility than the invisible institutions shaping the world he ran from and the underworld he encountered on the streets. In "Machi Ana," Muslim has it both ways—we feel sorry for the narrator but never accept his behavior, much less seek to emulate him. In fact, we can sympathize (not empathize) with the character because he disapproves of his own acts; we share his moral compass and are invited to imagine how easily we could act against what we know to be right.

"Machi Ana li Khtart" and similar songs are regarded as different than the work of Nass el-Ghiwane and their contemporaries in significant ways. Yet hip hop artists inherited from this era musical and poetic techniques that continue to move listeners and advance different kinds of arguments. By recalling the music of marginalized Moroccan groups, Nass el-Ghiwane invoked othered figures, heightening the nostalgia of their lyrics through sonic references to people and places constructed as part of Morocco's past rather than its path toward modernity. Instead of implying dissent through difference, the character speaking in "Machi Ana" embraces difference; he rejects the garden in which roses grow as he is rejected from it. In addition, his choice of electric piano to ground the story reflects Moroccan amateur musicians' transformations of a semiotic tradition derived from Western art and popular musics, often through self-taught techniques, outdated gear, and pirated software. The numbing repetition and anemic timbre of the arpeggios reference not only musical expressions of pathos, but the constraints many face in producing them. One might read the class position of the character through the degree of material access the electric piano indexes.

The nuance and indirection in Nass el-Ghiwane's texts are regarded as both artful and necessary. Muslim's character is quite direct in some places, yet allusive in others. As in "Es-Ṣiniyya," here a single person describes his losses, and during the chorus—a moment of peak expression that can contain multiple potential interpretations—he retreats to metaphor. As Rayya el-Zein notes, Arabophone hip hop frequently articulates the alienated community through the self, framing dissension and critique in "a mode of longing" for reincorporation or unification (2016: 157).[26]

Nass el-Ghiwane's legendary status and aura of protest continue to resonate through the often retold memories of those who experienced the band as groundbreaking in the late 1960s and '70s (e.g., Benjelloun 2010; Al Jazeera 2010). When "Machi Ana" was released, it fit into the interpretive frame of Muslim's album *al-Tamarroud Vol. 1*, as well as the frames audiences already held. Like the young man I spoke to in 2009, many explained to me that Muslim depicted the reality of Moroccan socioeconomic problems in ways they felt others would not. Public understanding of his religious devotion, along with his claimed responsibility to his generation, also factored into his fans' acceptance of Muslim as the conscience of hip hop during the 2000s.

Fans' appreciation for Muslim's consistency—the moral rectitude, passion, and embrace of a masculinist responsibility for the body politic delivered in song after song—demonstrate how perceived sincerity was read and rewarded among a growing community of practitioners. Other artists specialized more in expressions of sarcasm, parody, or dark humor. While these could certainly be received as sincere, they also contain a kind of doubleness in that they require the listener to decode—at least a little—the moral or political statement. This, in turn, produces an in-group knowledge that enhances the experience of listening for some while excluding others.

By contrast, the key aspects of Muslim's performances and reputation appear transparent and righteous, opposed to the strategic position-taking and ambiguity that both scholars and everyday Moroccans identify in their social interactions and arts. Muslim's most ardent fans found this refreshing precisely because it addressed their perceptions of hypocrisy by elders, elites, and other power-holders. Although the opposite of the Nass el-Ghiwane mythos, Muslim's lyricism is celebrated by his fans for similar reasons. In a sense, Muslim was beloved for returning his fans to themselves, much like Nass el-Ghiwane inspiring musicians and audiences to appreciate anew their cultural heritage.

Finally, like Nass el-Ghiwane and its fellow bands, Muslim's hip hop was not at all the most radical cultural or political movement of its moment (e.g., Tolan-Szkilnik 2023). Rather, the singular memorialization of Nass el-Ghiwane, who received the award of Chevalier in the French government's Order of Arts and Letters in 2010, not only crowds out the contributions of other Ghiwanien bands but also public recognition of '60s and '70s leftists. By narrating the band—and implicitly its 1970s audience—as at once progressive, resistant, and unitary, national media celebrate the achievements of the past in order to avoid the present. As one interviewee responded when I mentioned a generational link between hip hop and Nass el-Ghiwane, "Yes, but the subversive ones are dead" (interview, Paris–DC, May 2018). In a similar fashion, Muslim's work, and that of other first-wave artists, is already narrated by fans as a golden era of lyrical quality and authenticity.

In both cases, musical resources from beyond their local, national, or regional identities helped the artists perform a different relationship between the individual and the collective. While Nass el-Ghiwane performed a vision of a diverse nation in the face of oppression, they, or at least ʿOmar Es-Sayed, maintained they were not commenting on the relationship between the state and its subjects, but between the individual and their inheritance. As I argue in the next chapter, hip hop artists rarely draw attention to differences of ethnicity, lineage, or even religion in their performances. Instead, since the emergence of the genre, many have articulated a desire for translocal affiliation to hip hop while asserting the unity of national culture.

THE ANALYTICAL PURCHASE OF AMBIGUITY, OR THE INEVITABILITY OF COMPLICITY

In the introduction to this book, I related how, in 2018, audiences heard Muslim forthrightly defend his alleged decision to accept money to publicly support a state-sponsored music festival that opponents argued exacerbated class inequality. "Machi Ana li Khtart," and the benefit concert I attended in 2009, might appear to depict the upstanding underground rapper before his downfall. However, no great shift occurred in Muslim's public persona between 2009 and 2018. Instead, I argue that the entrepreneurial and moral commitments highlighted in these analyses go together. Intertwined, they express a locally meaningful neoliberal subjectivity cultivated by hip hop practitioners, a subjectivity whose conditions of possibility emerged from the events and memorialization of the 1960s, '70s, and '80s.

The previous generation's nationalism, debates, protests, and popular musics communicated a holistic view of citizens' deserved, if not conferred, rights and privileges. Much like Egyptians' 2011 calls for both "bread and dignity ('aish u karama)" refused to separate economic security from humans' intrinsic worth, postindependence activism responded to colonialist conceptual divisions between the economic, political, and social by stressing the unity of these domains. Whether *Souffles*'s pan-Africanist essays, the 1980s bread riots, the demands of political victims heard by the Equity and Reconciliation Commission in 2003, or unemployed graduates' recurrent demonstrations at Parliament, Moroccans framed recognition, accountability, and material needs as interdependent, seeking each through the others.[27]

Overlapping with this period, top-down neoliberal economic policy has also eroded perceived boundaries between the economic, political, and social from precisely the opposite ideological direction. Yet it is not sufficient to complement top-down neoliberalization by claiming a bottom-up version, as if these are not in a dialectical relationship. I also wish to avoid characterizing the diversely informed ideologies of my interlocutors as revolutionary on the one hand or reactionary on the other. Different incomes, exposures, educations, cultural and religious perspectives, and experiences of state power shaped the different stories my interlocutors told themselves about their economic and social precarity. Yet all recognized inequalities, and experienced feelings of precarity, in relation to forms of power that were reshaped during their lifetimes by neoliberalization.

Cultural neoliberalization, in ways informed by each person's specific circumstances, shaped a narrative about how to respond to inevitable collisions with past and present forms of exclusion. In songs, humor, comments, and behavior, my interlocutors lived their awareness that neoliberalization was not only simultaneously economic and political, but that it preserved—or enhanced—existing inequalities. Across vast regional differences, neoliberalization has enabled reconceptions of success as financial rather than social or ethical, individual rather than communal, to encroach upon prior discourses on what constitutes success and a good life. In this chapter's example, Muslim's entrepreneurship, his way of carving a niche in an emerging national market for hip hop, has always depended on expressing religious fervor and business acumen simultaneously. Recall that his 2010 album was widely anticipated precisely because he cast it as his return to music after exploring the notion that devout Muslims could not make hip hop. Similarly, when Muslim and the emcee Don Bigg were reported to have beef in 2007–9, most practitioners I spoke with stressed the free publicity both received, regardless of their position on whether the beef actually existed or not.[28] In accordance with the notion that ambiguous actions keep one's options open, artists, fans, and colleagues simultaneously appreciated the possibility of sincerity and the market applications of that sincerity.

Not all the artists discussed in the next chapters identify with their faith as explicitly as Muslim does in his songs, but they are nonetheless "moral neoliberals" who try to sensitize their audiences to injustice and suffering in order to encourage what they see as the appropriate relationship between the state, its citizens, and its economy (Meuhlebach 2012). Muslim's religiosity is not somehow absorbed or replaced by the realities of neoliberalization, but articulated to them. Exhorting others to more moral behavior supports, rather than contradicts, choices that maximize one's success or options—even at the expense of others— precisely because those choices can also be ethical, in the sense of being in what one understands as the proper relation to oneself (Foucault 1983: 238).

Actions that allow one to gather wealth, prestige, and opportunity rarely escape relations of complicity with existing power structures. Opposing some effects of those structures while reinforcing their fundamental qualities, as the hip hop artists I knew nearly always found themselves doing, leverages that unavoidable relationship for both potential gain and self-protection. For example, Muslim's invocations of traditional morality allow him to critique the state's treatment of the poor in ways that are both more impactful and less susceptible to censorship. At the same time, because political and religious leadership are united in the person of the king, arguing from moral authority ultimately reinforces the monarchy's authority. Since "Machi Ana li Khtart" expresses disappointment with everyone— the state that left the narrator in poverty, the everyday people who fear or ignore the degraded poor, and the narrator himself—the song places the state's and the citizens' responsibilities on the same rhetorical plane. In effect, Muslim points to complicity in a way that, paradoxically, decreases the perceived culpability of the state.

This chapter has attempted to sketch the cultural resources hip hop practitioners bring to their embrace of the transnational hip hop tradition and to offer a framework through which to think about artists' choices in the next chapters. Ambiguous actions, including listening, are not only strategic or pleasing, but necessary—perhaps for me as much as for Moroccans who must contend with the daily effects of authoritarianism. The pervasiveness and productivity of ambiguity as both sincere and complicit complicates my desire to elevate, much less fix, a single reading of any of the examples in this book. When, as Louise Meintjes describes, "ambiguity that appears to be a problem analytically is in fact the point politically," my role as a scholar making ethnographically grounded arguments is tested in productive ways (2017: 119). When I trace, and then retreat from, the crafted polysemy of musical compositions and performances in order to focus readers' attention on my own concerns and those of current scholarship, I am making what we characterize as the signal intellectual contributions of the researcher—and unavoidably linking my interlocutors and their work to some discursive relationship to existing depictions of Arab and/or Muslim difference. Whether that is a relationship of similarity or contestation may not change the effects, since, like the relations of complicity throughout this book, resistance and acquiescence are both forms of participation that recenter an unjust system. It is our desire—mine, my Moroccan interlocutors', and hip hop scholars'—for more that keeps the political purchase of both hip hop and ethnography alive.

2

———

A Moral Institution

Forming and Performing Hip Hop in the 2000s

Late one night in August 2015, I sat on a friend's balcony with a small group of hip hop listeners and aspiring artists. Conversations ebbed and flowed as we sipped tea, smoked cigarettes, listened to music, and scrolled through Facebook. A video was circulating; everyone but me had seen it. In the video, two young Moroccans sat in front of a webcam. We read them as young men posing for the camera in a way my friends saw as inappropriately feminine. Wearing eyeliner and lipstick, they tilted their chins so hair hung over one eye, or swept it back with a toss of their heads. To me, they looked supremely confident and very fragile at the same time.

"They're so stupid," my hostess groaned. It was clear the group assumed the two young people were gay men. Public harassment and violence against allegedly LGBTQ citizens had recently made the local news. As I watched, I felt the young adults in the video were brave and stupid in equal measure.

"This is not Moroccan," said one friend in English, aiming his remarks at me, the only non-Moroccan present.

"I used to think that," said my hostess. Once she met and listened to out gays and lesbians, she told us, she came to see that they were "born this way." Once you learn this, she concluded, you have to accept them, as you must accept everyone created by God.

Her friend agreed, but that was not his point. In the mix of French, English, and Arabic spoken all evening, he responded, "Yes, I didn't used to understand either—that homosexuals, they feel they are women on the inside. This is not their fault. But this is Morocco. They cannot wear these clothes"—he gestured to the video—"and walk in the street like this"—he raised his shoulders and wiggled his hips in his chair. "They can do this in their home. I will respect their privacy. Me,

I don't care. But for me, they have to be normal in public. The public will not accept it."

I sat silently as they debated, worrying about how to bring up the difference between sexual orientation and gender identity. As I rehearsed the phrasing to myself, our hostess sighed aloud. Watching the video over her shoulder a second time, I wondered what the parents and friends of these teens were saying to them at that moment.

"When we want freedom, we want free education—free health care—freedom to talk," my hostess said to me. "We wanted more speech. We didn't want it for this."

My friends didn't see themselves as anti-LGBTQIA. Earlier that day, some had criticized Moroccans' supposedly typical inflexibility around gender roles, relating audiences who reject women emcees to the assumption that men who enjoy feminized activities like cooking are gay. Coming from different educational and economic backgrounds, they collectively distinguished between accepting queer and gender nonconforming individuals, and withholding support for inclusive policy. Regardless of what I personally think of this distinction, my hostess and her friends believed this position maintained or facilitated social harmony. In this context, whether to "be normal" in public space was not about whether individuals have the right to be themselves, but about when individual rights and freedoms must be sublimated to the majority.[1] As my hostess suggested, for her, Moroccans' slowly increasing freedom to say what they think and feel, always won through action rather than passively awarded, came with increasing obligation to the greater good. That greater good, however, presumed the majority's passionate attachment to local forms of heteronormativity.

I thought about this exchange again and again in the months that followed. It came to illuminate how many of my interlocutors understood the individual's relation to the whole, and it invited me to rethink other questions and interactions.

Previously, I noted that hip hop artists inherited a holistic view of the rights and privileges of citizens as encompassing economic, political, and social domains. This chapter builds on artists' insights to explore how key musical texts and performances advance a theory of citizenship. This theory holds that despite authoritarianism, individuals and groups can have power, that their actions do matter. As hip hop practitioners gained competency in their art forms and built sociomusical communities, their texts and performances insisted on a relationship between personal ethics, national policies, and social outcomes. As the vignette above illustrates, however, this moral and affective commitment to efficacy was also exclusionary, hinging on practitioners' definitions of "the public" to whom they addressed their interventions. Why individual practitioners reinforce some conventions of Moroccan identity is, here, less salient than the complicit relations influencing artists to take some categories as natural, irrefutable, or beyond debate.

Throughout the 2000s and into the 2010s, hip hop artists and their fans—who were often the same people, gathering experience and expertise in each other's company—sought to wield influence through the state-market integrations that characterized Morocco's economic neoliberalization. While they typically shared their generations' post–Years of Lead apathy toward traditional democratic participation, these practitioners simultaneously critiqued some effects of state policies and embraced new possibilities opened by state interest in hip hop. At the same time, artists sought to convince their co-citizens of their own potential to change their lives and society.

Over this chapter, I discuss how practitioners use three practices common to both transnational hip hop and late capitalism in general—critique, commodification, and extraction—to build new discourses on citizens' power and capabilities. I frame these as producing "arts of citizenship" in multiple senses: as art that explicitly addresses or models a citizenship ideal; as art that speaks to its audience as a state might to its citizens; and as the state's arts, or techniques, of differential citizenship (Fredericks 2014; Appel 2019). Critique and commodification are not constructed as oppositional terms by me, my interlocutors, or many streams of the transnational hip hop tradition (e.g., Watkins 2004). Instead, they operate recursively, creating marketable material and market participants.

The first section introduces hip hop practitioners' vision of the proper attributes of a responsible citizen. In the second section, I discuss how leading first-generation hip hop artists promoted their idealized mentalities in recordings and performances for their and others' commercial gain. Practitioners borrowed highly visible practices from Morocco's heritage industry, creating popular songs that relied on the same techniques of folkorization and extraction, both to claim a moral position and to craft new forms of influence. While hip hop artists legitimized and were legitimized in the 2000s by "new state spaces," both physical and symbolic, their success in these spaces assisted in placing borders around a reimagined public (Bogaert 2012). The hip hop arts seemed to signify new freedoms on the horizon, yet its artists often upheld norms in service of deeply rooted beliefs about social harmony.

'AQLIYYA: RESPONSIBILITIES TO THE CULTURE

Some of the most visible hip hop artists in the 2000s took on the roles of educators, advocates, and philosophers. As networks of amateur artists grew and experimented in several Moroccan cities, practitioners codified values in emcees' lyrics and exemplified them in their interactions. Songs and conversations frequently focused on 'aqliyya, or mentalité—the "mentalities" or "worldviews" held by fellow citizens that needed to change, and those that ought to replace them.

'Aqliyya (pl. *'aqliyyat*) comes from the word *'aql*, which connotes the mind or intelligence in general. Likewise, the adjective *'aqli* describes someone sharp, quick-witted, or observant. Although several of my interlocutors had advanced degrees, and practitioners and their families often deeply valued education and educators, one does not need a lot of formal schooling to be *'aqli*.

Midcentury anthropologists highlight the ways that *'aql* is qualified through proper behavior, functioning to restrain and legitimize (generally male) public life (Eickelman 1976: 134; Rosen 1984: 31–32).[2] The noun *m'aqul* describes someone who puts their intelligence to respectable, moral use, often in service to their community.[3]

Judgments about *'aqliyya*, as shorthand for an entire group's modes of reasoning, have also policed the fault lines between Moroccan social classes throughout neoliberalization. Anthropologist Nadia Guessous recalls that, "in the 1980s and early 1990s, the occasional appearance of a hijab in high school was generally associated with custom and social conservatism and was folded into a larger dominant discourse about the problem of 'tradition' (*la tradition* or *al-taqalid*) or of *les mentalités* or *al-'aqliyyat*" (2011: 212). Among affluent Casablancans, "al-'aqliyyat" served as a synonym for insufficiently liberal or Western orientations. In 2001, political scientist Saloua Zerhouni interviewed an advisor to the prime minister who argued, "Change means that each Moroccan citizen considers himself or herself as a full actor of change on a daily basis.... We need to have citizens who assume their responsibilities; this requires a change in the mentalities" (2004: 76, 85n52).

From an opposing perspective, activists in the February 20 reform movement agreed that "Morocco needs two revolutions, *'thawra 'iqliya'* ('of the mind') and *thawra siyasiya* ('political')" (Aouragh 2017: 249). In each case, Moroccans with social capital leveraged al-'aqliyyat to critique the nation, framing their structural concerns as judgments of other Moroccans.

My interlocutors similarly focused on developing, opening, or freeing their own and others' *'aqliyya*. In the context of hip hop's transition from fad to officially condoned genre in the early 2000s, practitioners often described their preferred *'aqliyya* through the temperament, values, and work ethic needed to be an "artist" (Ar. *fnan*) rather than a mere entertainer. Those with the correct *'aqliyya* also invested in the future and its possibilities rather than passively accepting their current state. In addition, evocations of *'aqliyya* often reread the preference for ambiguity discussed in the previous chapter. Instead of protecting social harmony by maximizing one's options, my interlocutors were more likely to see ambiguity as promoting mistrust and instability. These three convictions resonated with Moroccans' needs in a neoliberalizing world, and they often converged in musical and everyday performance.

I interviewed the Casablancan emcee Magma shortly after his first year of law school. In a couple years, he explained, he would have his law license. Then, his expertise in contracts would allow him to start a record label. He also planned to earn or raise enough money to renovate his uncle's basement into the label's recording studio and office.

As we conversed with my Anglophone friend Fares, also an emcee, Magma answered questions in halting but correct English. I tried to use Arabic to make him more comfortable. "So in the future you want to have a studio," I summarized in Derija.

"Yeah. It's not a dream," he immediately replied. "It's—it's something I have in my mind. It's a . . ."

"A goal," supplied Fares.

"A goal," Magma confirmed (interview, Casablanca, July 2010).

My use of *fi al-mustaqbal* ("in the future") triggered a deliberate, if gentle, correction. Both Fares and Magma knew he was responding to the implications of the future tense in a typical Derija conversation. Plenty of things could derail his objective, yet Magma wanted to convey his commitment rather than highlight the unknowability of the future. Phrasing his plans in this way also opened him to future critique. In this way, his word choice modeled clarity and accountability.

Like the elites mentioned above, practitioners often revealed their preferred 'aqliyya by discussing or comparing other people. Magma's punchlines show off his erudition and work ethic while claiming a transcendent perspective: "Made my heart into a voicemail box, [put] my blood in the freezer / My mentality is 16:9 in a world at 4:3" ("1956" [2017]).[4] "16:9" refers to the internationally standard, wide-screen, high-definition aspect ratio for TV and film, while "4:3" refers to an earlier standard. Magma claims he can literally see beyond the frame limiting the rest of us, while boasting about the chilly determination this requires.

Magma occupied a similar socioeconomic place in Casablanca as Guessous had a generation before. Yet in my fieldwork, people across a wide spectrum of income, educational attainment, or family wealth used 'aqliyya in this way.[5] Hip hop practitioners' discourse signaled belonging to, and demarcating, the epistemic and aesthetic community they were building.

My deejaying teacher, DJ Sim-H, was a skilled performer and a passionate hip hop fan. Like other artists with whom I worked, he understood himself to be upholding standards of both conduct and taste. His most forceful condemnation came in the story of his breakup with a popular Casablancan group in the late 2000s. He had not heard from the emcees for months when they asked him, out of the blue, to play that evening. "Who calls 'their' deejay the day of the concert?" scoffed Sim-H as he told me this story.

Sim-H refused to perform and, after the event, he learned that an amateur at the concert volunteered to cue songs for their set. "Why did he want to go up [to the stage]?" Sim-H asked me, dripping scorn. "Just for a picture" (June 2010). This assumption served as the moral to his story. Worse than not maintaining relationships, he implied, was the desire to look like an artist without putting in the work to become one.

Sim-H's ideal of an artist, someone who brought his ideal community into being by acting as if his responsibilities to others, to oneself, and to the art form were one and the same, reappeared frequently in discussions of others' behavior. For him, both hypocritical behavior and insufficient knowledge of hip hop music were markers of inauthenticity and infidelity to the art. At times, these collided in the same person. After telling me the story above, Sim-H recommended artists to avoid during my research, as well as those I should seek out. The reasons people belonged in either category blended the aesthetic, the personal, and the professional.

While practitioners sought to influence each others' ʿaqliyyat through judgment and action, they also conceived of themselves as educating their public. Artists often described themselves, to me or in their texts, as teachers, advocates, or revolutionaries. Many recordings address the artist's expectations of Moroccan mentalities through explicit discussion or by confronting listeners with arresting images and analysis.

Don Bigg's "3a9lia (Mentality)" from *Magharba tel Mout* (Moroccan until Death [2006]) marks one of the first times a hip hop song centered the term.[6] In tune with critiques of ambiguous self-presentation, Bigg spends most of the song asserting that he remains true to his own and to hip hop's values despite his recent successes. Whether the people in his life "stood with me since the first day" or "changed on me even though I didn't know why," Bigg insists through both his words and the repetitive structure of his lines that he is the same person he has always been.[7]

Bigg underscores this argument through playful nostalgia. He begins with a winking shoutout to his audience:

> This song goes out to everyone whose mentality is ugly
> I can be [myself] because I'm one of them, you understand?[8]

The beat also indexes hip hop classicism. Throughout, the drum-set rhythm known as "boom-bap" interacts with a minimal triplet-based phrase, in minor thirds, played on an electric organ. Each verse is preceded by a few phrases of scratching on the words "Mgharba tel mout mʿa Bigg men qlbi kharja (Moroccan until death with Bigg, from my heart out [to yours])" by DJ Key, who was at this time one of few deejays in the country capable of this technique. Aimed at a relatively exclusive group of Moroccan fans who could locate these sounds and skills in place and time, Bigg's musical authenticity mirrors his stated personal authenticity. Whether you love or hate Bigg or hip hop's aesthetics, the musicians seem to suggest, they will remain. Read alongside other songs from this album, especially "al-Khouf (Fear)," the strategic deployment of ambiguity reemerges in Bigg's analysis as endemic, infuriating hypocrisy.[9]

Some years later, the self-consciously old-school group L'Bassline enjoyed a reputation for uncompromising lyricism and throwback aesthetics resting on the same commitments demonstrated by DJ Sim-H and Bigg. L'Bassline included four emcees, including Mehdi Lyoubi, the young man I met on Salé's beach in 2010 who performs under the name Mehdi Black Wind (see introduction of this book). With his homemade T-shirt, Lyoubi already held a preservationist outlook on Moroccan hip hop. L'Bassline depicted itself as purifying Moroccan hip hop, sweeping away the trends of the 2000s and beyond.

For example, in "Keep It Real" (2013), Mehdi Black Wind begins, "Genocide to all the slaves, those who make red and green rap." The original line reads, "Génocide l'gʿa lʿabid shab RAP ḥmar w khdar." The rhyming words "red and green" are the colors of the Moroccan flag. However, both words are also homonyms for more cutting terms: "ḥmar (حمار)" is a donkey, someone stupid or mute; "khdar (خدار)" communicates numbness. Mehdi and L'Bassline take direct aim at self-identified patriotic groups such as H-Kayne, which has advertised itself as *rap vert et rouge* ("red and green rap") since the release of its hit "Issawa Style" (2005). Yet the puns' layers suggest that patriotic rap is not simply complacent or trapped, but unoriginal.

Today a respected solo artist, Mehdi Black Wind recently told LaBase that "it's not necessary to use instrumentals from Mobb Deep. However, you must give a little importance to your text. Try to say something about [society's] failures. Connect it at a minimum to the realities of life."[10] Although he defines himself, and is defined by fans, in contrast to the nationalism of H-Kayne and similar groups, Mehdi Black Wind shares with such groups a commitment to educating his listeners.

In their actions, musical choices, and speech, my interlocutors demonstrated how aesthetic and moral dimensions of hip hop authenticity reinforced each other. Across diverse political positions, each performed a sense of responsibility to the art form, the audience, and themselves that forms a key part of Moroccan hip hop pioneers' ʿaqliyyat.

Woman Emcees: Responsibilities to the Nation

Far from being a site of "violence and delinquency," as "the uninitiated" were likely to assume in the 2000s, hip hop performances and their authors promoted personal responsibility as a means toward social harmony (DJ Key 2004: 12). Historically, visible and audible women artists have not been seen as encouraging harmonious relations, but as destabilizing public order (Kapchan 1996). Women hip hop artists deliberately upset deeply rooted boundaries between public and private, social and domestic, exterior and interior, "Western" and "Moroccan." In my late-2000s interviews and in early recordings, when hip hop practitioners often focused on constraints to making music, both men and women emcees responded to disbelief and hostility by emphasizing their resilience and determination to educate listeners. Since 2003, public discourse around hip hop has moved from rejection to acceptance, even celebration, yet women artists face nearly the same expectations and constraints as they did twenty years ago.

The women artists visible during the 2000s and 2010s self-consciously challenged the ʿaqliyyat of their families, fans, and nation. Women performed roles vital to the emerging culture, including as dancers, web designers, graphic designers, arts administrators, marketers, promoters, and managers. However, few women recorded hip hop music during the genre's first decades in Morocco.[11] Family and social pressure, rejection by male colleagues, recordists, or producers, an unwillingness to be in an all-male environment, and a lack of discretionary income or free time were all factors inhibiting women's performance.

From the earliest national and international recognition for Moroccan hip hop, journalists, researchers, and many practitioners regarded women emcees with particular curiosity. The documentary *I Love Hip Hop in Morocco* included Fati Show, a young emcee from the duo Mot de Passe ("password"), who acknowledged that "some say it's shameful for a girl to rap." At the film's climactic concert, filmed in 2004, she is booed by the crowd (Asen and Needleman 2007).

Moroccan media approach women emcees with similar assumptions about women's goals and men's values. Casablancan emcee Tendresse first gained recognition in the 1990s with the group X-Side. In the late 2000s, the Moroccan daily *Libération* asked, "How were you able to join a rap group [with young men]?" She responded with general advice: "One must make her own place . . . they must understand what you want to say. The boys know the street, unlike the girls, who must fight to be able to send their messages" (Alaoui et al. 2007). Tendresse placed the responsibility to overcome low expectations on women while making clear that she saw a present and future with multiple women artists.

Thirteen years later, when interviewed about her new EP *Lagertha*, the first question was nearly identical.[12] Again, Tendresse advised younger artists: "Everyone began somewhere, one must only have courage, and respect oneself before you will be respected" (Aziouzi 2020). As before, Tendresse was asked about her colleagues rather than structures or sounds. As before, she focused on personal responsibility, explaining that women must work by and have faith in themselves. Drawing attention to misogyny as one of the many social ills emcees tackle could be read as criticizing her peers. Instead, Tendresse celebrates women's achievements without naming men's discrimination.

Women emcees have used diverse strategies to appear on hip hop stages. During the late 2000s, multiple groups underscored their notionally equal citizenship by explicitly supporting the current order. The young leader of the group S-Girlz explained to me that their name stood for "*systeme* girls," arguing, "we truly need the system" (December 14, 2009). Bnat Lblad ("girls of the nation") likewise describe themselves in a press release posted to Facebook as "rapping for the nation," "while preaching peace, tolerance, but denouncing violence and debauchery" (June 2010). Male emcees quite often "rap for the nation." Yet, while women who depicted patriotism and moral order together may have overcome some of the general public's reticence, they were also seen by many hip hop devotees as inauthentic.

Tigresse Flow, the first all-women hip hop group in Morocco, was founded in the early 2000s. They won a national competition in 2008 with their song "Maghrebiyya (Moroccan Woman)." In the first verse, Soultana invites listeners to musical solidarity, asking, "Who's still with me? . . . In this song we are together, we arrive [together] through one voice." At the end of her verse, she declares herself a patriotic citizen through, not despite, her actions:

> I'm a Moroccan woman though I reveal myself among men [i.e., am not veiled]
> I'm a Moroccan woman though my clothes are crazy like they say
> I'm a Moroccan woman and I won't forget my country and those who love her
> I'm a Moroccan woman and I won't forget my peace to all her men[13]

Soultana and Tigresse Flow imagine a nation in which diverse cultures and politics are accepted, women take up space in public life, and religious justifications for discrimination have no force. With the final lines of this quote, Soultana also stresses her interior actions, implying that patriotic Moroccan women work on the affective dimension of citizenship for both themselves and "those who love" their country.

Rhythmically, this verse uses patterns that appeal to both hip hop fans and new listeners. Lines five and six use enjambment to continue the poetic line over two bar lines, showing Soultana's ability to keep a complex rhythmic pattern accurate until landing on a downbeat. By contrast, lines seven through ten, quoted above, fall neatly within their measures, using similar rhythms to enhance the parallel construction in the text.

After winning two national competitions in 2008, Soultana claimed on state-run television that the state-funded competition Mawazine Generation withheld the grand prize from Tigresse Flow. According to her, they were denied the advertised studio time and sponsorship because "it was as if they said 'they're only girls'" (Salois 2014). Tigresse Flow did not record an official EP or album, and twenty years into her solo career, Soultana has not yet been able to release her professionally recorded material as an album.

Ten years after this event, an up-and-coming emcee named Krtas Nssa ("woman's bullet") demonstrated the consequences of women's relative invisibility. In an interview with the YouTube channel Street Art, she described the Moroccan hip hop of the 2000s as having "one or two" female artists.[14] This is factually incorrect, but patriarchal narratives and YouTube algorithms make it difficult for even accomplished emcees to form a complete picture. With fewer recordings, documented performances, and space in local narratives, some of the earliest women practitioners have already fallen out of Moroccan hip hop's social and institutional memory (Almeida 2023). The local and national erasure of women hip hop artists has immediate practical effects for newer generations. Male musicians and culture industry personnel could more easily dismiss Krtas Nssa, as she and others describe experiencing, because few women were influential enough to provide meaningful support.

In my own interactions, I heard a variety of objections to the existence of women emcees. Over a decade, listeners of all genders told me they supported women's appearances on stage, or in public life generally, but that women's voices were inappropriate for the musical style. I understood this reaction to be simultaneously sonic and semiotic: if listeners associated the truth-telling and taboo-breaking of the hip hop they loved with male voices, women's timbres and registers would not convey the gravity their own texts demanded. Others explained that they disliked when women attempted to sound like men. Here, again, it was difficult and perhaps unnecessary to disentangle whether the act of rapping or the vocal quality led speakers to perceive these performances as too masculine.

Speakers also wished there were more and better women emcees, but claimed that, for one reason or another, the women available simply weren't ready to perform. Opinions here hinted at the feedback loop double standards create: as young women were held to different expectations than young men, their paths to and through the training grounds of the hip hop network were more difficult at every step. Local, gendered concepts of vocal sound and professionalism invoked strong affective responses in my interlocutors, in which even self-identified feminists doubted that women emcees could ever enjoy the same opportunities and appreciation as men.

During the 2000s and today, women emcees share their peers' concerns while using images, narratives, or moral characterizations understood as feminine. Today, several women have strong followings on Moroccan social media, and a smaller number have recording contracts or significant institutional support. Yet they are still less likely to secure live performances and still more likely to perform for non-Moroccan agencies with developmental or diplomatic missions. Simultaneously celebrated and dismissed, women hip hop musicians have been and continue to be policed across multiple regimes of respectability.

Futurity: Responsibilities to Oneself

The hip hop artists most circulated in the 2000s frequently located the solution to social problems they diagnosed in the self—specifically in individuals' responsibility to invest in themselves. While they described inequalities on a collective level, emcees rarely endorsed collective action (Salois 2014, 2018). Instead, artists envisioned political change stemming from individuals' simultaneous cultivation of intellect and affect. In performed texts and casual conversation, practitioners exhort each other to change their orientation toward change itself, encouraging faith in their abilities, risk-taking, and aspiration. As Soultana once remarked to me in a moment of optimism, "Change yourself first and then see what will change" (February 2018).[15]

Investing in oneself through education, religious commitment, entrepreneurship, or other ways was understood not only as taking care of oneself, but preparing to take care of others. As in "Machi Ana li Khtart," first-person narratives often depict the ʿaqliyyat of self-described loners—cut off from nourishing social ties by choice or by dispossession—as pathological (el Maarouf and Belghazi 2018). By contrast, as Tendresse implies in her interviews, self-investment cultivates the internal resources to reach others. Rather than imagining frictionless success stories, Moroccan hip hop artists promote responsibilization by incorporating beliefs about the individual's role into their social and systemic critiques.

In composing, emceeing, dancing, or listening, hip hop practitioners are working on both their ʿaqliyya and their *hal*—their dispositions and state of being. *Al-hal* (lit. state, condition) indexes local understandings of the relationship between the mind, the emotions, and the body. Within Sufi devotional practice, it refers to an altered state that assists adepts searching for oneness with the divine (e.g., Kapchan 2007; Haddad 2009).

Outside these practices, al-hal can describe a strongly felt interior state, accompanied by physical and affective expressions, somehow beyond one's rational mind (or ʿaql). Sound, singing, and music are understood to be profoundly effective vehicles for both the Sufi version of al-hal and a range of states in which "the agency of the individual is gradually relinquished in favor of something . . . more overwhelming" (Haddad 2009). Crucially, one can practice entering and maintaining these states, becoming more adept over time (Kapchan 2009).

Though Moroccan hip hop practitioners avoid relating their arts to Sufi devotional forms, narratives on the interactions of mind, passions, and body frame practitioners' simultaneously physical, affective, and intellectual reactions.[16] Practitioners also work on al-hal as they acquire embodied knowledge of the transnational hip hop tradition, whether that is how to nod one's head with the music, what gestures best punctuate one's phrases, or sequences learned by beginning b-boys and b-girls. Likewise, local knowledge indexed by musical choices underscores listeners' interpretations of the lyrics. Because engagement as a performer or audience member requires implicit and embodied knowledge, dispositions that link mind and body are at stake.

In addition, listeners are encouraged to take pleasure in simultaneously understanding the content on intellectual and embodied levels. Lyrics that use syntactic, sonic, and rhyming techniques to embody and enhance content underscore the holistic nature of knowledge valued in the transnational hip hop tradition. Just as this way of expressing an idea promotes the dissolution of a mind/body boundary in the listener, the musical cycles undergirding that delivery promote the dissolution of temporal boundaries. As Joseph Schloss notes, "As breaks are torn from their original context and repeated, they are reconceived—by performer and listener alike—as circular, even if their original harmonic or melodic purposes were linear" (2004: 33). During the first years that Moroccan hip hop culture took shape, the visibility of enculturated bodies moving, dancing, and listening in both everyday gathering places and large, outdoor concerts was important to practitioners' understandings of themselves as part of a collective with shared values—as a movement, as some claimed.

Throughout interactions I observed or participated in, and throughout Moroccan hip hop performances, the twin "revolutions" that Miriyam Aouragh mentions are consistently invoked. Both listeners and scholars debate the commitment, authenticity, or outcomes of emcees' calls for *thawra siyasiya*, or less drastic reforms—especially in the shadow of the 2011–12 Arab Spring (Caubet and Miller 2012; Slimani 2012). However, the widespread local assumption that changes in belief and worldview must precede or at least accompany material change, and that therefore one can and should critique another's mentality, has gone relatively unremarked. Yet through it, practitioners show that they take seriously their self-appointed roles as teachers and reformers. In this assumption, change must start with ordinary Moroccans. Thus, practitioners dedicated themselves, in their performances and through their lived examples, to encouraging listeners' belief in their own agency.

Practitioners' critiques demonstrated their belief that change is possible, even if the changes they envisioned stop short of any genuine upheaval of the political order. In fact, their mode of critique itself, their targeting of 'aqliyya, limited their ability to depict—much less advocate for—collective transformation.

SHOW ME MY COUNTRY:
NEW FORMS OF ENGAGEMENT

The debates that took place in the course of preparing this report were split between two principal visions: on the one hand, a generally positive appreciation of the values with great potential for solidarity . . . which form the foundation of [fondent] the Moroccan identity; on the other hand, a rather skeptical consideration of the slowness with which Moroccan society has shed a culture still dominated by irresponsibility, fatalism, and carelessness [laxisme]. . . . Therefore, the central role of the state appears in regulating values and in the consolidation of . . . the emerging values of citizenship, responsibility, meritocracy, and democracy.

(GOVERNMENT OF MOROCCO 2005: 33)

One evening in late July, 2008, I sought travel advice from the receptionist at my Casablanca hotel. I had planned to see a breakdance showcase, as it was called on my festival brochure, in a neighborhood several kilometers from downtown. The receptionist assured me I did not want to go. Instead, he insisted that I attend one of the highest-profile events of the festival that evening—a concert featuring hip hop and ragga artists from Agadir, Rabat, and Casablanca, headlined by Lebanese emcee and singer Rayess Bek with his live band.

Though Place Rachidi, a wide expanse of concrete across from the colonial-era government buildings at Mohamed V Square, was a short walk away, the receptionist called up one of the hotel's vans. Revealing himself to be the owner of the hotel, he drove me to the "backstage" entrance to the venue—a break in the metal fencing cordoning off the artists' tents, just meters away from the temporary stage—and harangued the young policeman standing there until he let me in. Moments later, I found myself in a very privileged position, alone in the empty space between the stage and a buoyant crowd of mostly male teens pressed up against the fence. With little knowledge of Derija and less knowledge of how to evade my determined host appropriately, I acted as a bystander to my own research.

I arrived in time to see Steph Raggaman, a singer who specialized in the dancehall-inspired raggamuffin style. Sharing the stage with MC Jo, Raggaman roared the chorus to "Bayda Nayda (Casablanca Get Up)," released the previous year and enjoying significant air play.[17] In the late 2000s, *nayda* (to move, get up, stand up) also referred to a self-consciously new cultural movement, defined by some artists and Francophone media sources as "an alternative culture" that moved of its own accord from the underground to the mainstream public sphere (Caubet 2011: 280). During the pre-chorus to "Bayda Nayda," the backing track articulates the chord progression with a bouncy triplet-like figure. Steph's dense chanting rides over the spacious rhythm, pausing at the end of every other line on the word "Casablanca":

> See the *nayda* in the *métropole*, and the Casablancans in the whole place
> This is the new style, they call it Casablanca
> This style is crazy, this flow is the favorite
> Steph Raggaman comes to you from Casablanca
> Blessings from the people's talk, blessings, no harm done
> Live and no limits to this state, Casablanca[18]

In the recording, Raggaman's voice and the music drop out at each ending "Casablanca," leaving MC Jo and other musicians on the track to whisper the word in rhythm. In performance, Raggaman paced exuberantly as he held his mic out to the audience, inviting everyone listening along to declare that the new style came from "Casablanca."

Unlike the rest of the song, the chorus of "Bayda Nayda" is sung in English. Reflecting the fact that, in 2008, few Moroccans outside an educated elite had access to effective English-language training, most of the chorus is directed at unnamed foreign listeners:

> Let me show you what we've got in my country
> Feel the flow, the soul of my family
> Everybody show some love to my homie
> Come on, Steph Raggaman *bayyan liya bladi* [show me my country]

Despite this and other songs positioning the city as the epicenter of a new musical and cultural moment, Steph Raggaman's set also took a stand on an issue of national and international significance. The entire stage wore matching T-shirts that read "Assa7ra FOREVER Maghribia (the Sahara is Moroccan forever)" in flashy gold-and-silver block letters. MC Jo, Raggaman's former bandmate and guest that evening, was marketing these tees alongside his recent song of the same name.

MC Jo's song "Assa7ra FOREVER Maghribia" is built on the melody and chorus of "L'Ayoun 'Ayniyya (Laayoune [in] My Eyes)," by the Ghiwanien fusion band Jil Jilala, who wrote the original for the 1975 Green March. King Hassan II organized this successful nationalist mobilization, in which over three hundred thousand Moroccans trekked across the country to "claim" the Western Sahara from Spain and the Sahrawi independence movement, to draw attention away from critiques of his authoritarian regime (Mundy 2006).[19] Susan Gilson-Miller notes that women figured prominently in the march, which underscored its nonviolent nature and the apparent depth of popular support (2013: 180). According to MC Jo, invoking memories of the Green March produced rap that both skeptical adults and their hip hop–loving children could appreciate (Akalay, Bennani, and Hamdani 2011). He also successfully tested the market for patriotic hip hop. As he recalled, "When the directors of Maroc Telecom heard the single, they signed me right away for the tours they organized that summer" (Akalay, Bennani, and Hamdani 2011).

The state-run telecommunications utility helped launch Jo's song into national circulation, while the Société National de Radio et Télédiffusion produced its official video. Though MC Jo did not have a set of his own at the performance that night, his T-shirts and presence demonstrated how effectively diverse agents used Morocco's signature nation-building issue. In keeping himself relevant and promoting his new clothing line, MC Jo kept a key nationalist symbol, and the state's historic role in popular culture, visible on stage.[20]

Scholars of Moroccan hip hop and popular culture more broadly have focused on the lamination of the state and the cultural spheres, the public and the nominally private. Some highlight the state's authoritarian presence and its limiting effects (Boum 2012a and 2012b), while some emphasize how individual agents respond to those limits (Almeida 2017; Salime 2015; Salois 2014). Zakia Salime and others have, in particular, turned to the notion of citizenship to make sense of the impacts that young musicians working in Western-identified genres have made since the turn of the twenty-first century (Salime 2022).

In part, each of us has followed the framing of artists themselves, who in the 2000s often explicitly depicted themselves as speaking to and for the nation. As Steph Raggaman notes in his final verse to "Bayda Nayda":

> Reach out, here's the mic, they speak in mono not in stereo
> Listen to my words, yo, the frequency is Moroccan
> I represent, my brother, for this ragga style session
> I represent my country Morocco, it's my nation
> Enter with me the melody of this style's vibration[21]

FIGURE 2. Steph Raggaman, currently known as Mustapha Slameur, and his deejay wearing shirts that read "Assa7ra Forever Maghribia" in concert, Casablanca, 2008. Photo by author.

FIGURE 3. MC Jo wearing a shirt he designed that reads "Assa7ra Forever Maghribia," in concert with Steph Raggaman, 2008. Photo by author.

However, Raggaman and other artists offer a more nuanced analysis of their lived experiences of citizenship than scholars, including myself, have presented. Like Tigresse Flow in "Maghrebiyya," Raggaman claims his Moroccanness, and thus his right to represent and be represented, through multiple verbal and musical translations. By voicing their claims to citizenship through successful foreign genres, artists configured their critiques not solely as a response to state domination, but also as an adaptation to Morocco's top-down economic and cultural policies at the turn of the twentieth century. When Raggaman paired his musical and political allegiances in the lines above, arguing his new style is more, not less, expressive of Moroccanness, his forms of consumption performed his nation's participation in global circuits of culture and capital.

Artists professing their national identity through musical and cultural forms from elsewhere can be read as flipping the script on Europe's, and the global north's, historic appropriation and consumption of Moroccan culture. Yet, at the same time, songs like "Maghrebiyya" and "Bayda Nayda" served the state's need for new expressions to shore up its international reputation as a modern nation that is both Arab and sufficiently "Western." Though observers of the creativity of the 2000s often stressed the new Western-identified Moroccan popular genres' independent origins, and the low socioeconomic status of some of their leading figures, the very mediatization of hip hop and other genres in that decade depended on the state's material and political support for burgeoning private media and sites of popular culture. The way Raggaman's and others' work circulated demonstrates that this ability to seek out, consume, and inhabit musical and expressive forms from valued locations outside Morocco—something that was much easier for urban youths with stable family incomes—were seen as important attributes.

Morocco's authoritarian neoliberalism made it possible, and productive, for hip hop practitioners to commodify their assertions of citizenship in at least two ways. First, as MC Jo noted in the quote above, artists' engagement with issues traditionally seen as political helped them become visible in state-supported media and live performances. Yet, up to a point, even political statements read as oppositional were effective in garnering positive state and public attention.

Second, becoming—or aspiring to become—a certain kind of consumer and producer continues to be a favored way of understanding one's citizenship. In the live performance described above, MC Jo's T-shirts linked the cultural capital of hip hop, state and municipal sponsorship of the concert, and his own entrepreneurial savvy to a red-line issue that has aroused passionate defenses of Morocco and Moroccanness for over forty years. Throughout the history of Moroccan hip hop, state-sponsored media, advertisements by publicly and privately owned entities, and live performances combine and recombine to create statements about what issues citizens should care about, what industries they should focus on, and what products they should consume.

The way I was ushered to this performance was instructive in this regard. Since the 1990s, tourism has been one of the key ways in which the state seeks a post-colonial, economically competitive international position.[22] In turn, the tourism industry and its rationales support the serial exploitation of Moroccan cultural practices as resources for cross-cultural connection. By rendering some of the most memorable parts of the song in English, "Bayda Nayda" precedes many other artists doing the same in an effort toward international recognition. Through the final phrase of its chorus, "bayyan liya bladi (show me my country)," it also defines knowledge of one's country through the eyes of the consuming foreigner—a practice familiar to Moroccans since the colonial era.

Once hip hop performances became a feature of publicly funded live events across Morocco's major cities in the 2000s, the links between market participation, musical belonging, and acts of citizenship that live events illuminated quickly strengthened and grew more complex. Nearly two years to the day after watching Steph Raggaman's set at Place Rachidi, I attended a different event at the same location. Place Rachidi had been renovated as part of an overall effort to spruce up the parks and government buildings at the heart of Casablanca's downtown. In place of the crumbling paving stones and bare, flat expanse of the old square, the new Place Rachidi appeared designed for live events with large audiences; a gentle slope from the sidewalk to the interior gave way to a flat space big enough for a mobile stage and backstage area.

On this Sunday evening, I noticed novel additions to the typical setup. Neat rows of red-upholstered chairs were set up directly in front of the stage. A second fence behind them separated the ticketed attendees from other listeners or foot traffic. Two buses promoting LG phones were parked on the street next to Place Rachidi. Instead of the usual police and security guards, staff at the entrances wore LG polos, handing out branded visors while refusing entry to those without tickets.

On stage, audience members stood behind podiums, competing to text the fastest on their new phones. The event had been billed as a concert by the "Casa Crew Family," both on the circulating flyers and by the two emcees who had invited me. I had expected a show by the beloved local quartet and a select group of their friends. Instead, the "concert" was actually a combined game show, lottery, and product launch, with a punctuating performance.

I found Soultana backstage with friends and a DJ. The members of Casa Crew had invited her to perform along with them as part of the "family" in addition to two younger local acts.[23] She handed over a ticket she had saved for me. At the top, next to the LG cartoon mascot, it read in English and then French:

> Mobile Worldcup Morocco Championship 2010
> LG MWC Championnat National du Maroc!
> Casa Crew Mini Concert
> Présentateur DJ Momo
> Le participant selectionné parmi les spectateurs pourra gagner "un super
> portable LG" dernier cri ainsi que la mascote officielle du MWC.
> Ce billet gratuit vous permet d'entrer par order d'arrivée.
> Donc, il serait impossible d'entrer s'il n y a plus de places.[24]

A tear-off portion of the ticket left space for contact information, in case one's ticket stub was pulled during the phone lottery.

While milling around backstage, I asked Caprice, one of the emcees of Casa Crew, how long they had been waiting. He shrugged, saying the organizers had asked all the musicians to arrive at the beginning of the event to make sure the night went smoothly. "But have you ever seen a hip hop concert with chairs?" I asked him. He smiled and, gesturing to the VIP space just in front of the stage, assured me that Casa Crew would get people up and moving during their set.

After the games, speeches, and a local dance troupe, Casa Crew finally climbed the steps to the stage with practiced energy. As Caprice had promised, they immediately called their audience to the empty area at the foot of the stage. Despite the warning on the ticket, their enthusiasm apparently influenced the ushers and ticket-takers: by the third song, friends I had seen in the unticketed audience appeared next to me on the makeshift dance floor.

I was waiting to hear a recently released song, "Kayna Fawda (It's Chaos)," which I'd seen Casa Crew perform multiple times in late 2009 and early 2010.

"Kayna Fawda" applies the infectious danceability of its beat to a scathing critique of economic inequality. Each emcee's verse compares the haves and the have-nots in creative ways. J-Ok opens the song focusing on the misery of unemployment and the drive to emigrate:

> There's chaos everywhere you go, it's disorder
> In the waves of the sea, you can see a crowd on the ship
> There's no order in this time, only joblessness
> The head rings [like a bell] and the chaos comes up in the banks[25]

In his own verse, Caprice paints a stark image of class differences, arguing that "this country has been cut in two / Some live by the remote control and control [us] / And some live on the sidelines." In the third verse, Chaht Man expands on the idea of control by asking:

> Where are those responsible?
> Where are the trustworthy people [*nass m ʿaqulin*]?
> We won't keep being humiliated
> By "reasonable cuts"[26]

Finally, Masta Flow's verse proceeds at twice the density of the other emcees' texts. In a rapid-fire flow made crystal clear through his diction and nasal timbre, he moves from his bandmates' focus on economic inequality to moral condemnation.

> There's chaos during Ramadan
> What's wrong with you all?
> I'm not with those who are doing it
> I believe in God and the Qur'an
> The world's hour is appearing [i.e., the world is coming to an end]
> Young man and young woman are the same
> We got lost in the deluge
> There's chaos, and that's it [*u kan*]![27]

Taken together, the verses of "Kayna Fawda" usher listeners through a clearly organized argument. First, they observe some consequences of inequality. Then they analyze who and what have caused the chaos, and, finally, they link economic disorder to moral disorder, as Masta Flow gives examples of behaviors that appear to him to signal moral and social decay.

As Chaht Man makes clear in his verse, those who are "responsible" aren't "trustworthy (*m ʿaqulin*)," and cuts to public services, subsidies, and other supports aren't "reasonable" for those who depend on them. He continues by specifying officials who routinely betray their obligations, including the police, city employees, and doctors in public hospitals. In this portrayal, as in the commonplace use of the term *massa ʾoulin,* or *les responsables* in French, those responsible wield power that touches economic, political, even bodily domains. They are opposed to ideal leaders, the *m ʿaqulin*, who would exercise control in wise and moral ways. In the final verse, the band moves from wordplay to short, straightforward phrases to deliver their conclusion, which situates the analysis again at a national level: "We need to fix the country / we need to turn on the light for our children."

Alongside the intricacy of the lyrics, Casa Crew and their audience focused in the moment on generating an affective co-presence through movement. Each time I watched Casa Crew perform this song, I witnessed an outpouring of energy from both the artists and their audiences. At each show, the four emcees relied on "Kayna Fawda" to renew audiences' energy through the forms of call-and-response built into the song. Over bell-like arpeggios and a bouncy bass line that emphasized the lowered second scale degree, the quartet reinforced each other's rhymes, traded measures, and led audiences in shouting "kayna fawda!" throughout the chorus. As they urged their crowds to chant and dance along, each emcee pinballed around the stage in his own style of movement.

To an uninitiated observer, the crowds of mostly young men jostling, jumping, and shouting to "Kayna Fawda" during the largest shows of the season might appear chaotic in itself. Yet the unified attention this song captured added an important dimension to Casa Crew's critique of the failure of public order. As the lyrics led audiences through missing components of a smoothly functioning society—employment opportunities, social and economic equality, normative performances of devotion to Islam—plazas and parks full of mostly young men moved together, physically supporting one another despite the likelihood of significant differences among them. When "Kayna Fawda" provoked joyous condemnation in state-sponsored concerts and televised performances, the audience endorsed, and perhaps exercised, "the emerging values of citizenship, responsibility, meritocracy, and democracy" that the government report cited above sought to promote.

Given how impactful this song was within their typical set, I was surprised when the LG showcase performance didn't include it. Instead, at the conclusion of their "mini concert," Masta Flow thanked LG and "the whole Casa Crew family. Unfortunately we don't have any more time tonight but thank you Soultana and thanks everyone." The most energetic song in their set was cut. In addition, the only woman on the bill, Soultana, had been dropped from the evening's schedule without explanation to the audience or the artist herself.

The use of Casa Crew to draw crowds to a product showcase at this particular site, in the heart of downtown Casablanca, demonstrated the speed with which hip hop took on its unique role as the music most often associated with the changing market-state complex of the 2000s. In this performance, the musicians and their peers acted within what we might call neoliberalized expectations of the state and its citizens—expectations that not only took into account the sweeping socioeconomic changes wrought over the 1990s and 2000s, but performed the responsibilization encouraged by state policies and their effects, even as hip hop practitioners were critical of some of these effects.

One could see this in the conditions of musicians' labor that evening. That some, or all, of the artists performing that evening were not informed of details critical to their work was not unusual. Throughout the evening, as in many other concerts I attended, artists and audiences were confused about who was performing when and for how long.

That some artists were asked, or chose, to manage the others was also not unusual. According to Caprice, the organizers had asked Casa Crew to perform, and they in turn asked to include additional artists whom they designated as the Casa Crew Family. Originally, each of the guests had been told to prepare two songs, after which Casa Crew planned an hourlong set. None of the performers, however, were aware of how long the "championship" portion of the evening would take, or how much time would be left for them, until their moment on stage occurred. Casa Crew's role insulated the event organizers and gave the band the risks and responsibilities of managers.

One could also see artists' neoliberalized expectations in their analysis of and attempts to manage public order. As the lyrics to "Kayna Fawda" and many other songs from this period explain so clearly, the state and its agencies were (and are) frequently seen as abandoning their commitment to maintaining public order. Not because state agents are absent—the police and other authorities are consistently cited in these critiques—but because they were widely experienced as doing their jobs corruptly or not at all. As "Kayna Fawda" also exemplifies, the synthetic scope of critique posits economic inequality as integral to any analysis of the state's failure to provide public order. In a context where the state's hold on the market is correctly assumed to be quite powerful despite decades of selective privatization and trade liberalization, Casa Crew's critiques argue that failures to build or maintain a safety net are failures of the state, not a self-contained machine known as "the economy." At the same time, individuals are also presumed to have agency and a role in maintaining social harmony and equality. While each emcee's verse depicts ordinary Moroccans as victims of forces much larger than themselves, the song simultaneously critiques citizens for failing to live up to their obligations to each other.

The scale of analysis in "Kayna Fawda," and the way in which it allowed live audiences to see each other move in accordance with that analysis, was similar to other powerfully popular songs from this period that analyzed issues in relation to their listeners' national identities rather than their class status or ethnic background. In this way, hip hop served to promote a sense of national unity through, not despite, its practitioners' arguments. This was as true for songs that expressed devotion to tenets of national identity mythologized by the state, such as the status of the Western Sahara, as it was for songs that focused on avoidable suffering.

As hip hop practitioners took for themselves the power of naming disorder and disunity, a highly audible move that occasioned widespread commentary on urban artists' determination in the 2000s, they also took on the responsibility of critiquing and educating the public they addressed.[28] In interviews and conversations, practitioners were often passionate about the role they ascribed to themselves and their desire to raise expectations for their musical colleagues and their audiences. Caprice, for example, was one of several emcees who defined hip hop to me as a "movement," and like Magma, Don Bigg, DJ Sim-H, or Tendresse, he depicted self-education and self-motivation as a matter of artistic and personal integrity (interview, Casablanca, June 24, 2010).[29] Interviewed that year, Masta Flow told a journalist that "when one is an artist and a rapper, one is responsible and . . . one is automatically conscious [*engagé*]. In fact, without desiring it, we become it, we are sometimes obligated to be it when . . . we comment on what is happening around us" (*Le Matin*, January 12, 2009).

Casa Crew's role advertising for LG that evening was a particularly direct example of how performances like Steph Raggaman's pitched an image of the nation to its citizens. In music, advertisements, and festivals of the 2000s, that image was of youths with leisure time, disposable income, and eager familiarity with European and US fashions. A touristic image of youths in Casablanca and, to a lesser extent, other major cities came to index Morocco as a forward-looking yet distinct place that could still be valued for its difference from the global north. (Masta Flow's remarks to his 2009 interviewer could have been an advertisement for Royal Air Maroc or a five-star hotel: "Our style is Casablanca with all its differences and all its contradictions . . . anchored in tradition, displaying an unrivaled modernity" [Le Matin].) At the same time, citizens were encouraged to hope that Morocco would increasingly converge with Europe and North America economically. Casa Crew's values and goals were equally, if not more, compelling when articulated within a commercial domain.

Like the LG event and many similar promotions held by private companies internationally, the Steph Raggaman concert I saw in 2008 also used hip hop to attract desirable audiences. My status as an unwitting VIP at that concert, where I was granted unearned access because of my whiteness, Americanness, and potential affluence, was reproduced many times over—including at the LG showcase.[30] Both private and public entities instrumentalized hip hop to welcome those who might benefit them in some way, and to normalize attributes that were associated with both the nation's development and material success.

Over a short period of time, Place Rachidi became a physically and symbolically central location from which the municipality and the state could legitimize hip hop and be legitimized by it. Steph Raggaman's performance took place during the Casamusic festival, later known as the Festival de Casablanca. Directed by Hicham Abkari, a former employee of the city's state-sponsored youth centers who was an early institutional supporter of hip hop in the 1990s (personal communication, July 2010), the festival articulated state, municipal, and corporate funding. Each year, the festival locates artists like Steph Raggaman—hip hop and other

Western-identified popular musicians—at Place Rachidi, while other, more "local" genres are sited in less central neighborhoods across the city.

LG's unorthodox concert-showcase leveraged expectations that "modern," "Western" genres belonged at this site, across the street from highly visible expressions of state power, at the heart of Morocco's economic center. When private companies used the same spaces to produce similar events and similar publics, they both benefited from and contributed to its established associations. In the case of Place Rachidi, this meaning sedimented from the actions of multiple actors that were loosely coordinated, if at all. As Bogaert describes, "new state spaces" frequently bring together state agencies and private interests in ways that allow corporations to deploy state power (2012: 262). In a context where most believe that little occurs without state approval, hip hop practitioners' articulation of traditional exhortations to maintain public order with novel aesthetics of critique became a link between corporate and state power that strengthened both.

In the examples above, hip hop artists promote an understanding of citizenship that centers market participation. Producing and consuming objects, as well as live music, are presented as strengthening national unity and citizens' values. Artists consistently eviscerate the idealized notion that Moroccans' desire and ability to access the political—to vote, to protest, to educate themselves—exists independently of their wealth or class status. They recognize, comment on, and act within markets' imbrication with the state, in solidarity with those listeners who interrogate the relationship between the economic and the political.

Throughout this chapter, hip hop artists try to lead by example, demonstrating belief in themselves and in their co-citizens' capacity for action. The actions they encourage and take sometimes uphold, rather than challenge, the ways that authoritarian governance and market incorporation have reinforced each other and reshaped Moroccan life since the 1980s. Yet this does not evacuate the force of their faith in themselves and each other, especially compared to the ways that the state expresses its contempt (*hogra*) for its subjects (El Maarouf and Belghazi 2018: 298). The potential for reorientation toward the present as united with the future, the self as united with its body, and the body as united with a collective could be mobilized as a fundamental epistemological challenge to the existing order—or it could stop at oneself.

Hip hop practitioners envisioned, and continue to envision, a holistic citizenship in which the state acknowledges economic rights as inseparable from political ones. However, this vision can come from artists who are otherwise aesthetically and politically opposed to one another. The most explicit examples of pro-state hip hop come from the Marrakesh-based pop-rap band Fnaire. First promoted by Moroccan producer and entrepreneur Abel Damoussi in the 2000s as a vehicle for his nationalist poetry (interview, Rabat, June 29, 2018), Fnaire marketed their combination of locally specific sounds and elevated Derija verses as rap *taqlidi* or "traditional" rap (Almeida 2016: 121). They originally rose to prominence in 2004 with the song "Matkitsch Bladi (Don't Touch My Country)," written in response to the May 2003 suicide bombings in Casablanca. Throughout their nearly twenty-year career, their best-known songs have defended the state during moments of political upheaval.

Fnaire and Damoussi crafted an effective formula in which each song show-cased one or two different regions or groups, often through the use of women's traditions. Examples from their collaboration include "Lalla Mennana" (2007), which repurposes a children's song to celebrate the 2004 passing of the Mou-dawana, or new civil code. While they no longer collaborate with Damoussi, the band has continued to compose in this pattern. Nine years later, "Chayeb (Old Man)" (2016) borrows from the repertoire of the Houariyat—songs composed and performed by the women of the Houara tribe—to make a statement against child marriage.

Yet the success of Fnaire's messages depends, in part, on extracting value from the groups they represent by repurposing musical indices of their difference within the logic of Western popular song forms. Their video for "Yed el-Ḥenna (Hand of Ḥenna)" (2007), in which director Ivan Herrera and executive producer Damoussi famously staged scenes reminiscent of the 1975 Green March, dem-onstrates their cultural nationalism and explicit celebrations of state policy. The album version of "Yed el-Ḥenna," the title track of their 2007 album, opens with an uncredited female Sahraoui vocalist and guitarist. A portrait of King Mohamed VI is propped up against a pole of the tent in which people in traditional dress have gathered for tea. Footage of the vocalist cut from the official video for "Yed el-Ḥenna" shows her watching for people on the horizon as she sings, finally smil-ing as a flag-waving crowd, led by Fnaire, crests the nearest dune.[31]

Consistent with the song's theme and the Moroccan government's refusal to recognize the Western Sahara as a separate entity, at no point does either video or the song itself acknowledge the forty-year resistance to Moroccan occupation. Instead, the Green March is represented as a welcomed gift to the Saharouis and a metaphor for the national unity with which Moroccans face contemporary chal-lenges. Like other work in Fnaire's career, "Yed el-Ḥenna" benefits from the assets of a given group or location—in this case, the improvisatory vocal and guitar tra-ditions of the Sahraoui, so profoundly influenced by Mauritanian and West Afri-can musics—while silencing those groups' actual concerns.

Compare the narratives that Fnaire promotes to Chaht Man and Muslim's "Fin Ḥaqna?" (2009). A few years after changed policies brought select hip hop musicians to a broad national public, Chaht Man and Muslim sought to estab-lish an underground sensibility through musical and vocal semiotics, branding themselves rebels and revolutionaries. This song—translated as "Where are our rights?" or "Where is our share?"—generated significant academic attention to its explicit denunciation of privatization (Almeida 2014: 159; Miller and Caubet 2012: 8–9; Salime 2022: 13). Its anticorruption discourse connects hip hop to perennial critiques of Moroccan and SWANA governments leveled by both citizens and global north observers.

At the same time, when Chaht Man and Muslim use the language of rights in their lyrics, they limit these almost exclusively to a share of measurable, material wealth. Unlike, for example, the character Don Bigg depicts in "16/05," who seeks the political recognition, freedom of education, and freedom from police corruption that might emerge from reduced inequality, the demands named in "Fin Ḥaqna?" narrow to a share of profits from the nation's agriculture, fishing, and mining. In this narrative, privatization and global market sales have denied Moroccans access to their country's own goods at prices they can afford. Industry leaders enrich themselves while "selling" and "stealing" citizens' goods and their rights.

In Chaht Man's third verse, immaterial demands for mobility, freedom of expression, and the recovery of Morocco's former territories of Ceuta and Melilla are placed alongside the potential for oil wealth, framing all of these as similar objects whose value can be revealed or affirmed through the same methods.[32] Just as the responsible parties, which include both corporate and government actors, are depicted as one and the same, so too are the nation's exports and citizens' rights. In turn, without explicit remarks on how citizens can reject the effects of global market integration, the rights-holders imagined in the song are defined by their ability to consume.

The musical choices and verbal delivery in "Fin Ḥaqna?" belong to hip hop's traditional sonics of opposition, strengthening Muslim's and Chaht Man's public images. However, the rights Muslim and Chaht Man mention are envisioned as similar to the privileges Fnaire promotes in specific ways. Both ensembles speak as if their visions include all citizens; both align with the developmentalist rhetoric Moroccans have heard since independence. In this rhetoric, citizenship means sharing the wealth created by the nation-state's eventual accession to global market participation and the "developed" world. As in the larger transnational marketplace, however, citizens' access to the benefits of wealth is and would be unequal by design.

In examples throughout this chapter, artists understand market participation, whether as consumers, advertisers, or creators, as an act of identification with the nation. In this way, they associate citizenship with economic progress as much, if not more than, ideas about national identity or fealty to the state and monarchy. Paradoxically, this has occurred through, not despite, the state's retraction of postindependence forms of economic security.

This chapter's examples differ widely, yet all cultivate an ʿaqliyya that proposes a particular relationship between the personal, social, economic, and political. The focus on personal responsibility allows critique to flourish without disturbing the way power circulates and is maintained in Morocco. However, this observation tells us little about how individual listeners understand or incorporate the critiques they hear.

Nadia Kiwan calls the critical, yet regime-supportive, stance of many hip hop and fusion artists "alternative nationalism" (2014). Others have argued that musical participation, as well as texts, enhanced desires for and performance of participatory citizenship over the 2000s and 2010s (e.g., Belyazid and Mettour 2007; Salime 2015). These formulations speak to North African and Arab world studies' focus on population-state relations without asking how market rationalities intersect with the changes scholars observe. The examples of personal and musical commodification here render explicit links between national politics, musical and social belonging, and market participation. The intellectual and aesthetic community that early-2000s hip hop practitioners built shared its emphasis on individual responsibility, education, and empowerment with politically disparate sources, including old-school French and American hip hop and twenty-first-century technocrats. That such different currents embrace these values indicates how vital centering the individual as the basic unit of society has been to Morocco's relatively smooth transition into social and economic neoliberalization. Success in Morocco's marketplace for national(ist) media and performances has been vital to promoting hip hop practitioners' ideals of citizenship and their vision of citizens' power.

CONCLUSIONS:
RESPONSIBILIZATION AND COMPLICITY

This chapter analyzes moments when musicians addressed individual responsibility in place of collective action. Rather than rejecting the collective, the stress many placed on responsibility expressed a shift in the imagined relationship of the individual to the society. As practitioners perform arguments about what should fall within personal responsibility—as they reframe collective (moral) judgments in terms of personal responsibility—they also shift the imagined relationship between action in the public sphere and in political structures. In this way they function like intellectuals who, for Said Graiouid, must balance political engagement with moral and ethical limits on their intervention: "The Moroccan intellectual tends to avoid engagement with radical politics that aim to create social disorder (*al-ṣiba*) or unrest (*fitna*), and embraces instead hybrid approaches that alternate resilience and resistance, dissent and compromise, critique of the ʿamma (the general public) and state politics, and advocacy for endogenous 'reforms from within' over drastic social change" (2021: 1221). As in Graiouid's examples, hip hop practitioners claim "the capacity . . . to intervene imaginatively and critically in their social environment" yet "legitimize . . . a hegemonic . . . narrative" (2021: 1224).

First-generation artists' citizenship praxis emphasized real and important differences with how previous generations related to political and social institutions. At the same time, their work often legitimized the state's emerging discourses on Moroccanness—not only because they had to speak and act within limits, but because core aspects of their vision aligned with the state's goals for the nation. Whether urging listeners to voice their own critiques, developing a "both sides" analysis in which personal responsibility could counter state power, or reinforcing the instrumentalization of othered cultural practices, hip hop musicians often performed and continue to perform an "integrative function" (Graiouid 2021).

At the end of the August night that opened this chapter, when my friends implicitly discussed what rights and freedoms should be curtailed for the sake of the majority, the group agreed that LGBTQIA Moroccans were safest in the closet until *mentalités* changed across society. Each speaker cited some other Moroccans, on some other balcony, as harboring prejudice. While claiming a progressive point of view, the speakers' dim view of "the public" nonetheless placed the responsibility for LGBTQIA citizens' protection on that group.[33] In this logic, the public is presumed unable or unwilling to change their ʿaqliyyat and behavior, lacking the agency to learn even as they disproportionately control public space.[34] For the hip hop practitioners I worked with, the responsibility to educate and better oneself was seen as congruent with, even necessary for, public order. Across political positions and degrees of piety, they imagined a society in which citizens freely prioritized order, harmony, and care for others, even as they placed boundaries around whose concerns were worthy of care.

Hip hop creation, performance, and consumption in Morocco's major cities is, as Xavier Livermon puts it, "as critical a site for political practice as any political and economic institution or action" (2020: 4). Over the 2000s, a certain section of Moroccan hip hop production and performance became an institution of its own. The artists and aspiring artists with whom I worked cultivated hip hop as praxis, an activity that allowed them to embody values they felt were insufficiently present in their lives and society. They developed a normative vision in which public order is no longer defined solely by corrupt state forces, but remains paramount nonetheless. In encouraging themselves and their listeners toward "positive" attributes of the neoliberal subject, artists performed freedom to be both moral and individualist, rather than a freedom from obligation. As a dimension of the agency so often denied to practitioners' parents during the Years of Lead, personal responsibility was often valorized as a practice of freedom. Yet that practice conformed to some parts of the state-market nexus even as it sought cultural, political, or aesthetic liberation.

While musicians frequently challenged state policies and their unequal outcomes, they also reinforced a deeper alignment with normative neoliberal values that both transcends and conforms to the ideal entrepreneurial citizen promoted by the state. These values lay beyond the debate between practitioners and among commentators over which nationalisms or royalisms belong in hip hop music and culture. Instead, musicians and other practitioners played a highly audible role in the governance project launched by Morocco's global market integration and its accompanying financial, cultural, and political norms.

3

The Ethics and Aesthetics
of Competitions

The dazzling sunlight seemed to illuminate this July Saturday in Casablanca inside and out. Tucked away in a paved lot between apartment blocks, several kilometers from downtown, the street art festival Sbagha Bagha was closing a week of activities with its second annual graffiti battle. As Soultana and I climbed out of a petit taxi at the corner, a tiny Renault puttered past. "It's this way," yelled Khalid, the organizer of the Block Dix open-mic series, from the driver's-side window. We strolled after him, talking about people we used to know.

"The guys from Rime Fire Crew used to live in these apartments," said Soultana. "You remember them."

"Oh yeah, we saw them at the Tremplin all those years ago. Are they still together?"

"No way. They are doing nothing with music," laughed Soultana.

"I looked up Bellops on Facebook this morning," I said. Bellops had belonged to an emcee duo named Dirtyfaces. They had won the Jil Mawazine competition's hip hop category in 2009, and I ran into him at seemingly every concert in 2010.[1]

"I think he went to Paris. To study *les audiovisuelles*."

"Yeah, I think so. His latest photo is from a control room at Mawazine." In the picture, he was sitting in front of a bank of televisions during that May's Mawazine festival, each feeding one camera from performances broadcast live on 2M.

"That is the best thing," exclaimed Soultana, suddenly energized. "It is the best thing when people realize they can't making a living from rap and they go study." We passed Khalid's Renault, parked next to others just like it, and entered the concrete courtyard.

By 4 p.m., six contestants had been narrowed to two. Two pristine gray boards in wooden frames, the size of a lecture hall chalkboard and about four feet off the ground, sat in the center of the lot. Roped off from the crowd, the finalists—MEVOK, from Tangier, and SAKO, from Casa—sat hunched over sketchbooks on plastic crates. As they plotted their final images, two deejays a few meters away traded samples foundational to the hip hop arts. Using a vinyl controller, DJ Rasch scratched over unison bass and guitar from Incredible Bongo Band's cover of "Ina Gadda Da Vida" to texture his transition to Arthur Baker's "Breaker's Revenge," a track many older participants would remember from bootleg copies of *Beat Street* (1984). "Khouya, ay! (my brother, ay!)" exclaimed the day's *animateur*, our microphone-wielding host, as the familiar bass line emerged from the noise.

Standing next to Rasch in front of his CDJs, DJ Sam Noise simultaneously prepped his next song and decorated Rasch's mix by scratching, releasing the disc into a single measure of the iconic percussion break from Incredible Bongo Band's "Apache" precisely on beat. Rasch nodded his approval, and on the third release, Sam Noise kept spinning while Rasch faded out his mix, arriving at complete silence at the guitar strum heralding the call-and-response horns of "Apache."

While Sam Noise scratched the "p" of "party people . . . Can y'all get funky? / Soul sonic force" into "Apache's" guitar theme, the host continued to layer over the music. "Maximum du bruit pour MEVOK et SAKO (lots of noise for MEVOK and SAKO)," he called out over the guitar line, now sandwiched between two-bar chirp scratches. "Ça, ça, ça, le finale." Together, the three improvised a dense texture that recalled generations of dance battles, soundtracking the afternoon with American recordings nearly fifty years old.

Music for the day's battle was provided by Block Dix, an open-mic event held at the Boulevard Festival's headquarters in Casablanca. Rasch and Sam Noise were its main deejays, returning each month to support young emcees. In addition to entertaining the artists, spectators, and neighborhood children milling about the lot, Block Dix broadcast Sbagha Bagha live through its web radio setup in the adjacent tent. On the other side of the graffiti battle, the visual artists' collective Skefskef had set up booths with merchandise and a used book table. And all around us, the walls of the apartment buildings and garages glowed with portraits, fantastical imagery, wildstyle lettering, and tags—the work of artists from Sbagha Bagha's previous competitions and murals. They made perfect backdrops as fresh-dressed participants posed for friends, the publicist, or the professional photographer roaming the lot.

As soon as the competition concluded, the *animateur* opened the stage to Block Dix participants. After three teen regulars performed original songs, an up-and-coming young emcee from Rabat named Lionbad took the stage. The sun had barely dropped below the high rise next door at 7:30 p.m. when his set ended. As volunteers wrapped cables and broke down tents, clusters of friends straggled away from the lot, a long summer evening still ahead.

The contours of this event are similar to countless events across Morocco and the world since the hip hop arts spread internationally through competitions,

FIGURE 4. Emcee Lionbad posing for photos, Casablanca, 2018. Photo by author.

concerts, and recordings starting in the 1980s. Throughout the day's activities, the tension between individual expression and convention that powers the hip hop arts generated opportunities to differentiate and compete, to learn and mentor.

Layers of formal and informal competition were built into the day across the elements, as well as in the ways people dressed, reacted, and socialized. Some, like the graffiti contest itself, were overt, synchronous, and interpersonal. But some were potential, asynchronous, and self-directed. For example, the artwork surrounding the lot and the videos and photos taken that day may endure for years to come. For aspiring writers (graffiti artists) and muralists, the painted walls offer a standard to hold oneself to; for everyone captured in a photo or video, those documents offer entry into possible future contests over credibility and social capital. Likewise, while the open-mic participants weren't officially judged, they could expect critique from their peers and audience members that might impact their social status, just as they would use someone else's performance to hone their own craft and aesthetics.

Although the graffiti artists on view that day competed for substantial amounts of money and bragging rights, as with musicians, winning was unlikely to open up professional opportunities. They could not even expect to judge the next year's competition, since Sbagha Bagha's foreign judges were a key way they attracted top participants (La Rédaction 2018).[2] In the absence of paying gigs, getting in front of well-respected artists for constructive feedback was as meaningful as prize money.

This chapter could have opened with many other examples of formal competitions, where aspiring artists prepare recordings and performances to enter in order to win other opportunities to record and perform. Why have these been so central to the culture of Moroccan hip hop practitioners? Since at least 2000, Moroccan hip hop artists have embraced juried competitions to hone skills, share music, and strengthen social ties. The cyphers, battles, and discourses of self-improvement fundamental to transnational hip hop culture provide not only opportunities for mastery, but for solidarity across stylistic and social difference as practitioners recognize their competitors' commitment. At the same time, the hip hop arts' forms of competition, and the differentiation they promote and circulate, have intertwined with existing markets—and enabled new ones—since their inception.

This chapter explores how musicians' competitive ethos and practices help to produce their understandings of markets and of themselves as market actors. While state-sponsored and independently organized competitions are opposed to each other in many ways, in practice, organizers and musicians depict both as a prelude to and substitute for an idealized market in which artists make a living wage. I suggest that for my interlocutors, competition is both an acceptance of and a solution to ways practitioners' lives are dominated under Morocco's authoritarian neoliberalism. Because my interlocutors conceive of markets as both natural and necessary, competing in a way that sustains, rather than weakens, social bonds becomes a form of care for oneself and others.

To make this argument, I define markets not solely as sites where products are exchanged, but as domains where actors circulate tangible and intangible goods and compete to create and obtain various kinds of capital. I define market actors here as heads of self-designed projects of circulation who seek value and mobility. My interlocutors were savvy participants in both a material market for musical products, including recordings, performances, and expertise, and an intangible market for personal values and modes of being. Both kinds hold the potential to enable desirable change in one's life; both sometimes operate in the same moment. Both circulate hip hop cultural expressions and, in so doing, generate social and sometimes material value through other practitioners' recognition.

From the perspective of neoclassical economics, hip hop practitioners' informal markets might appear unhealthy (or inefficient). However, many artists understand themselves to be collectively pursuing more formal markets, which would behave similarly to textbook capitalism and in which they could be more effective entrepreneurs. In order to promote a more secure formal market, practitioners simultaneously cultivate their audiences' willingness to pay for things like recordings and performances, and they act on themselves to become something worth paying for. Throughout the chapter, I argue that the ways artists work on both themselves and their artistry blur analytical lines between self and labor, individual and community. They also bring to the surface practitioners' alignment with the state's ideologies of "development," in which the goal of global market integration drives decisions across regions, decades, and forms of governance.[3] Since thriving markets of any kind are understood as closer to the situation of the global north, both material and intangible markets have important ethical and political ramifications.

Practitioners' embrace of development paradigms speaks to the unavoidable complicities my interlocutors faced. As creative workers and entrepreneurs, they pursued their goals DIY or in bottom-up ways, in opposition to the top-down approach of the state, its provinces, or its municipalities. However, actors carrying out plans from both orientations desire similar outcomes. To oversimplify, DIY and state actors may start from different perspectives, hold different politics, and prefer different methods yet effectively pursue the same thing—increased visibility and mobility in a transnational marketplace that has historically structured North Africa as a source of exotic artifacts, sunny vacations, agricultural products, and low-skilled labor. Critically, my interlocutors were well aware that appearing to align with state ideologies could backfire among their peers, yet there was little to be gained in doing otherwise.

Twenty years of independent competitions have built the hip hop arts community and taught many to view competition as self-improvement, as a moral good, and as a site of solidarity. At the same time, as I will show, neoliberal realities situate competition as both a sincere form of collective care and a way to build individual mobility and capital. Viewed in conjunction with the personal responsibility discourse described in the previous chapter, the expressions of care and solidarity performed through competition supported profound feelings of community without a disposition toward collective action in a traditional political sense. Instead, they solidified norms around building and participating in markets not only for recordings and performances, but for as-yet-unknown opportunities.

In what follows, I position hip hop's emergence and transnational spread as a story of artists' simultaneous rejection of and success in racial capitalism, showing how musicians promote care for themselves and one another through competitive contexts. Then, I offer a brief history of Moroccan hip hop's emphasis on formal competitions in order to contextualize the divergent visions of musical labor, artistic success, and professionalism put into practice by the two largest independent and state-sponsored competitions of the 2000s and 2010s. Finally, the chapter returns to the idea of solidarity by discussing practitioners' hopes for mobility. As Moroccans' possibilities and methods of migration are polarized by inequality, solidarity can take the form of seeking social and geographic mobility in order to care for one's community, but also to help imagine productive futures for the hip hop arts.

COMPETITION AS CARE FOR THE CULTURE

Shortly after 5 p.m., Sbagha Bagha's host strolled into the center of the graffiti artists' circle. People gathered around the competition area while MEVOK and SAKO stood back to observe the full effect of their finished panels. Each had painted the same letters with distinctive shapes, colors, shading, and background. At the host's shout of "*trois . . . deux . . . un . . .* STOP!" the artists put down their cans and brushes, the deejays quieted their music, and the judges stood up behind their makeshift table.

Each judge said a few words, in French, in front of the artists and audience. With phone and video cameras rolling, the first judge noted that MEVOK's sweeping, fluid serifs were "a little too complex compared to the other one." The second congratulated both writers but concluded that "SAKO has better used the full space of the panel." The third stressed that he "really enjoyed both styles. MEVOK, it's super as always, but that 'A' has lost the style a little." A cheer went up as SAKO struck a half-joking prize-fighter pose then gave MEVOK a bear hug before shaking the judges' hands. While each of the judges brought out a different detail in his comments, they showed a clear preference for SAKO's simpler, more angular style, featuring a classic gradient that drew one's eye from the lighter-colored, thinner forms at the top of the panel to the darker, broader limbs of the letters at the bottom. SAKO's way of shaping and using space upheld canonical forms; in contrast, as one judge said to MEVOK, "you are making another [kind of] graff."

Competition is baked into hip hop's history and culture. Informal and formal contests are foundational to b-boying/b-girling and deejaying in the form of battles, emceeing in the form of cyphers, and graffiti in writers' jockeying for status (Austin 2016: 224). Practitioners and historians often make the competitive drive itself sound as natural and unavoidable as the tides. In a characteristic example, art historian Maia Morgan Wells presents graffiti's development as self-explanatory: "As an increasing number of teenagers added their own twist to what they saw on the subways, competition ignited rapid stylistic innovation" (Wells 2016: 467). Celebrated flyer maker Buddy Esquire described the desire to compete in sensory terms: "'It's like an itch,' he says, 'a drive to want to do it, to want to get better, to want to work hard at it'" (Smith 2010, quoted in Ewoodzie 2017: 131). Mark Katz describes competition as a vital force propelling deejays: "It motivated them, gave them direction, and structured their daily lives" (2012: 44). The deejays and dancers that Katz and Joseph Schloss interviewed frequently describe their competitive feelings as both primal and cultivated, a natural resource to be harnessed (Schloss 2009).

These narratives celebrate competition's benefits for individuals and for the collective improvement of the art form. For each person, devotion to craft and thus to competition with others and oneself is a virtue, a practice with moral force. It defines the person as she refines her abilities; it invites a habit of self-interrogation on what, when, and how to achieve.[4] Gigging musicians in hip hop and other genres adopt entrepreneurial discourses, citing competition against oneself as continuous self-improvement and self-care (Hesmondhalgh and Baker 2010; Scharff 2016).[5]

Competition within the hip hop arts thrives on the differentiation, commodification, and entrepreneurship that powers contemporary capitalism. Yet, while competition has grown from and energized individuals' capitalistic labors, individual competitions can sustain profoundly meaningful sociality. Throughout transnational hip hop history, competitions produced and continue to produce solidarity as the flip side of the individualization described above.

Competitions exhibit artists' dedication to their art forms, traditions, and mentorship. In Joseph Schloss's work, b-boys and b-girls describe battling as "sharing," as "topping the next one and going to the next level," to collectively build better dancers and dance forms (2009: 108). Producers would compete to find obscure breaks, "[establishing] a canon of records . . . that a producer had to be familiar with, an expectation that still stands to this day" (Schloss 2004: 37–38). Today's international competitions in deejaying and dancing allow competitors and fans to draw connections between uniquely talented performers and national or regional trends. Assertive individuality makes possible continually expanding genre boundaries and higher expectations for performance. Discernible differences—of technical ability, aesthetic preference, regional style, etc.—are required, in this view, for artistic advancement to occur. Competition strengthens bonds across difference by reinforcing the sense that everyone can and should contribute to the development of the art form.

Competition also passes on cultural memory as performance conventions. Older artists remain relevant by mentoring, judging, and sustaining unwritten rules of conduct. Joseph Ewoodzie Jr. cites an early deejaying battle in which Afrika Bambaataa noticed that Grandmaster Flash was using rented equipment. Feeling this violated unspoken but established standards for fair play, Bambaataa coached Flash's opponent, the young Grandwizzard Theodore, in real time to beat Flash (Ewoodzie 2017: 117). Approximately two decades later, Marcyliena Morgan described LA's Project Blowed open-mic nights as "a space of hard work, skill, approval, and dreams . . . an uncensored yet scrutinized space where [freestylers'] discourse is meticulously monitored, judged, and applauded or ridiculed based on their skill and ability to express their lives" (2009: 5). When mentors set standards for performance and behavior, competition becomes a crucial site of technical, aesthetic, and ethical education.

Hip hop's competitive practices are fundamentally shaped by US racial capitalism, which leverages racialization to generate saleable difference (Melamed 2015: 77). With some exceptions, most of Morocco's hip hop artists do not explicitly link success under neoliberal racial capitalism with ostentatious displays of wealth. Instead, they celebrate ordinary individuals making a living under systemic political and economic constraints. Further, many conceptualize success as accessing a formal market like those they understand to exist in Europe and North America. My interlocutors' frequent critiques of the informal state of Moroccan popular music markets referenced their desire to participate in what is represented as capitalist modernity.

Prior to the hip hop arts' emergence in the 1990s, regionally and nationally known art forms had their own competitive traditions. *Ḥalqat* (sing. *ḥalqa*, lit. "throat" or "link in a chain") are audience circles assembled around live performances in markets and gathering places. Ḥalqat vary widely, from storytelling and live music, to magic tricks, healers, and clairvoyants (Kapchan 1996: 30; Schuyler 1984: 96). Caprice, an emcee from the first-generation Casa Crew group, recalled the ḥalqat in his neighborhood of Hay Mohammedi, suggesting that cyphers took their place for hip hop fans of his generation (interview, June 24, 2010). While performers usually do not jostle for airtime within a single ḥalqa, they incite a competitive atmosphere as they coax audiences away from nearby artists.

Cyphers and ḥalqat were also conceptually linked in their supposed distance from respectable activities. At least in the first decade of Moroccan hip hop, emcees, dancers, and their audiences could be sure that people outside the cypher were, at best, indifferent to their art. As a foreign practice associated with Afro-diasporic populations, poverty, and urban decay in the United States and in France, hip hop was often understood as a sign of moral and economic degradation among Moroccan youths, inviting surveillance by their neighbors and the police (Cestor 2008).[6]

For Deborah Kapchan, *ḥlayqiya*, or halqa performers, remind their fellow citizens that markets have both winners and losers: "Ḥlayqiya (pl.) are socially devalued because their goods are often intangible or ephemeral and because their activities challenge dominant notions of what constitutes value in society. Performers . . . are excluded from a material economy whose primary value is the generation of capital, yet included in it as an example of refuse" (1996: 40–41). Both ḥlayqiya and early hip hop artists were seen, at least by some, as the surplus that reminded observers of the dominant culture's comparative value.

From hip hop's emergence in Morocco in the mid-1990s to the late 2000s, the vast majority of performance opportunities were in formal and informal competitions, from cyphers to juried exhibitions. Recalling musicians' and dancers' practice in the 1990s, sociolinguist Dominique Caubet invokes an anticommercial discourse: "There was no money involved, there were no festivals, no venues, and the artists were all playing . . . for the pleasure of it" (2016: 251). While Caubet describes a lack of infrastructure as positive, implying that "playing for the pleasure of it" is opposed to playing for financial gain, emerging artists tell stories of competing against each other and against their own achievements during this period. As groups of friends grew in their abilities, they linked to others, creating networks and relations that would circulate and assign value to styles, techniques, and trends—creating, in other words, a market for intangible practices.

Some of the earliest practitioners still active in the 2010s recalled how young aspirants built off each element to develop their competencies in the others. Amine Snoop described to me how, as a young teen, he would sit near b-boys' late-night practice sessions, composing rhymes to the beats from their boom box (July 29, 2015). When sharing her origin story, Soultana often mentions hanging out with boys her age in her sprawling apartment complex, joining the emcees' cypher between pickup basketball games. Yoriyas, who competed as a b-boy before becoming a professional photographer, agreed with my theory that his experience with the layered rhythms of hip hop shaped the visual rhythm of his compositions (July 5, 2018).

In the years before widespread internet access and self-produced videos, aspiring musicians and dancers had to attend competitions to see each other work. Deejays unable to afford their own equipment could practice by accompanying emcees on someone else's decks during dance or musical competitions. For emcees, more formal competitions were not only a place to hear rhymes and flows beyond those of their closest friends, but also a way to gain experience with performance practice they could not reproduce in a courtyard cypher, including how to hold a microphone and move onstage. Dance crews' rehearsals, whether in state-funded youth centers or on the smooth floors of abandoned lobbies after hours, took the form of cyphers where learners simultaneously shared, advised, and competed.

To the best of my knowledge, the earliest formal competitions were established in Casablanca. In 1999, Hicham Abkari, who would become the artistic director of the annual Festival de Casablanca and head of Casablanca's Mohamed VI municipal theater, was working at a state-funded cultural center in the city. He organized a dance battle "like those that exist, for example, in Germany" (Cestor 2008). "Everything happened in a little room in the Sidi Belyout cultural complex. . . . I worked in the site as an assistant director. I had an easier time than someone from outside [the complex] . . . because it was not viewed very well at the time" (Cestor 2008). As someone charged, in theory, with supporting urban youth culture, Abkari became an early supporter of the new trend (personal communication [p.c.], July 24, 2010). Knowing that many Moroccans learned about hip hop through the racist discourses that often accompanied it in US and international media, Abkari thought competition would legitimize teens' passion. Inviting TV crews and explaining that dance battles were already common in Europe could "give a little visibility and diminish the suspicion that this genre of dance and . . . [rapping] might create" (Cestor 2008).

Fez emcee L-Tzack began dancing in 1999 and entered formal competitions almost immediately. "We [went] to an *achiri* competition at that time in Casablanca for free. At that time you go, you work, and you dance the whole day, no Red Bulls, no water, no nothing," he recalled in a 2010 interview.[7]

> And I did this like first time, second time, the third time we win. . . . The third time the year is like 2002 . . . And then we just like—win, the battle, and then we just like leave the whole shit, like leave and take the bus and go back to Fez [laughter]. . . . They were like "wait we gotta give you, we gotta give you something!" And it was just like an *achiri* thing, you can buy it from the medina. I can buy like a collection [of trophies] for myself (interview, Fes, January 2010).

L-Tzack laughed as he remembered his first plastic trophy, but he also stressed his team's dedication, describing their efforts as "work" and noting that they had to pay their own way to Casablanca. "You pay all, and at that time you were more poor because you were more young. And you don't work [a job]," he explained. For L-Tzack and others, neither education nor available jobs could guarantee a future worth having. While early competitions also provided little, they did offer challenge, growth, and a sense of belonging.

MAKING MARKETS, MAKING ONESELF

During the final round of the graffiti competition, as small circles danced and chatted to James Brown tunes, the originator of the Block Dix open mic took a break from his web radio duties to stand in front of a sprawling mural for an interview. I asked Khalid, a professional musician and producer, why he started the series. Khalid knew exactly what he wanted to say. "In 2011 or around then, I did a tour in Germany," he began. "The idea came to me when I went to Berlin. . . . There were . . . these beautiful open mics I enjoyed. And I had a little [jealousy] *fi hal*, like why don't we have these in Morocco? And it was just in their circles, it's not that the state did it or something. Some kids who are friends, between them, they do this thing . . . *Donc* that's how the idea got in my head. And that's the beautiful thing about traveling in life" (July 2018).

Khalid continued to recount a capsule history of Block Dix, offhandedly mentioning the series' achievements. Yes, it had been held every month without fail since 2011, he confirmed. Yes, it was the only open mic in Morocco that had continued for so long. He was almost bored by my amazement.

"So from 2011 until now we did a lot of things, a compilation, a [TV] program, a web radio specializing in hip hop, we partnered with Boultek on this thing Sbagha Bagha . . . but this had been our idea from 2011." Here, Khalid dragged out his statement in a knowing fashion, pausing between each word with a conspiratorial smile. "With it, we create a hip hop industry in Morocco."[8]

We both laughed at his exaggerated delivery. "In order to do anything, we had to have so much money. It's normal if you know the history of rap in America, how it worked, you understand me? . . . Our way is from our cheap standard of living [*min al-ɣaiya economique*]."

Khalid explained that Block Dix's first goal was to create a label under which to organize all their activities—releases, concerts, tours, merch. But he was also contending with young artists' desire to build their reputations quickly by posting all their music on YouTube. Khalid was sympathetic, but he also hoped to convince them to play a longer game.

> Now that we've arrived at a certain level, I advise kids to be wise. They post their releases for free so that Moroccan youths, the Moroccan public is with them. Now the public is used to something for nothing . . . they're used to getting something for a dirham. You understand? *Donc*, I told them post the music on YouTube, put one post there, and later we'll find some way to sell it to a fan. . . . [If you can sell] this CD or this original title, then you found a real fan. A good fan. And then they have a lot of views and it will bring you to them, and we can listen to music like it's their job, you understand? We don't say "ah, we need the state to do this for us," we don't have a problem [doing it ourselves].

As the next sections will show, Khalid's justification echoed those of his elders. As a professional several years into his career, Khalid conceived of Block Dix as a way of building infrastructure for the next generation of artists. Throughout our interview, he framed his thinking and labor as mentorship, as caring for the future of the field. His generational solidarity is the ground in which productive competition could occur and young emcees could flourish.

From the late 1990s through the 2000s, organizers, funders, and participants used formal competitions to determine collectively the boundaries and expressions of professionalism. Rather than denoting paid versus unpaid performers, professionalism discourse emerged as a way practitioners identified gaps between desired and actual conduct. Through discussing and holding themselves and others to "professional" standards, practitioners located, critiqued, and took responsibility for structural inequalities between their informal markets and those they imagined to exist in Europe and North America. Dancers, emcees, beatmakers, and deejays understood learning professional-level musical, technical, and physical skills as a necessary step toward competing in a transnational marketplace.

Markers of professionalism were both business and personal, public and private. They included practitioners' efforts to circulate their work and the ways they treated others and themselves. Artists frequently complained about the unprofessionalism of venue owners, event organizers, and even colleagues who devalued musicians' skills and time through disrespectful acts. For example, my teacher, DJ Sim-H, once told me a cautionary tale about a former friend. When their event fell through and they owed money to a nightclub owner, his partner drove off with their shared equipment and left Sim-H alone with an angry creditor (interview, July 26 2010).

More prosaically, artists complained in public and in private about handshake agreements that left them vulnerable to last-minute changes, or about event organizers that refused to pay for decent sound and lighting equipment.[9] Salé-based emcee K-Prime summed up his advice to his fellow musicians in the following way: "Not all Moroccans are artists. 'Cause you know some people, you just call them and say 'Can you come? There is a concert.' . . . He doesn't know that he has to be professional and he has to think before answering yes. Which kind of concert? Which microphones? Which speakers? . . . If you are a professional, [if] you do professional work, you have to get paid to get on the stage. If we all do that, people, they gonna pay us to get on stage" (interview, Salé, March 26, 2010).

In these and other examples, practitioners sought to cultivate a reputation for being a *fnan*, or artist, rather than simply a singer or entertainer, hoping that acting as if one deserved proper treatment would encourage event organizers to provide it. Convincing oneself of one's own value was not simply good for one's mental health, but a necessary step to convincing others. Collectively acting on these beliefs could, ideally, transform behaviors among those doing the hiring. As K-Prime assured the group listening during our interview, "If we all do that, people, they['re] gonna pay us to get on stage." The tangible and intangible dimensions of efforts to professionalize their market were equally important to artists' potential future success.

Professionalism discourse also generated difference along existing socioeconomic fault lines. For musicians like Don Bigg, who characterized himself as "middle class" in our first conversation in 2009, postsecondary education, access to resources, and exposure to formal markets in other sectors enabled specific interventions (p.c., October 21, 2009). In order to circumvent the pervasive piracy of CDs, he placed official copies of his 2006 and 2009 albums in a single store in each major Moroccan city. Unlike the majority of CDs one could find at the time, these "real" versions looked, felt, and sounded "professional"—they came in new jewel cases, included a glossy booklet, and sported the statement "all rights reserved" as if they had been produced in the United States. More importantly, his recordings were professionally mixed and mastered. Most Moroccans purchased music in local boutiques where the seller made a profit by copying music onto CDs or tapes, often on demand. Bigg's strategy, instead, emulated the buying experience found in cities' most upscale neighborhoods. In a moment when most emcees pursued a full album as a personal and artistic milestone, using it as a credential to attract performance opportunities like musicians in other popular genres, Bigg invested in an attempt to re-value recorded media.

By contrast, a much larger group of practitioners, including full-time musicians, lacked the resources or knowledge to do more than critique the market as they experienced it. L-Tzack had left his successful first-generation group Fez City Clan shortly before I first met him in 2009. After his father passed away when he was young, he grew up in a low-income neighborhood in Fez's old city with his mother and younger brother. By 1999 he had fallen in love with b-boying.

> *LT:* I was just like going *inside* this hip hop. No competition, no radios, no TV show, no nothing. And I'm poor, I don't have a father. I was just like, just doing this, I don't know why. I was just like, "I found my thing. I found what I love in this *achiri* country." . . . I leave my school for this.
>
> *KS:* You left school?
>
> *LT:* Yeah, I didn't—it was like coming to [the] bac[calaureate], and I didn't go the day for the final exam . . . I just, like, go to dance a competition in Casablanca and forget about it (interview, Fez, January 2010).

In late 2009 and early 2010, L-Tzack leveraged a seemingly free resource—his Facebook network—to build support for his forthcoming album. Using a tactic he observed from multinational recording companies, L-Tzack released a series of freestyles to generate excitement, hoping that audience interaction on his posts would become an attraction in itself. By February 2010, his series had failed to increase his network or provoke invitations to perform. In a somewhat cryptic Facebook post, he complained that musicians couldn't "do it big" in Morocco. When I messaged L-Tzack, his reply listed all the ways the country lacked essential market infrastructure, but he also demonstrated how he understood the forces at work.

[I]'m mad about my co[u]ntry i'm real[l]y tired of all this thin[gs] work[ing] incorrect[ly]. . . . no music tv, for people to [see] faces of rappers . . . no stores to [sell] music CD[s], no industry, no marks to support bands, no sponsoring . . . so what [do] we have [for] the big event of hip hop . . . one day of hip hop in boulevard festival??? . . . come on it's really not [enough]. A lot of collaboration[s] ask [emcees] to travel in Europe to make concerts and promotion there, but here they say rap is nothing, so . . . we will never have this normal support from people.

In L-Tzack's view, until "they" expressed respect for hip hop music through material interventions, "people" would not respond with "normal" behaviors like purchasing CDs or paying for tickets. Attempts to advertise and normalize hip hop music would make little difference without the kinds of structures in place in Europe, structures that Moroccans lucky or rich enough to travel could learn about by collaborating with European musicians and organizations. At the same time, despite his former group's experiences performing at state-funded events, L-Tzack cited only the annual Boulevard festival as a "big event of hip hop." Standing outside the emerging networks and funding sources in Casablanca and Rabat, L-Tzack saw independent and state-sponsored festivals as part of the same system. He also made it clear to me that the formal market he desired could not be built by practitioners alone: "We need really to jump right now to the professionalism step. I mean this every fucking *responsable* in this country have to do something for all young [people]. They have to stop to think . . . about [how] to make all this lost energy go in [the] right way, and let all [these] artist[s] make [their lives] and dreams . . . and [e]specially not like the old artist[s]. I mean not [spend] all my life in music and in the end finish [poor]" (Rabat–Fez, February 7, 2010).

L-Tzack's message ignored the state's increased platforming of hip hop in the mid-2000s. But these opportunities affected only a handful of artists who were well positioned to take advantage of the efforts of the state and international recording companies. His analysis reflected the experience of the broad majority of emcees, who might achieve gratifying local recognition yet have no means to convert that popularity into something more enduring.

L-Tzack's background, and the experiences with the repressive side of state power that accompanied his poverty, also shaped how he viewed potential solutions. His use of the French *responsable*, which could invoke either government officials or business owners, aptly demonstrated the necessity for a specialized term. Calling for only businesses or only local officials to exert influence would not capture Makhzenian power to maintain the single government/economy nexus. Despite the rhetoric that surrounded him from practitioners, major venues, and the lyrics of hip hop songs he loved, L-Tzack identified the state's role in creating and maintaining new markets precisely because, in his lived experience, it was little different than the government's historic control over the economy.

While much has changed for working artists since 2010, some assumptions in both Khalid's and L-Tzack's arguments have stayed the same. Khalid's assertion that practitioners will eventually build a functioning market, one that by definition attracts consumers from the global north without the aid of the state, appears at odds with the logic deployed by L-Tzack in our decade-old conversation. Both socioeconomic positioning and the age of the speaker contribute to those differences. However, as Khalid's remarks above demonstrate, practitioners continue to conflate the idea of being professional with being competitive in global north markets. This is not only because they are surrounded by an ideology that prizes the structures, resources, and rewards that appear to exist in Europe and North America, but because their analysis of the limits of their market is still correct. For practitioners, as long as they lack a formal market—with all its rapaciousness and opacity—they lack a fundamental similarity with the global north, a difference that literally and figuratively powers the "developed" world's perceived monopoly on "modernity."

In addition, both Khalid and L-Tzack make their arguments for themselves and others. Khalid has coached aspiring emcees for nearly a decade. L-Tzack compares "all young people's" chances to those of artists from previous generations, who often had little security when they were too old to work.[10] In the chain of associations within professionalization discourse, links between individual moves and community well-being—between posting boastful freestyles and creating a training infrastructure—appear and reappear. The discourse surfaces deeply held concerns about material sufficiency and prestige, but also beliefs in musicians' worth. A "modern," "professional" market would confer on its participants society's "normal support," as L-Tzack put it, rather than the tolerance, bemusement, or even dismissal that Moroccans outside of practitioner communities often expressed toward hip hop culture in its first decades.

In the late 1990s and early 2000s, multiple competitions emerged from artists' networks in Casablanca, Rabat, and Meknes. In one of these, amateur rock musicians Mohamed "Momo" Merhari and Hicham Bahou created Le Tremplin ("springboard") in Casablanca. The nonprofit that grew to produce Le Tremplin and the Boulevard festival would become profoundly influential for "Western" musical genres in Casablanca and throughout Morocco. From its earliest years, this association paired skill- and network-building with a professionalization discourse in which entrepreneurship was linked to the ideal of aesthetic and political independence.

Le Tremplin grew out of an informal series of concerts organized by Merhari and Bahou at a community theater named Le Fédération des Oeuvres Laïques, or F.O.L., in Casablanca's upscale Gautier neighborhood. At the time, Bahou ran the Association for Artistic and Cultural Education, itself a part of the F.O.L., in addition to still working his day job at an ad agency (Callen 2006: 124; p.c. with Bahou, Casablanca, July 2, 2018). Merhari and Bahou sought to provide a laboratory for unappreciated, even persecuted youth musicking (Callen 2006: 125–26). From their inception, Le Tremplin and the Boulevard festival were designed to bring scattered practitioners of alternative musics into regular dialogue and to build mutual support.

The first annual Tremplin included several rock and metal bands and three fusion bands (EAC-L'Boulvart 2008: 37). In 2000, hip hop was added to the competition, and it soon became the category with the largest number of applicants each year.[11] Merhari has claimed that "2000 was the birth of rap in Derija," rather than English, because "groups had to include in their application tapes [*maquettes*] some tracks in Arabic" (Berrada 2015). By 2001, the three-day event included workshops for participating musicians. These included instruction in beatmaking software, preproduction and postproduction musical effects, recording technology, and sometimes instrumental technique (Callen 2006: 23).

By 2003, Tremplin relocated to Casablanca's rugby stadium to accommodate the hundreds of young people who came to the free four-day event (Caubet 2016: 251). By 2008, the enterprise had grown into two separate events: the spring Tremplin and its companion, the fall Boulevard festival, four days of invited domestic and international acts in rock and metal, fusion, hip hop and rap, and electronic musics (Harmach 2009a). By the late 2000s, the winner in each genre at Tremplin performed at the larger Boulevard festival months later. Depending on the year's sponsorship, winners also received additional training, access to a recording studio, and/or money.

Throughout the 2000s, Tremplin and Boulevard festival were funded through an ever-changing combination of municipal, NGO, and corporate gifts, including funding from the Institut Français and the American embassy and consulate.[12] In 2008, as the organization was building out its new headquarters in the basement of Casablanca's Technopark, it received a check worth two million Moroccan dirhams from the personal funds of King Mohammed VI. Widely reported in the media at the time, this gift acted as "a stamp" of approval (p.c. with Bahou, Casablanca, July 2, 2018) that insulated the Tremplin and Boulevard festival from conservatives' and Islamists' criticism.

Over time, Boulevard's corporate and governmental funding has enabled it to conduct year-round programming. Today, the umbrella organization EAC-L'Boulvart oversees many additional events in and beyond Casablanca, including Sbagha Bagha and other street art events, concerts, artist residencies, and partnerships with foreign festivals.

By the late 2000s, annual Boulevard happenings were understood as central events in the temporal, spatial, and social dimensions of the regional and national hip hop network. Tremplin in particular educated performers and audiences in the social and musical skills to be considered a competent participant.

I attended the Tremplins in 2008 and 2010. The 2008 competition took place in a large, traditional auditorium in Rabat that held several hundred people. It offered competitors experience on a proscenium stage, with the typical lighting, sound, and audience interactions of that experience. As one of the largest theaters in the country, the venue was likely the most prestigious any of the competitors had played. However, it offered the audience few of the opportunities to interact with performers that were critical to later editions of Tremplin.

In 2009 and 2010, Tremplin was held at Les Abbatoirs, the site of the former city slaughterhouse. Maintained by the city with several Casablancan cultural associations, Les Abbatoirs had recently been rescued from redevelopment and was serving as an all-purpose cultural center and event space. According to the estimates of the Boulevard Festival, ten thousand people aged between sixteen to thirty-five years old visited Tremplin daily in 2009 (EAC-L'Boulvart 2009: 7).

In 2010, Les Abbatoirs made an intriguing and sometimes disturbing site for an event at the leading edge of Casablanca's musical cultures. Tremplin stages were placed throughout a crumbling multibuilding complex in which signs of its former use were slowly being papered over—literally—in the form of tags, posters, murals, and advertisements. At the same time, the drains in the floor and giant hooks dangling from the ceiling of the huge, colonnaded halls allowed one to trace the path of generations of cows and sheep through the complex. The competition stage was located in a courtyard near the back of the available portion of the complex; later in the evening, the audience moved to a smaller space near the main gate, where another stage was set up for the invited artists. The former offered competitors and audiences the opportunity to circulate, to come and go, to cluster near the stage or to hang back. The latter, more crowded as people poured in to watch the headliners, ensured an atmosphere of sweaty electricity. Both spaces enabled moments of introduction, reacquaintance, or collaboration.

The daytime competition courtyard was small enough for well-known artists to be clearly visible in the audience or in the crowd socializing behind the sound technicians' tent. Throughout the day, moments of mentorship, critique, and mutual support undergirded the competition. The youngest competitor was just eight years old while the oldest were in their mid-twenties. Their approaches ranged from hard-hitting social commentary to the skits, group dance moves, and *rap comique* of Rime Fire Crew. The most comfortable performers simultaneously played to the live audience and the cameraman, prompting cheers from an audience that recognized their skill and enjoyed watching emcees lean into the camera. Several groups inserted practiced moments of audience interaction in their four-song sets, including classic call-and-response patterns. One coached the audience to wave their hands from side to side in time with the music, shouting "Limen! Lisr! Limen! Lisr! (Right! Left!)" as if we were marching in unruly formation.

As groups left the stage, they would join the audience, watching their competition with a mixture of appraisal and enjoyment. Competitors and audience members watched each other for indications of how groups were doing, noting the difference between clumps of fans who came to support their friends and those who moved when inspired by the music. Those circulating in the audience compared preferences and opinions, forming shared narratives about the performers in real time. When I remarked to a friend that I enjoyed one group's instrumentals, she scoffed, pointing out the American artists each track was taken from. Others would turn to me when their favorites appeared, making sure I had my camera ready.

As younger aspirants competed on stage and connected in the audience, established musicians from hip hop's earliest years in Morocco reconnected with each other. I witnessed people who knew each other only by sight, by conversations over Facebook, or by reputation meeting for the first time. Older musicians arrived singly or in small groups to the delight of younger competitors and audience members. Their investment in the event added legitimacy and excitement to the competition. The judges themselves were deeply embedded in the formation of the network unfolding in front of them. And while the competition portion of Tremplin was not televised, the evening's invited performers were broadcast live on the 2M program *Korsa* (p.c. with Younes Lazrak, March 18, 2010).

First-wave artists and event organizers scattered about the audience and dispensed photo ops and advice to enthusiastic amateurs. When Muslim crossed the courtyard, he was mobbed by fans of all ages. Masta Flow and J-Ok, from Casa Crew, were at the center of a circle of well-wishers, constantly shaking hands or greeting old friends. As the afternoon stretched into evening, a small but steady stream of young women approached Soultana. At one point, she coached a young girl on her flow, showing her how to keep her original lyrics in time by stressing the same beats on every line. While Tremplin did not impose stylistic or technical rules on its competitors, as I noted in other competitions, the elder musicians and younger audience members collectively built expectations for performers' musical and stage skills, forming a sense of the day as a critical event for the future of Casablanca's hip hop.

The effects of Le Tremplin and the Boulevard festival on performers of "Western" genres, in Casablanca and throughout the country, over the past twenty years cannot be overstated. The organization's many staff and volunteers consistently focused on supporting the basic infrastructural needs of aspiring artists. Their events functioned as key opportunities to circulate diverse styles, enhance young people's networks and reputations, and build capacities, all outcomes that continued in later events like Sbagha Bagha. The organization also popularized its own beliefs about meritocratic competition, freedom of expression, and professionalization.

FAKE MARKETS AND REAL COMMODITIES

The day after Sbagha Bagha's closing battle in 2018, I met Hicham Bahou for coffee at Boultek. Le Tremplin, EAC-L'Boulvart's original program, had met goals far beyond its original purpose. In their first year, Bahou and Merhari told a journalist they hoped their fledgling competition would inspire state support for "young artists" (Dades 1999 quoted in Callen 2006: 125–26). Nearly twenty years later, Hicham noted that when the national Jil Mawazine competition ended in 2014, people expected him to be pleased because state-sponsored competitions had "stolen" their format. But they were wrong, said Bahou—it was good for the musicians. Plus, there was nothing to steal. "That's not our idea. It's just a competition," he remarked to me. "It's no one's idea" (Casablanca, July 2, 2018).

As we talked, he took a call from WeCasablanca, a city-run event-planning agency. Earlier that year, the agency had asked to partner with L'Boulvart on their own mural project around el-Hank, an impoverished coastal neighborhood named for the lighthouse at its center. According to Hicham, L'Boulvart agreed to help find walls to paint and artists to invite. They also suggested adopting other aspects of the Sbagha Bagha program—spending weeks, not days, in the neighborhood; inviting young people to watch artists work and to join workshops with muralists; ensuring that residents felt the art was for them as much as for others. In the end, the city agency invited four or five artists to spend a week painting murals, then left the neighborhood. Now, they were ready to announce the completion of the murals and wanted Hicham's assistance with outreach. "The murals were finished two months ago . . . and now they will invite people to tour them next week?" related Hicham after his call, eyes narrowed in exasperation. WeCasablanca had benefited from L'Boulvart's unpaid legwork and expertise but ignored the values behind their work.

The success of Tremplin inspired regional and local competitions across the country. The state has acted both within and parallel to this tradition of musician-organized competitions. Between 2006 and 2015, the nonprofit association Maroc Cultures held a tournament-style popular music competition known as Jil Mawazine ("Mawazine Generation") alongside the international Mawazine festival. Jil Mawazine was the largest and most influential popular music competition to receive state funding during that period.[13] Like Tremplin, it was open to applicants from across the country. With greater resources, however, Jil Mawazine created a multilevel live application process in which applicants performed at five regional competitions before the finalists competed in Rabat. For over a decade, through Jil Mawazine and similar regional competitions, the state both underwrote the emerging popular music market and played a defining role in what musicians interested in these competitions wrote, rehearsed, released, and performed.

While the competition created value for the Moroccan state by attracting favorable media coverage, for most winners Jil Mawazine failed to make the signal contribution it advertised: to lead to a viable next stage in one's professional career, ideally via exposure to international markets. The market Jil Mawazine and similar state-funded competitions created was "fake," in that it promoted ways of composing music, performing, and promoting that were driven by competition rules instead of by listeners' or artists' preferences. Yet winners became symbols of the government's preferred narrative of the country and its citizens, a commoditization that simultaneously exoticized winning artists and tamed their appeal to national and international consumers.

Jil Mawazine consistently reaffirmed the state's vision of itself as the ultimate arbiter of opportunities for Moroccan youths. Statements from Maroc Cultures often assumed or asserted the musical, technical, and cultural underdevelopment of the competitors. In 2007, then-president of the festival Abdeljalil Lahjomri described the competition's goal as "to push [young artists] toward quality and to impose upon them certain professional requirements [*exigence professionelle*]" (Chabaa 2007). The competition's head judge, musicologist Ahmed Aydoun, frequently cited "the opportunity to play . . . in professional conditions" as important to uncovering talented musicians (Harmach 2008). Ten years later, looking back at Jil Mawazine, the festival's official press booklet characterized exposure as support: "As a concrete aid to launching their careers, the winners were offered the opportunity to play during the festival" (Maroc Cultures 2017: 13). The 2017 edition continued to imply that Moroccan acts needed the increased exposure the festival could provide. Moroccan musicians' stages "offer[ed] conditions equivalent to the stages reserved for international stars. During the nine days of the festival, Moroccan groups and singers also benefit from collaboration with . . . true event professionals at every level: technicians, logistics, communications, etc." (Maroc Cultures 2017: 16). During the years Jil Mawazine ran, in order for competitors to enjoy the benefits advertised by the festival, they had to meet vague but exacting standards for how to represent Moroccanness in sound.

The competition changed in many ways over its nine years, but general outlines were maintained. Musicians competed in several "Western" genres, including hip hop, rock, fusion, and electronica. Competitors submitted an application described as imitating a professional dossier, including a CV, photos, a press blurb describing their biography and musical style, and two recordings on CD or cassette.

During the live competitions, each act played two to four songs. A multijudge panel assessed and ranked each act. A second round was held in each city approximately one month later, and from there, one ensemble in each genre of music was chosen to compete at the national finals in Rabat. Winning ensembles usually performed the following year at the Mawazine festival's stage on the beach at Salé.

Over the years, Jil Mawazine winners were rewarded with forms of professionalization in various forms and amounts. The first year's awardees received new instruments and "the possibility of being produced" (Chabaa 2006). In later years, advertised awards included a three- to five-year contract with Maroc Cultures, a professionally recorded and promoted debut album, and a music video to be played on national TV (Jadraoui 2009; Bouithy 2010; *Libération* 2010).

By the time journalist and musician Jihane Boughrine published her inquiry into Jil Mawazine in 2014, the advertised prize had expanded to "a management contract of five years"; musical and technical training; recording, producing, and promoting an album with professional staff; and the expectation that each winner would perform during the Mawazine festival in 2014 and during the next competition in 2015 (Boughrine 2014). Regardless of their performance history, winners were amateurs in the sense that they had not released a full-length album.

In practice, awards usually included time in a professional studio with a producer and sound engineer, the opportunity to produce a music video, and promotional placements on state-sponsored TV and radio. Execution of these awards varied widely. In at least one year, King Mohamed VI gifted personal funds to winners, solidifying the appearance of unified monarchical and governmental support for "Western" genres (Ghayet 2008).

Musicians who matched the competition's preferences, often by returning with refined entries every year, could move to finalist and eventually winner status. In 2010, I met with the members of Hakmin ("rulers" or "wise ones"), who had won the second Jil Mawazine competition in the hip hop category in 2007. Their beatmaker and vocalist, Rachid, invited me to his family apartment in Meknes. We said hello to his mother in the spacious living room before he showed me the group's studio—his emptied bedroom armoire, lined with blankets and outfitted with a mic and a plastic-covered window cut into the side. From his desk next to the armoire, Rachid could see the occupant of the recording booth simply by glancing to his left. Two other group members perched around the tiny room as we talked.

At the time, the group was writing songs for their projected second album. During our conversation, they told me the group formed in 2006 and entered the first Jil Mawazine competition that year. Disqualified because the youngest member was not yet fifteen, they entered again in 2007. Their second try won praise from judges and press for including indices of Moroccan genres in their performances. Rachid described the group to me as "rap *en fusion*," noting that they adopted this term after a journalist applied it to them in 2006. "Rap was waiting for this concept," said Rachid, as he played fragments from their 2009 album, *Besm Allah* (In the Name of God), on his MIDI keyboard. "Our development at Mawazine took us to a professional level" (interview, March 17, 2010). With their mix of sung harmonies, ragga-inspired chanting, rapped verses, and melodies that recalled *malhun*, 'Aissawa, and Gnawa repertoires, Hakmin understood themselves as expressing national pride in a fresh, innovative way.

By the time they won in 2007, Hakmin was already part of a discourse that rewarded the transformation of select Moroccan genres into forms of recontextualized heritage.[14] The first Jil Mawazine winners, a boy-band-inspired group named Tiraline, combined tightly choreographed dance moves with rapped verses and sung references to 'aita, traditional song whose transformation from a controversial, if beloved, genre to national folkloric asset had begun only in the 1990s (Kapchan 1996: 209). In the years following their wins, both groups' rare performances were linked to the state or non-Moroccan state entities like the US Embassy.[15] In 2010, I attended Hakmin performances like the closing concert for L'Université de l'Été (the Summer University), sponsored by the ministry of foreign affairs, in which college students with Moroccan heritage spent two weeks in Morocco.

Jil Mawazine produced a stable of ensembles whose repertoire consistently recalled genres already considered beloved folklore and whose opportunities rarely went beyond concerts at state-sponsored regional festivals. Competition winners were also unable to effectively contest any breach of their planned awards or contract by Maroc Cultures. By 2008, Hakmin were promoting an upcoming tour "in Morocco and abroad" in support of their album.[16] To my knowledge, the album was released and promoted through a music video produced as a result of their award, but no tour occurred.

The choices of Tiraline and Hakmin set a precedent that would recur in 2010 and 2011, when the solo singer/emcee AZ Flow and the group Rwapa Crew, both of whom had competed multiple times, won using similar tactics (Salois forthcoming). In between, Morocco's first all-woman hip hop group, Tigresse Flow, won their category in 2008. The song that received the most attention did not feature musical indices of Moroccanness, but instead celebrated their identities as Moroccan women in their lyrics.

The 2008 and 2009 winners' awards included the recording and promotion of a full-length LP (Harmach 2009). According to Soultana, who launched her solo career in 2009, Maroc Cultures declined to produce Tigresse Flow's album despite doing so for the all-male ensembles who won the rock and fusion categories that year. Since it was widely assumed that young women musicians would stop performing once married, Soultana surmised that the festival team thought they were a poor investment (Salois 2014). However, the appearance of an all-female hip hop group enabled much positive coverage of Morocco in 2008 and 2009 (e.g., Pfiefer 2009; Raiss 2009).[17]

In practice, the Jil Mawazine competition effectively underdeveloped its musicians and potential national market in several ways. First, the competition's disproportionate impact on the otherwise self-organized hip hop network provoked the formation of groups whose central goal was winning competitions and who disbanded after that goal was met or when they gave up trying. Though some of the artists I met during this period saw little distinction between competing at Tremplin, Jil Mawazine, or other festivals, the state's resources, reach, and narratives set expectations and shaped the conditions of possibility for performing opportunities in a way no other institution could do.

Jil Mawazine also incentivized musicians to adopt certain musical and textual choices by selecting musicians who chose options like these, year after year, in a program explicitly advertised as identifying musicians ready for professional careers. Cumulatively, the competition communicated that the state supported a narrow range of styles or approaches to each genre. More importantly, it communicated that the judges and organizers of Jil Mawazine could only imagine music that essentialized Moroccan identity within the framework of transnationally popular "Western" genres as internationally competitive. While for many musicians this was irrelevant, the significant number of repeat competitors suggests that for some, at least, the market vision Jil Mawazine advertised was strongly attractive.

Though I cannot confirm this, the competition's preferences may have made a bigger impact on those without a deep network of fellow practitioners or access to a wide variety of international media. In the small mid-Atlas town of Ifrane, regional competitions backed by both governmental and corporate sponsors help young hip hop artists legitimate their practice to their skeptical parents (Seilstad and Essiffi 2015: 82). Of the winners in Jil Mawazine's first six years, only the two from Casablanca—Tigresse Flow (2008) and Dirtyfaces (2009)—performed tracks without explicit musical markers of Moroccanness. The other four were from smaller towns in the greater Casablanca region (Tiraline and AZ Flow), from Meknes (Hakmin), or from Fes (Rwapa Crew), none of whom had a community of hip hop practitioners of the size, depth, or resources of Casablanca.[18]

Finally, once a musician or group won the competition, Maroc Cultures maintained a high level of control over musicians' sounds and winners' postcompetition performances. This control intensified in 2008 or 2009, when musicians were required by contract to perform only at the invitation of Maroc Cultures for three to five years after their win. Regardless of gender, the market that Jil Mawazine constructed for its winners in the hip hop category offered few—or in Tigresse Flow's case, no—stepping stones to opportunities outside of state-sponsored events.[19]

During its nearly ten-year run, Jil Mawazine had a far-reaching impact on how career-minded musicians in Morocco's hip hop, rock, and fusion networks thought about their work. In a fast-moving stylistic environment in which most competitors were in their late teens to late twenties, and in which competitions were difficult and expensive to run, its state backing and seemingly unlimited budget made Jil Mawazine appear especially stable. Its organization and the preferences of its judges profoundly shaped popular musics throughout its tenure, making it an excellent site to explore how hip hop artists understood the state's role in the genre and its market.

In the introduction, I noted that the Mawazine festival incurs criticism from a wide range of voices on both moral and financial grounds. Hip hop artists of my acquaintance frequently added that the festival underpaid Moroccan artists relative to those from Europe, the United States, or the Middle East. Jil Mawazine's effects on the professional horizons of hip hop artists during the 2000s and 2010s became another way that, through state-funded and state-aligned projects, the government maintained the underdevelopment of youth culture while claiming to support its eventual transformation.

Throughout the 2000s, the large number of small, independently organized competitions inspired by the Tremplin model—as well as Tremplin itself—offered ways for local musicians to build working relationships with each other and to practice solidarity across difference and despite personal and professional jealousies. The smallest competitions gathered and activated local networks by cobbling together borrowed, rented, and volunteered equipment, spaces, and labor. In a very real sense, the awards offered by these competitions enhanced this effect since they were usually small amounts of money paid for out of the competitors' entry fees.

In contrast, the small number of hip hop musicians who earned the state's overt approval by winning a festival competition, of which Jil Mawazine was the largest, could count on being paid for a handful of performances every year for a few years. But of the hip hop musicians who won the first six years of Jil Mawazine, only Soultana was able to continue performing at the national level after this relationship ended, albeit at an attenuated pace.[20] Winners rarely returned, or were invited to return, to stages they might have played pre-award; as Hicham Bahou told me, these artists might reasonably see themselves as having outgrown all but the biggest national stages (July 2, 2018).

Despite this, aspiring musicians continued to hope that national-level performances live, on TV, or on the radio would offer wealth as well as convertible prestige. While some state-sponsored competitions attract amateurs from their specific region, the largest have the budget and infrastructure to reach beyond the major cities, drawing young musicians from the largely rural south and east. Their status as government-funded entities with access to national media outlets also adds legitimacy to the idea that winning ensures entry into a national or even international market. While I cannot say what effects the lower levels of the Jil Mawazine tournament may have had on participants who did not ascend to the final round, I suggest its advertised prizes made striving to appear successful all the more important for the awardees. The way the state disburses funding, including occasional high-profile gifts from King Mohamed VI, extracts value from youth cultures by creating a sense of competition spurred by scarcity rather than solidarity.

National competitions like Jil Mawazine, and today's competitions attached to regional festivals, are often described by Moroccan theorists and others as a tool to police popular musicians and hip hop artists in particular. Early in the 2000s, Taieb Belghazi described the impacts of the Fes Festival of Sacred Music as the "festivalization" of that city. Instead of an opportunity to turn social relations upside down, as Turnerian theorizing emphasizes, this and other elite-led, state-sponsored festivals "[reproduce] the dominant[-]power political structures in Morocco" (Belghazi 2006: 97). Said Graiouid and Taieb Belghazi point out that the small and densely connected network that controls access to national platforms depends on royal patronage to do its work.[21] This has "enhanced state dominance, 'naturalized' art's ties to the market, curbed the development of the public sphere, and accentuated forms of inequity among cultural workers" (2013: 264).

Aomar Boum holds that the state's actions have successfully co-opted some hip hop artists and events. Implying that state support invalidates artists' present or future critiques, he describes the King's 2008 gift to EAC-L'Boulvart as "soft surveillance" through which sponsorship "succeed[ed], if only partly, in turning protest music disseminated primarily through YouTube into a profitable industry and weakening rappers as a political force amidst the Arab uprisings" (2012a: 25). He suggests that "we can identify a number of artists who became close to political parties or state agencies while creating a false consciousness of state contestation. . . . The fragmentation of the industry of hip hop demonstrates the structural strength of the Moroccan system and its power to weaken these protests" (2012b: 6).

Boum's argument resonates with analyses of the Moroccan state's successful divide-and-rule strategies (e.g., Cavatorta 2007; Maghraoui 2020). However, to make this argument, Boum suggests that the development of a "profitable industry" will chill rappers' speech, and he asserts the existence of an industry in order to describe the state's disruption of it. In his first example, focusing on the king's gift alone obscures the long-term support the Boulevard Festival has enjoyed from the municipality of Casablanca, the ministry of culture, and from non-Moroccan state entities like the Institut Français and the US Embassy and instead posits a clear line between a state of independence and one of corruption. It also avoids consideration of artists' and event organizers' possibilities and limitations. For example, for the state, the fact that the Boulevard Festival's founders literally could not refuse a gift from the monarch surely heightens the effectiveness of the donation. Yet in our conversation, Bahou chose to highlight how this helped his organization rather than constrained it. Precisely because it was described as an unsought "gift" in national media, EAC-L'Boulvart could disavow any alteration to its beliefs or commitments.

While it is beyond the scope of his argument, Boum also does not note that for EAC-L'Boulvart, DIY artistry and aesthetic diversity express a politics of freedom that aligns the organization with "Western" narratives about the affordances of art and civil society. Tremplin, Sbagha Bagha, and other events build spaces in which colleagues' desires to learn and to experiment are seen as natural. "The objective of Boulevard has never been to organize a simple music festival for three or four days each year, but to continually . . . defend a principle: the freedom of expression," claimed EAC-L'Boulvart President Braham Bihi in the pages of the organization's annual journal, *L'Kounache* (The Notebook). Bihi cites article 27 of the Universal Declaration of Human Rights, noting that "access to playing an musical instrument is considered an intrinsic right of mankind" (Bihi 2009: 18). In the context of EAC-L'Boulvart's ideologies and objectives, the King's 2008 gift could be—and has been—read as support for cultural "westernization," consistent with the state's goal of promoting youth cultures post-2003 while simultaneously cultivating loyalty to the monarchy.

Academics' responses to state power in the cultural field, and its expression in festivals, frames the intertwined nature of the monarchy, the state, and the country's primary economic actors in ways that legibly intervene in existing social science discourses. To do this, scholars paradoxically both underplay and overplay the historic and pervasive power of the Makhzen. On the one hand, each framework conforms to unexamined expectations to separate states and markets analytically. This minimizes the power the state wields through its imbrication into all parts of the supposedly postprivatization economy. On the other hand, each framework starts by imagining a state that is not only unitary but successful at controlling citizens through surveillance, patronage, or the threat of reprisals. While the state certainly does deploy these tactics, such analyses do not include the ways that the state undermines its own control by appearing fragmented, contradictory, or simply ineffectual. Nor do they leave room to think through the roles of citizens who are neither co-opted nor militantly resistant. Further, describing the state as a singular, canny actor in this way takes for granted the effect that the monarchy and the Makhzen seek to perpetuate.

While scholars have described hip hop practitioners' interactions with state-sponsored and state-aligned projects as an inevitable process of co-optation, a more capacious question is how state sponsorship furthers—rather than inspires—citizens' complicity. How do we account for the fact that EAC-L'Boulvart accepted funding from Casablanca and various postcolonial states for over fifteen years, yet there was no widespread discussion of their "independent" status until they received a gift from King Mohamed VI?[22] How can we account for the motivations of amateur hip hop groups like Hakmin, who originated with the goal of competing in Jil Mawazine and defined themselves through the styles its judges found most attractive? These are questions that a diagnosis of co-optation does not seek to answer, precisely because the diagnosis imagines prior separation from the state and its ideologies. Yet many of these actors were not outside those ideologies in the first place.

Pervasive yet insufficient state funding contributes to a lack of genuinely private funding options. Moreover, these forms of funding set expectations for what is to be supported, so that corporations without financial ties to the state might be less likely to fund activities without direct or indirect seals of approval. Further, Jil Mawazine and similar regional competitions successfully presented themselves as benefactors to Moroccan youths, appearing to cultivate a national audience for Moroccan performers in "Western" genres by offering access to platforms that could be reached in no other way. Yet they simultaneously appealed to existing desires for transnational mobility and recognition. Such state-funded competitions thus represented most of the avenues of ambition a young artist might reasonably imagine.

In both financial and discursive ways, then, state sponsorship makes it more difficult to imagine oneself outside of the current cultural field. Even an entrepreneur like Khalid, the Block Dix organizer who counsels his mentees to seek multiple ways of reaching international listeners, encounters a gray area between "post the music on YouTube" and "later we'll find some way to sell it." The premise of Jil Mawazine, and of more recent state-funded initiatives, seems to fill that gap by positing an audience for those whose music conforms to the state's long-term vision of saleable Moroccan culture.

The environment I have described here renders complicity with the state's norms, goals, and practices nearly impossible to avoid as musicians reach beyond their immediate neighborhoods. The state's successful strategy of inserting support into developing realms of the musical market has continued into the present, with the emergence of state-supported recording studios like Studio Hiba and events like Visa for Music, a WOMEX-like annual showcase sponsored in part by the ministry of culture. In these ways, and in addition to older forms of support, musicians from across the socioeconomic spectrum find that state funding is implicated in the structures that best meet their needs.

While I have attempted to show how unavoidable state interventions have been, it is equally important to consider how complicity works differently across diverse levels of income, wealth, education, or social capital. While L-Tzack, for example, argues for the state's responsibilities to its citizens precisely because of his experience of the state's repressive powers, those with greater affluence find that state-sponsored interventions constrain and benefit them in more subtle ways. The women of Tigresse Flow, all of whom were young, unmarried, and from working-class neighborhoods at the time of their 2008 Jil Mawazine win, had few options when they were denied their award except to leverage the short-term notoriety of being females in the public eye to complain to the press. Even for internationally famous EAC-L'Boulvart, simply maintaining core events still requires financial support from multiple levels of the state, constraining the way the organization can act. "We are like the goldfish—[every year] we forget all the last years and we return with a smile," Bahou joked to me about EAC-L'Boulvart's municipal sources of funding (July 2, 2018). Across socioeconomic differences, actors were highly aware of both the limitations and affordances of state support, even if they were unsure of which agencies contributed what amounts. Entering a market for performances, images, or reputations required understanding the influences at work or, equally importantly, those perceived to be at work. In turn, responding in ways that asserted one's values—regardless of one's field of choices and eventual actions—was critical to maintaining one's personal and professional connections, and to potential future collaborations.

CONCLUSION:
IMAGINING MOBILITIES, IMAGINING FUTURES

Early in the afternoon of Sbagha Bagha, before the deejays had finished setting up, MC Dalim and I chatted about his background. Dalim was a longtime mentor at Block Dix. He earned a degree in African American studies while perfecting his craft as a rapper, he told me, writing a thesis on how the Harlem Renaissance influenced Malcolm X, Louis Farrakhan, and Martin Luther King Jr.

We found a freshly painted wall for a backdrop, and I asked him the same question I would ask "elders" all day: What advice would you give your younger self?[23] Dalim could sum it up in a single word. "Study!" he urged.

"Study, study, study well," he insisted. "Why? Not to work. To toughen yourself [*bash tw3ir rassik*]."

"But you already have your degree," I responded.

"Even though I have studied up to a certain level, you have to study to the next level," he said to his hypothetical teenage self. "If you study, you won't be afraid. You'll understand things I don't know." You have to enlighten yourself if you want to enlighten others, he stressed. Dalim concluded by opening up his remarks to the present. "If we want society to go forward, people have to become a little more *intellectual*," he said, using the English term.

Later that day, I watched Dalim coach his young mentees during the open mic. I watched them pour energy into their performance personae, lifting their chins, straightening their shoulders, angling their elbows sharply outward as they stepped

FIGURE 5. MC Dalim during an interview with the author, Casablanca, 2018. Photo by author.

out from behind the deejays. At the edge of the stage, Dalim quietly checked in with each performer before and after their set, offering praise, feedback, or just a clap on the shoulder.

Perhaps because I asked him to give advice, Dalim's remarks were normative rather than specific. He referenced several values I understand as widely shared among first-generation Moroccan hip hop artists. One is a belief in education as good for the self. Another is a belief that the right kind of person, with the right kind of mentality, is good for society and the nation. Instead of being afraid of what you don't know, you'll have control over your own self (*rassik*), allowing you to contribute to society instead of being swept along with it or held back by it. As a mentor, Dalim puts these beliefs into action, encouraging others to take charge of their own learning within hip hop culture and supporting institutions in which young emcees could grow.

I was unable to return to Sbagha Bagha the following year. Watching for glimpses of it on social media, I noticed that Dalim had posted a reflection on his work to Instagram. Under shots of himself with young artists in the web radio tent, laughing with Khalid and that year's Block Dix performers, he had written in English: "ambition is doing what u love."[24]

This chapter has positioned solidarity, expressed as deeply felt commitments to mentorship, fellowship, and artistic excellence, as vital to the competitive practices that form the social and musical foundation of Moroccan hip hop culture. In turn, those competitive practices make it possible for participants to think of their social and musical labor as interventions into different kinds of markets and to think of themselves as entrepreneurs in those markets. Competition is routinely understood as core to neoliberal subjectivation, as the primary way one interacts in a world made up of increasingly intimate cost-benefit analyses (e.g., Feher 2009; Read 2009). Yet solidarity is equally necessary to our picture of neoliberal subjects precisely because it helps sustain that competition. It offers competitors opportunities to feel morally upright, emotionally fulfilled, and socially connected even while they live with or embrace a zero-sum approach to both material and immaterial questions. These sentiments and sensations continue to affect practitioners when competition is conducted against physically distant, invisible, or unknown competitors, or even—perhaps especially—against oneself.

Most of my interlocutors embraced the informality and precarity of their market even as they noted its shortcomings and worked, when they had the means, to reform it. They also enjoyed formal and informal competitions as important and common sociomusical events. And critically, my interlocutors treated and continue to treat competitions as a form of care for oneself and one's community. Caring labor, differentiated by socioeconomic status and by gender expression, often took the form of mentoring across artistic generations.

Likewise, self-care often took the form of preparing oneself for informal and formal competition. Striving in competitions and markets brought a sense of pride for both "winners" and "losers," for both individuals and their communities. L-Tzack sounded a note of wonder when he reflected on how much he had learned through his decades-long love of hip hop culture: "I can make beats, I can record, I can mix it and master it. Me. I can do so much" (interview, Fes, January 2010).

When Moroccan b-boy Fouad Ambelj, known as Lil Zoo, became the world champion of Red Bull's BC One competition, his former teacher Yoriyas posted a joyful tribute on Facebook in October 2018. "10 years ago at mid of night I was practicing alone at a park of street of Casablanca 04 district, a 12 years kid was watching me dancing, for few min i asked him: yo kid!!! it's too late what you are doing here," he began.

> After 4 years I play against this kid in final of Morocco championship and I lose (I was happy to lose even i did my best to win) . . . Yesterday I was drinking a tea and watching a live of the number one world championship of breakdance called @ redbullbcone [. . .] in the end a great dancer won it and he become the new world champion this guy is the same kid I meet 10 years ago his name Foad we call him Lilzoo!!! Congratulation bro, thanks for the inspiration!!!

Competitions act simultaneously as markets for styles and skills, movements toward "development" and professionalization, expressions of care for others, and allegiance to something bigger than oneself. Markets were and are seen as something that could free practitioners from inheritances, expectations, or stagnations they lived with, even as informal versions could heighten old inequities or impose new ones.

By demonstrating the degree to which the state intervened in the growth of hip hop music-making over the 2000s, but also the ways in which practitioners themselves shaped that growth, I argue that practitioners' identities as market actors can be read as both an acceptance of and a solution to forms of domination under Moroccan neoliberalism. As David Scott describes this dynamic, recalling Talal Asad and Stanley Diamond, market aspirants are "coercively obliged to render themselves its objects and its agents" (2004: 9).

My interlocutors conceived of markets as enabling their desired futures. In both material markets for music and intangible markets for personal values, immediate benefits were as or even less important than the speculative value—the potential future value—of market participation. This chapter has sought to show how these material and intangible markets are inseparable from one another, and how the value "discovered" by them is oriented toward the future, whether the participant imagined sales, physical mobility, or simply a time and place in which they felt supported, proud, and accomplished.

The solidarity I have described throughout this chapter does not necessarily extend to musicians' political beliefs. However, it does permit a shared calculus of what success might look like. For many of my interlocutors, regardless of their family's income, mobility is the most valued "thing" one can obtain from one's market actions. Geographic, social, or financial mobility amounts to a potential for all other kinds of capital and, in turn, other futures. Moulay Driss El Maarouf summarizes the ever-present belief in this potential, located within the mobility of people and various forms of capital: "The west, as an idea traded across local markets through music and fashion, might represent precious opportunities for local cultural economy to thrive and become richer with time" (2014: 263).

Geographic mobility in particular allows a person to circulate in markets elsewhere, markets for labor, music, or otherness imagined to be better—bigger, busier, more lucrative. Thus, solidarity can also take the form of feedback on practices of differentiation as individual tactics for mobility, from one tactician to another. When the judges of Sbagha Bagha described MEVOK's entry as insufficiently canonical, or when MC Dalim argued that young artists must study to "move society forward," both were encouraging individualization within community norms. Both spent energy on a project in which individuals might contribute to a better future, but they did so by supporting competition against others or oneself.

David Graeber returns to the perennial question of whether "value" and "values" are the same (2001: 78). My contention is that among my interlocutors, the latter is now often understood in terms of the former—not as an amount of currency, but in conceiving of personal values as part of one's market value alongside one's education, skills, or social connections. As the next chapters elaborate, many of my interlocutors find themselves in markets that circulate people who are seen to embody valued qualities like resourcefulness, determination, or resilience. The emphases on personal responsibility and community, meritocracy and solidarity, that appear throughout this book underpin people's desires to form markets. They also make them marketable persons in a community that defines itself partly through its mentality about the future. The markets my interlocutors sought to build did not always circulate money, but they did have to hold the possibility of change.

4

Embodying the Urban Poor

ʿAyoun al-Ḥak (الحق عيون, "eyes of truth") wanders through deserted downtown Rabat in the middle of the night. A slight man lurks nearby, hunched in an oversize T-shirt and shorts, a cap pulled low over his face. As he walks, al-Ḥak tugs at the lapels of his crisp black suit and perfectly knotted tie and shoves his hands in his neatly tailored pockets. The camera closes in on his face as he describes the life of the homeless from an empty park bench; it pans out as he shuffles down familiar sidewalks. Finally, after six lines in a rhythmically compelling pattern beginning with the phrase "I saw (*shuft*)," he stares directly into the camera for the punchline: "I saw my life in that long boulevard full of hurrying people / People don't recognize others, I will befriend [them]: one of them am I."[1] In the next shot, the other denizen of the night—the R & B vocalist Toxi—bursts into the hook, arms outstretched in the empty street.

In "Boulevard" (2013), ʿAyoun al-Ḥak interprets hip hop's charge to represent the street quite seriously. Though born and raised in a middle-income neighborhood in Rabat (interview, Rabat, July 31, 2015), he speaks both *as* and *to* the most impoverished in his city, taking responsibility while playing a character who struggles to understand himself "class passing" as a professional ("I'm one of them," he reminds us, jabbing a finger at his chest). Listeners who have seen al-Ḥak's other music videos or read his public statements will likely recognize that al-Ḥak hasn't actually experienced homelessness. They also expect to accept his narrative as "real"—an aesthetically appropriate expression of his own observations, intentions, analyses, and politics (Jackson 2005: 192). Throughout the piece, lyrics, musical choices, and visuals underscore the conflation of truth, sincerity, and realness, all in the service of sensitizing al-Ḥak's listeners to the struggles of the urban poor.

This chapter demonstrates how Moroccan hip hop practitioners, across varied socioeconomic positions, depict poor and powerless citizens as objects of governance in concert with the state. By deploying long-held assumptions about the *oulad sha'ab*, or "children of the people," as an authentic source of national identity, musicians claim the authority to speak for the politically and economically disenfranchised. At the same time, their actions align with the state's views of the urban and rural poor, aiding in framing these citizens as a category of concern and a target for action.

The first section explores how the idea of the oulad sha'ab has changed over time. As generations of rural migrants arrived to Morocco's major cities, the postindependence celebration of traditional identities originally indicated by the term has been tempered by the increasing association of new migrants with abject poverty and state-sanctioned dispossession. Next, I move to contrasting ways leading artists speak for and about poor, isolated, or marginalized subjects in their music. While these examples use divergent tactics, they perform similar assumptions about "the people" and intervene in similar ways. Finally, I describe a recent, significant outcome of this discourse: a hip hop training program that encourages "resilience" among poor youths in Sidi Moumen, home of the suicide bombers of the nation's worst terrorist attack, in 2003.

Even when artists critique state corruption and its abandonment of poor citizens, the narratives and initiatives described in this chapter discursively—sometimes materially—reinforce policies and effects that target the poor. These interventions institutionalize an empathetic response that expresses deeply held attitudes about the relationship between poverty and authenticity. As in other examples throughout this book, such interventions accomplish this reinforcement precisely because the practitioners involved sincerely believe in their work's potential for good. As a whole, then, this chapter asks: Can hip hop artists' attempts to humanize the urban poor escape the complicities that shape them and in which they intervene?

WHO ARE THE *OULAD SHA'AB*?

In *sha'abiyya* (lit. "popularity") discourse, poverty must be ameliorated, but it also keeps people closer to their core values and to an idealized Moroccan character. As the emcee Amine Snoop mused, "The poor people . . . they have the pure inspiration" (personal communication [p.c.], May 9, 2018).

The noun *al-sha'ab* ("the people") has signaled a political constituency since the beginning of modern Moroccan nationhood. While those who wield the term often claim to be using it inclusively, its effects are often exclusionary. The definition of al-sha'ab—who is hailed by the term and who most properly represents the Moroccan nation—has been contested throughout recent history, whether by nationalists in the 1920s and '30s, Marxist-Leninist artists in the 1960s, Ghiwanien bands of the 1970s, or the leadership of today's political parties. Prior to the end of the French protectorate in 1956, nationalists invoked the people in rhetoric "that emphasized Morocco's Arabo-Islamic dynastic history as evidence of long-standing national unity," refusing colonial insistence on cultural and ethnic difference between Arabs and Berbers (Wyrtzen 2015: 137). In the mid-twentieth century, political actors frequently adopted a populist discourse, similar to that of other Arab nations, in which al-sha'ab continually progressed toward greater unity and prosperity (e.g., Sabry 2010: 55). Following his father's and grandfather's practice, King Mohamed VI continues to address citizens as *sha'abi al-'aziz* ("my dear people") in his speeches. The related words used to describe people, practices, and musical genres still reverberate with some of the rhetorical grandeur they absorbed during the heyday of the pan-Arabist and Moroccan independence movements, but they can also evoke intersecting distinctions by class, origin, education, or income.

Today, the adjective *sha'abi* ("popular") is potent precisely because it can celebrate authenticity and index the lower classes at the same time. A valued traditional item, practice, or person can be called sha'abi, but the term can also evoke rural and urban poverty that is associated with isolation, backwardness, lack of education, and narrow tastes. Regardless of the positive or negative valence, sha'abi practices "contribute to the definition of . . . Moroccanness and Moroccan identity" (Simour 2016: 7).

As a noun, sha'abi identifies interrelated indigenous popular musics. Applied to popular musics from the 1940s, sha'abi genres have been associated with rurality since the 1970s. This remained true even as urbanization continued to intensify and even as the leading practitioners of sha'abi genres have routinely come from urban backgrounds (Callen 2006: 337; Aydoun 2014 [1992]: 161). Until the advent of private commercial radio and television in the early 2000s, state-controlled media preferred to play more prestigious genres, contributing to the discursive association of sha'abi with rurality, poverty, and lower classness. At the same time, urban and rural performances of sha'abi styles flourished on cassette. Musicologist Ahmed Aydoun argues that urban migration birthed contemporary sha'abi, writing, "In the . . . popular quarters situated in the medina or on the periphery [of major cities], the music you will hear most often is sha'abi [*le cha'bi*]. . . . This population comes from different regions [and] consumes, in addition to folklore [*folklore*], a middle genre drawing on all the popular styles and exclusively privileging rhythms for dancing" (Aydoun 2014 [1992]: 161–62).

The negative associations with migrants, cultural stasis, and pastness surrounding sha'abi as both a term and a genre are echoed by musicians across genres and socioeconomic locations. Writing in 2006, Jeffrey Callen noted many 1990s fusion bands participated in this discourse, viewing sha'abi as "mediocre and conservative music" (2006: 5). Throughout the earliest years of my research, in 2008–10, hip hop artists often positioned their music as a response to sha'abi, complaining the genres were meaningless, repetitive, or simply boring.

In recent decades the increasing immiseration of rural migrants in Morocco's major cities has transformed the figure of the oulad sha'ab in popular discourse. Unable to afford city housing, many settle in *bidonvilles* (lit. "oil-drum towns" or "tin towns"), informal homes on the urban edge.[2] Others move to the *medina* ("city"), the preprotectorate sections of major cities, which often lack the services and amenities of the French-built or postindependence *villes nouvelles*.[3]

Elite perspectives on rural migrants have colored the available meanings of oulad sha'ab over time. A professor and former minister of culture voiced the prevailing sentiment: "At the level of mental structures, the inhabitants of the medina still occupy the countryside. . . . New arrivals to the city use inappropriate mental structures—tribal, traditional, and rural—to cope with urban reality" (Haddad 2001: 105). In interviews, Koen Bogaert learned that "public officials generally seem to believe that the slum dweller is not capable of engaging in public life, that he needs to be re-educated, and that he himself is responsible for his situation" (2011: 726). Such responses fold descriptions of slum dwellers, and the assumptions of their economic and moral deviance (Zaki 2007), into the meanings evoked by sha'abiyya discourse. In this telling, uprooted rural Moroccans are unable to transform themselves into successful urbanites as much because of their mentalities as their poverty.

As sha'abiyya discourses became more firmly associated with low- and working-class Moroccans in the 1980s and '90s, they were rhetorically opposed to Westernization and affluence. Yet because oulad al-sha'ab also index tradition, the concept also valorizes when used by, or between, Moroccans of greater social standing. While from the 1960s to '90s, calling someone *would sha'ab* ("child of the people"; *would* is the singular of *oulad*) emphasized his patriotism, today its use often reflects a belief that "traditional" populations possess the greatest cultural authenticity and the least ability to succeed at "modern" life.

HIP HOP ARTISTS AS OULAD SHA'AB

Hip hop artists draw on the positive and negative resonances of sha'abiyya discourse to discuss political belonging. In "Bladi Blad (My Country Is the Country of)"—a 2006 track from Don Bigg feat. Kolonel—Rabat emcee Kolonel calls out corruption among the Makhzen with the line, "They ate the people's money until you shook as they passed."[4] In the song that precipitated his first arrest, "Klab al-Dowla (Dogs of the State [2011])," Mouad "al-Ḥaqed" Belghouat uses a formal tone to indict the government: "In the name of the people who are in my heart, I pour it out to you, you infidels."[5] That same year, Don Bigg responded to the February 20 protest movement with "Ma Bghitch (I Don't Want It)." While he uses "al-shaʿab" in a traditionally political way in the line "They give beans to the people so they can't sharpen their teeth," he also complains that "the people don't exist, they don't look out for themselves," perhaps using the term to question the assumptions of coherent social class and mass solidarity.[6]

In her song "35.28," Soultana makes a similar move, naming "the people" but refusing to celebrate them:

> Stop being so cold, the whole world is saying it
> My silence and your silence leaves those responsible to the people insolent
> My voice and your voice count, but my point is in the final line
> Whether one speaks or not, they buy [us] with flour, oil, and sugar[7]

Here, the punchline depends in part on Soultana making the legacy of nationalist uses of al-shaʿab explicit through her denunciation.

The phrase, and figure, of oulad al-shaʿab can also make a point by its absence. For example, in "The Tears of the Neighborhood (Dmou3 al-Houma [2016])," Muslim uses *would al-houma* ("child of the neighborhood") throughout. When one expects to hear "would al-shaʿab" instead, this emphasizes that poor neighborhoods where young men are inevitably drawn into drug use and crime are isolated from sources of power, dislocated from the supposed political force of the people.

The subject defined through hip hop artists' use and deformation of oulad shaʿab is also depicted visually. Artists position themselves as, or as speaking for, oulad shaʿab by visualizing themselves within terrains of authenticity in their videos. They also evoke shaʿabiyya discourses when repurposing traditional musics. Pro-state pop and hip hop artists like Fnaire[8] celebrate the diverse sounds and figures of Moroccan cultures while aligning with the goals of the state. Their oeuvre depends on a powerful strand of shaʿabiyya discourse in which rural lifeways are the source of shared Moroccan identity and values. Few artists defend state policies as explicitly or consistently as Fnaire, but many use this dimension of shaʿabiyya discourse to legitimize their own narratives and critiques.

In the 2015 track "T-JR feat. Ahmed Soultan" ("Toujours" or "Toufik Jr.," 2015), Don Bigg and his son leave for the countryside so Bigg can clear his head, reflect on his life, and return to moral certainty.[9] Throughout, shots of Bigg and Ahmed Soultan, who sings the chorus in the Tashelhit language, interweave with the visual story of a man growing up in a tiny rural hamlet.[10] In the first verse, Bigg raps the story of his son's birth as the camera pans over mud-walled buildings. Outside one door, a father-to-be waits anxiously while his laboring wife moans. Then an elderly woman ululates, signaling a baby boy's arrival. In the second verse, the baby becomes a curious child learning to read while, in the lyrics, Bigg recites his hopes for his own son's future.

In the third verse, the child becomes a man with a small daughter of his own. "Bring me a pen and paper," says Bigg to his son. "I'll record for you the seven things I'll remind you of every day that I live."[11] As Bigg enumerates his fundamental lessons, both protagonists—he and the rural man—take the children to pray at their grandparents' graves. Soultan's chorus underscores the idea that across cultural, economic, and linguistic differences, Moroccan parents believe in passing on elders' wisdom. Mixing Tashelhit and Derija, he concludes, "I hope that your children will see your parents / and your path."[12]

Throughout, the camera frames the rural family's faces and interactions tightly, focusing viewers' attention on the warmth and strength of generational ties. We see that the paint is peeling and the sparse furnishings are worn, but the family is portrayed as simple and dignified rather than deprived. Though Bigg visits a grave topped by a marble headstone in a graveyard at the edge of a modern town, and the rural protagonist visits a grave marked with rocks in a field, their understandings of a vital form of identification—how to raise Moroccan children—are the same.

In other videos, artists travel through the countryside to find themselves, presenting its inhabitants as authentic Moroccans to learn from. In "Kue Passa" (2015), Mr. Crazy rhymes about his dissatisfaction with his life as he hikes alone through mountains. "I'm watching my life passing by like it's going on sale [*gha promo*]," he laments. "I found myself, I'm one of the ugly ones, my life needs some Omo [a popular laundry detergent]."[13] His backpack and bedroll suggest this character faces a long journey, perhaps to the Mediterranean. Together, the lyrics and visuals extend the metaphor of the countryside as a place that reveals truths, and of migration as a search for personal transformation and fulfillment.

While hip hop musicians claim cultural authenticity via rural landscapes and impoverished rural citizens in these examples, a separate video trend explores the flip side of sha'abiyya discourse. 'Ayoun al-Ḥak's "Boulevard" is one of many videos that demonstrate musicians' commitment to the urban poor by placing emcees in or adjacent to visible poverty. Al-Ḥak goes further than most, empathizing onscreen through his character's homelessness.[14] More commonly, emcees use Morocco's crumbling urban infrastructure and bleak shots of citizens experiencing hardship to assert their critical acuity and willingness to take a hard look at inequality. Through these tactics, artists claim the moral authority to speak for, and less often with, the urban poor.

In SiSimo's "'Eid al-Faqr (The Poor Person's Holiday [2013])," he and codirector Mehdi Ouldsouilem open poignantly with a man and a woman—perhaps a father and his adult daughter—in happy times.[15] They are superimposed over a scrolling shot of the elegant apartment buildings lining Boulevard Zerktouni near the Twin Center mall, located in the most famously upscale neighborhood in Casablanca. As a single 'oud concludes a meandering melody, hinting at the chords of the chorus with a sound linked to both tradition and power, the man gives the woman a beautiful necklace and kisses her on the forehead. The screen fades to black on the woman's smile. Next, a wailing infant and a reprise of the 'oud melody accompany the camera, panning from feet on Zerktouni's crowded sidewalk to that same woman—now in a modest traditional robe—huddled against a streetlamp. Nearby, the man lurks. Though he is drunk and desolate, he keeps a tearful eye on her as she begs from passersby.

SiSimo expands out, lyrically and visually, from one family to the stunning economic disparity on display in Casablanca. Shots of the city's bidonvilles are intercut with gleaming buildings; luxury cars pass garbage collectors steering donkey-driven carts down major thoroughfares. Close-ups of indigent individuals of all ages pair with repetitive statements in the chorus. Each mouths the beginning of each line: *hna al-fuqara* ("here are the poor"). Yet SiSimo is not a character in this narrative, but the narrator. Though his voice emanates from their faces, he is only seen with his hard rock band. Though SiSimo is from Fez, his use of Casablanca's architectural signatures signals to Moroccans the simultaneity of concentrated wealth with the social and political abandonment of the poor.

Like SiSimo, in "Anti" (2018), trap artist LBenj acts as a keen observer rather than a participant.[16] The opening shots closely track a distraught, hoarse-voiced man shouting incoherently in what appears to be the dead of night. His ranting contrasts with the delicate electronic timbres and high ranges characteristic of Moroccan trap, shading the autotuned falsetto voice in the background with a sense of foreboding. He gesticulates and stumbles as he crosses Avenue des F.A.R. (the Royal Armed Forces), a four-lane road separating Casablanca's tiny medina from the imposing protectorate-built structures downtown. His face is pixelated, giving the impression that he is a real person and not an actor.

During the verses, LBenj details the urban poor's challenges while demonstrating his distance from them. A few shots of him in rain-slicked streets late at night, when no one but the homeless and the intoxicated are out, legitimate his knowledge. Otherwise, he perches on a stool in a fancy pub, his untouched martini communicating worldliness and wealth. LBenj may be a denizen of the street, but he speaks as a *flâneur* rather than as a member of the group he characterizes.

Sha'abiyya discourse allows Moroccans across social classes to voice their belonging to the nation through their identification with the rural or urban poor. Even when hip hop artists follow the genre's visual conventions on consumption, displaying luxury cars, homes, and fashions in their videos, their texts on inequality and injustice identify their wealthy and successful characters with the social body. For some artists like Amine Snoop, who publicly claim their impoverished origins, celebrating the people in this way also recuperates his upbringing among Casablanca's working poor. For others, it legitimizes their right to critique and authenticates their moral arguments.

Emcees' texts on poverty encourage listeners to feel responsible for themselves and others without promoting specific policies to redress inequality. First-generation and younger artists frequently envision a society where individuals care more for each other not only because they see this as morally correct, but because they expect change to flow from individuals rather than from a government perceived as having abandoned the poor. Today, musicians participate in or even design diverse efforts to help poor youths, including the workshops in the next section.

THE STARS OF SIDI MOUMEN

On a scorching day in August 2016, I sat alone outside just after Friday prayer at a musty midcentury cafe on the rondpoint Mers Sultan in downtown Casablanca. As I waited for Anas, I plucked my espresso from its saucer from above to avoid the table's baking surface.

Anas had agreed to travel together to his workplace, the Centre Culturel les Étoiles de Sidi Moumen. Universally referred to as Noujoum Sidi Moumen or simply Noujoum ("stars"), the center opened in 2013 in the neighborhood of Sidi Moumen on the outskirts of Casablanca. Anas, a baby-faced emcee in his late twenties, was Noujoum's first full-time hip hop specialist. That summer, he taught its first workshop on emceeing known as "Positive School." This day, the twelve students, aged twelve to twenty-two, would hold their closing concert for family and friends.

Once I spotted Anas, I met him at the corner trying to flag an empty taxi. His younger brother Abdou nodded companionably at me without removing his headphones. In the taxi, I handed Anas books I had brought at his request.

"I . . . want some [books] that I can read to have more knowledge about hip hop and DVDs [and] videos about hip hop story . . . that I can show to my students," he had explained over Facebook when we got back in touch the previous month (p.c., July 8, 2016). He was delighted at the foreword by DJ Kool Herc in Jeff Chang's germinal *Can't Stop Won't Stop*. "I'm happy to know I'm teaching them the right things," he told me in his careful English. He'd already delivered a lecture about the founders, he said, including Herc and Afrika Bambaataa. I mentioned Grandmaster Flash's appearance in the book, too, casually referencing the legend-driven history Americans and Moroccans often retell.

"And Grandwizzard Theodore," Abdou piped up from the front seat. "His little brother who invented scratching by accident."[17] I could hear the overdriven bass from the buds still firmly lodged in his ears. Anas beamed and high-fived his brother for remembering the lecture.

As we maneuvered toward the southwest edge of the city, Anas explained how much he enjoyed teaching, telling a new generation about hip hop's founders and what he believed they stood for. Like other artists I worked with, he relied on occasionally fictionalized depictions of places like the Bronx or Compton to understand what influenced his favorite emcees. I recalled how the previous year, he diligently followed news of the NWA biopic *Straight Outta Compton* and Dr. Dre's album *Compton: A Soundtrack*, scoring digital bootlegs the same weeks they were released.

Anas was fond of telling the "something from nothing" origin stories of his favorite American artists.[18] Although these biographies seemed to contrast with his own life—he and his brother grew up with their parents in a comfortable apartment in downtown Rabat, and both had some postsecondary education—he often returned to how hard emcees worked before fame, how inner resources and dedication carried them when they were just long-shot amateurs.

His emphasis on transformation was well suited to Positive School and the goals of Noujoum Sidi Moumen. Founded shortly after the tenth anniversary of the May 2003 suicide bombings in central Casablanca, Noujoum was established to provide youths in the bombers' home neighborhood with alternatives to Islamist extremism. Anas's story was rapidly becoming one of the testimonials to hard work and commitment he enjoyed sharing. The previous summer, he assured me that "if we have a good spirit and clean mind . . . no one can stop us" (July 30, 2015). Now, he coached underprivileged children to deliver uplifting rhymes. As he said during my visit that day, "I never expected to make a salary doing rap music."

My visit to Noujoum Sidi Moumen, and the performances of Positive School No. 1 that I witnessed, demonstrate how narratives about the relationship between poverty and extremism have transformed the neighborhood of Sidi Moumen, Casablanca's nonprofit sector, and sha'abiyya discourse. Hip hop artists have contributed to these narratives since shortly after the bombings occurred, releasing songs that, like the vast majority of Moroccans, refused the moral and geopolitical ideologies the bombers are believed to have held. Volunteering—or in rare cases like Anas's, getting paid—to share both their musical expertise and their 'aqliyya has also given practitioners legitimacy in a new arena.

As I discuss below, Anas and his coworkers embraced resilience as a goal for their young students. As a desirable result of personal responsibility and self-care, resilience depicts poverty as an individual challenge to be overcome rather than an injustice to be fought. Today, resilience-building projects are a significant response to the national and international understanding of suicide bombers. In what follows, I discuss Moroccan responses to the attacks that killed dozens in Casablanca on May 16, 2003. I contextualize Positive School No. 1 and Noujoum Sidi Moumen as part of an outpouring of concern for "slum dwellers" after 2003, and I discuss how Positive School No. 1's curriculum replaced hip hop's tradition of critique with "positivity." This promoted resilience discourses already shared across local, national, and international state and private agencies. Finally, I return to Anas's and others' attraction to stories of resilience when discussing 'Ali Sawtek (Fr. Haut et Fort, En. Casablanca Beats), the 2021 full-length fiction film based on Positive School directed by Noujoum cofounder Nabil Ayouch.

The multiple assumptions in sha'abiyya discourse ground Positive School, with its aim of training young people to be resilient despite generational poverty and systemic inequality, in Moroccan culture. The energy and sincerity with which young cultural workers like Anas promote resilience, the degree to which this value aligns with the kind of person they encourage themselves and others to become, is just as important to the workshop and students' flourishing.

May 16, 2003

On May 16, 2003, fourteen young men staged a coordinated suicide bombing in Casablanca. Targets included a Spanish restaurant, a branch of the Golden Tulip hotel chain, and a Jewish cultural center. Thirty-four bystanders and eleven attackers died.[19]

The attacks were the first suicide bombings against Moroccan targets (Alonso and Rey 2007: 572). They generated instantaneous condemnation across the mainstream political spectrum, from the Francophone press to the Islamist Justice and Development Party's newspaper.[20] Postattack demonstrators adopted the slogan "Matqish Bladi," or "Don't touch my country," shown in a hand of Fatima symbol (Rogers 2012: 458).

While it is not clear who trained or bankrolled the bombers, national press and historians alike have highlighted the role of "foreign" Wahhabist doctrine in inspiring the attacks. According to Pierre Vermeren, the royal prosecutor alleged that two Saudi-trained Moroccan imams "were the inciters" of the attacks; they were subsequently jailed (2009: 173). Moroccan security forces have accused al-Qaeda of ultimately ordering the attacks and similar foiled plots (Alonso and Rey 2007: 581).

At the same time, astute observers noted seeds of the attacks were planted decades earlier. Alonso and Rey point out that foreign-trained imams led increasing numbers of mosques across Morocco from the 1970s through 2003, explaining the influx of Islamists through the monarchy's "very close ties to the Wahhabi regime in Saudi Arabia . . . [it] was accepting financial support in return for fostering Wahhabism" (Alonso and Rey 2007: 573). They argue that an "endogenous" Salafism, loyal to neither the Moroccans nor the Saudis, grew among Moroccan followers after both states cooperated with the United States during the first Gulf War (Alonso and Rey 2007).

Editor and journalist Abdellah Tourabi, by contrast, dates Moroccan strains of extremism from the independence movement, arguing that early nationalists borrowed from Mashreqi Salafism to build rank-and-file support (2008: 214). In this view, Saudi-trained Moroccan imams of the 1970s and '80s merely heightened existing strands of extremism. Tourabi and others argue that in the late twentieth century, the state leveraged Wahhabist or Salafist imams against native antimonarchy groups, and only sought to reestablish control over the popularity of these doctrines after the 2003 attacks.

As more information emerged, it became clear that all of the suicide bombers were from the same place—*Karian Thomas* (or *Toma*), a bidonville within Sidi Moumen.[21] Formed by waves of rural migrants, the karians of Sidi Moumen were at the time cut off from the rest of Casablanca geographically, culturally, and economically, with few or no services provided by the state.

From at least the 1990s, Islamic charities have filled gaps left in housing, public health and hygiene, education, and even security. According to Lamia Zaki, "The state is at once absent from the *kariens*, since they refuse to introduce to them the most elementary forms of infrastructure . . . (running water, electricity, sewers, trash collection, public transport stops, maintenance of order . . .). Yet it is still present, since it attempts to maintain every day the precarity of the site" (2006). Tourabi offers shocking, unverified numbers: "In a city—Casablanca—where more police surveil the American consulate than assure the order and security of neighborhoods filled with more than 100,000 inhabitants, the state had de facto delegated its responsibilities in policing to . . . groups of zealots" (2008: 220).

In the years after the attacks, the Moroccan state, national press, and international counterterrorism commentators aligned around what I call the "vulnerability narrative": that economic and political disenfranchisement leave the poor *as a group* vulnerable to radicalization. Implied within this emphasis on inequality is an exclusion of other explanations. In other words, one could readily withstand the internal consistency and claims to authority in jihadist doctrines were one not already broken down by poverty and discrimination, which disables critical faculties people would otherwise deploy. The state's response to its own diagnosis has been an array of reforms safeguarding affluent public places and the state's reputation, secondly, if at all, alleviating the suffering of its poorest citizens.

After May 16, journalism, commentary, and artistic reflections across the political spectrum cemented the vulnerability narrative as the way to understand how deeply deprived youths could kill themselves and others. The monarchy's widely publicized counterterrorism efforts promoted assumptions that radicalization was primarily a problem of inequality, not discourse, even as the state quietly arrested thousands and launched extensive surveillance efforts. According to Mustapha Hamil, "Two weeks after the 'May 16 attacks,' King Mohamed VI visited Sidi Moumen and promised to improve its housing conditions but nothing concrete on the ground was accomplished, except perhaps that Sidi Moumen got the reputation as a hotbed of fanatic kamikazes" (2010: 566). In a sweep, about five thousand Moroccans "were arrested and interrogated in subsequent days [after May 16 and] . . . eighty-seven were accused of complicity" (Park and Boum 2005: 334).[22] The National Human Development Initiative "was launched 'with the aim of combating poverty as a means to combat radicalism and terrorism'" by the end of 2003 (Bartolucci 2010: 127).

Morocco's national and regional governments used the attacks to launch an ambitious urban renewal program known as *Villes Sans Bidonvilles* (Cities without Slums). Karian residents were induced with low-cost loans to move to apartments in new high-rises far from their homes (Bogaert 2011; Atia 2019). Alongside existing assumptions that karian residents could not assimilate to urban life, "the bombings of 2003 reinforced the objectification of the slum *population* itself as a calculable target for a general strategy of government, trying to convert the slum dweller into a responsible citizen" (Bogaert 2011: 712, italics in original).

One could invoke the vulnerability narrative whether discussing individual responsibility or state policy. Former Minister of the Interior Driss Basri, infamous overseer of King Hassan II's surveillance and repression during the Years of Lead, described karian residents as "poor people with very little who can easily get entangled in the mysticism around Islam, which makes them willing to do anything in order to get to paradise" (quoted in Alonso and Rey 2007: 575). At the same time, leading liberal commentators like the editor of independent *Le Journal Hebdomedaire* held that "the suicide bombers are a home product . . . the inevitable consequence of 'specific socioeconomic conditions, an inadequate education system, wrongful religious policy, the failure of political parties, an obsolete system of government and an inappropriate media policy' [Jamai 2004]" (quoted in Hamil 2010: 557). In this way, commentators from opposite sides of the political spectrum appeared to agree on the credulity of the very poor.[23]

Conditioned on the negative dimensions of sha'biyya discourse, the vulnerability narrative displayed commentators' unwillingness to engage the attackers as unique individuals with considered moral, political, or intellectual positions.[24] This narrative allowed Moroccans to understand the state's post-2003 policies of forced resettlement and counterterrorism policing as protecting, rather than abusing, the urban poor.[25]

Attempts to prevent or provide alternatives to radicalization assumed that economic and cultural deprivation mutually reinforced each other. These attempts sought to address the perceived lack of education, exposure, and urbanization of karian residents. For those who saw Casablanca's disparities as a temporary consequence of Morocco's global market integration—rather than failure to redress the permanent effects of that integration—the answer lay in expanding that integration by bringing new opportunities to the karians.

The Centre Culturel les Étoiles de Sidi Moumen, opened in 2013 by painter and novelist Mahi Binebine and filmmaker Nabil Ayouch, follows through on the responses implied by the vulnerability narrative. As leading figures in Morocco's national and international arts scenes, Binebine and Ayouch both encapsulated and led elite opinion on Sidi Moumen in the years after the May 16 attacks. In 2010, Binebine published *Les Étoiles de Sidi Moumen* (The Stars of Sidi Moumen), a novel that focuses on four young men's trajectory toward martyrdom. Ayouch released *Les Chevaux de Dieu* (Horses of God), a film based on the novel, in 2012. Each depicts political and economic inequality as inescapably intertwined.

The Centre, also known as *Noujoum* ("stars" in Arabic), is a project of the Ali Zaoua Foundation, a nonprofit incorporated in London. Ayouch created the foundation in 2009, naming it after the titular character in his 2000 film. Ayouch had already been working in Sidi Moumen, "in the streets, in the slums," to film

Ali Zaoua (p.c., April 2023).[26] In several different interviews, Ayouch described his shock in 2003 upon learning the suicide bombers were from a place he had spent years making documentary films. This realization changed his relationship to the neighborhood. "I investigated in the bidonvilles [over] two years in an almost anthropological fashion. I informed myself by meeting sociologists [and] political scientists who were interested in radical Islam," he told one interviewer (Aubel 2013).

Noujoum offers classes and workshops in several genres of music and dance, photography, foreign languages, and other skills. According to Sophia Akhmisse, the director of Noujoum and manager of the Ali Zaoua Foundation, preparation for the permanent cultural center began in 2013 when Ayouch and Binebine screened *Horses of God* in Sidi Moumen. They arranged for families of victims and suicide bombers to watch the film together (interview, August 5, 2016). A cover story on Noujoum from 2017 set the scene: "[*Horses of God*] was shown throughout Morocco, except in Sidi Moumen, which lacked a cinema. Nabil Ayouch contacted the governor. . . . The showing took place on May 16, 2013, ten years to the day after the attacks. Ayouch invited the families of the victims and two mothers of the kamikazes, in niqab, were present in the hall that night. There were a lot of tears" (Charon 2017). After this profound encounter, Ayouch and Binebine rented the building in which they showed the film. Through their relationships with Moroccan artists, sixty of whom donated paintings for an auction, they raised enough for a cultural center (Akhmisse, quoted in Bouithy 2014). They continue to fund through donations and a partnership with the municipality (Fondation Ali Zaoua; interview with Akhmisse, August 5, 2016).[27]

According to Akhmisse, when she was hired to create programming in 2014, she visited neighborhood homes asking what people would like the center to offer. An overarching theme emerged: instead of one-time workshops that left attendees with no way to apply their new knowledge, people wanted structured classes that built toward mastery in domains—foreign languages and music—that required extensive practice and increasing skill. In response, Noujoum offers more than one level of each language. Courses in instruments, singing, dance, and visual arts range from a month to three or four months each.

Just as the state and municipality moved quickly to build formal infrastructure for the neighborhood after 2003, nonprofit associations showed much interest in Sidi Moumen shortly after the attacks. By 2014, some residents characterized the associations' typical behaviors and funding models as exploitative. As Akhmisse described it, residents saw the same short-term interventions over and over again. These yielded photos with which associations could fundraise, but little concrete change for residents themselves (interview, August 5, 2016). Noujoum's permanent physical presence and longer classes were not only more effective teaching, but communicated respect for residents' needs and desires.

FIGURE 6. One half of a graffiti mural in the courtyard of Noujoum Sidi Moumen, 2016. Photo by author.

Ayouch and his colleagues surveyed Sidi Moumen residents before opening Noujoum and learned that "art and culture was really the thing that was needed the most. Because lacking also the most in those neighborhoods" (p.c., Nabil Ayouch, April 2023). Yet Akhmisse indicated that the focus on the arts at Noujoum was not solely a result of its founders' professions and beliefs. Not every Sidi Moumen resident accepted music and dance classes as appropriate for their children, but many saw the arts as a valuable way to build students' skills and intellectual capabilities. The press booklet I received during my visit offered a typical week's schedule filled with "nearly eighty-five hours of classes" for children, teens, and adults, including English and French, theater and fashion, guitar, drums, and piano, zumba and yoga, and classical and hip hop dance (Fondation Ali Zaoua: 7).

At the same time, I knew from years of interviews with first-generation hip hop practitioners that many felt their parents and even their peers did not respect their love of the genre in the 1990s and 2000s. I asked Akhmisse why Noujoum would run a two-month emceeing workshop alongside a full complement of instrument and dance courses. Why did she think it was valuable?

Seated behind her paper-stacked desk in the tiny office she shared with two other staff members, Akhmisse opened her eyes wide and exhaled. "I think it builds self-confidence," she said, after a pause. These students have already chosen to pursue hip hop, she continued. We show that we support their choice.

Given Noujoum's founding and the role it sought to play within the neighborhood, the support of the institution and its staff could carry significant weight for students and, perhaps, their families. When I asked if they planned to hold more Positive School workshops, Akhmisse answered unequivocally: we will do them for as long as we have interest.

In August 2016, Positive School No. 1 had thirteen enrolled students—four young women and nine young men—but Anas, the young emcee hired to lead the workshop, already spoke excitedly of his plans for Positive School No. 2. Nearly forty children had already enrolled for the next class. The new, expanded version would run the entire academic year and hold a concert every three months (interview, Akhmisse, August 5, 2016). Perhaps they could even have a "level A" and a "level B" (p.c., Anas, August 5, 2016). On top of that, Noujoum hoped to expand in the coming year to Tangier, where they would run the same programs.

The Positive School project came from hip hop artists themselves, who pitched it to Noujoum leadership in the spring of 2016. According to Anas and his original collaborator, they proposed developing a hip hop musical with students at the center for its annual May 16 commemorative event. In the eventual plot, students played victims of the 2003 bombings. The concert performance, held on May 17 as the second evening in a week of events titled "Creative Explosion," was considered such a success that Anas was hired full-time to lead the first, and then subsequent, Positive School workshops (p.c., August 5 and 7, 2016).

The first Positive School's students ranged in age from twelve to twenty-two. Each student had paid about two hundred Moroccan dirhams (about twenty dollars) for the eight-week day-camp-style program. According to Akhmisse, the fee communicated the commitment the center expected of its students more than it covered costs. Each weekday, Anas met with his students in the classroom normally reserved for English instruction. In the corner of the whiteboard at the front of the classroom, a paper *khamsa* read "Try to speak English—Avoid speaking Arabic."

Part of each week was dedicated to the history of US hip hop music. Since many students had little to no education in French or English, Anas would show music videos, documentaries, and movie excerpts, then summarize in Arabic. Students also developed a persona, including an artistic name, a song topic, and some lyrical and musical ideas. Anas told me that he created the beats students used, helped write the lyrics for each song, and formed ensembles by pairing the students into duets or placing a chorus singer on students' tracks.

By July, the students were ready to record their songs. For most, it was their first introduction to studio recording equipment and interacting with a microphone. The resulting compilation was advertised along with the closing concert and handed out to attendees in exchange for their fifteen-dirham ticket to the event.

As the early August date of their closing performance drew near, Anas introduced considerations that might go into a professional performance, including the order of songs and whether and how to provide visuals on stage. Finally, students were coached in performance practice, including how to hold the mic, listen for the onstage monitors, and move onstage in a way appropriate for their genre. Their final class sessions were spent in Noujoum's black-box theater, becoming accustomed to the proscenium stage, the lights in their faces, and their voices bouncing off the walls and concrete floor.

Throughout the course, Anas had ample opportunity to reinforce "positivity" and to implicitly ground the value of the concept in the disciplining force of sha'abiyya discourse. By their nature, the origin stories he provided of hip hop's early innovators focused on select individuals whose achievements we now frame as transcending their circumstances. When helping students identify and describe issues important to them, he offered suggestions or alternatives fitting interrelated goals: to create uplifting, family-friendly material, and to debunk misconceptions students' families might hold about hip hop.

For example, Anas told the story of a duet he coached between two students stuck on what to write about. At his suggestion, they both wrote to their mothers. The resulting song, "Yo Mama" (spelled "Yo ماما" on the compilation), included parallel verses in which the young men imagine what their parents would like to hear. In the first verse, the youngest student at Positive School begins, "Mama, don't be scared that you won't like what I'm saying." The second verse, recited by one of the oldest students, begins, "Mom, don't be scared, I understand what you're telling me."[28] The youngest emcee addresses fears that rap introduces children to bad words and vulgarity, while the second verse acknowledges parents' fear that young men simply ignore them as they move toward adulthood.

One important goal of the summer course was promoting social bonds and emotional health across differences of age, gender, ability, or religiosity within the group. The afternoon of their final performance, a dress rehearsal channeled the students' nervous energy and boosted more reticent students' confidence. I watched from a corner of the auditorium as the group ran through the set, with Anas urging each student to move quickly and with authority onstage. When he asked students to act like the audience they wished to see, they crowded the foot of the stage for each song, dancing jubilantly and half-jokingly cheering at the top of their lungs.

At one point, rehearsal broke down when a young girl stepped forward to perform her solo rap. This song was the only moment in the set entirely in English. A few measures in, she lapsed into silence; her small frame, draped in a pink hijab and matching long cardigan, seemed to shrink toward disappearance. Anas hoisted himself onstage and bent deep at the waist to look into her eyes. For a few bars, they rehearsed a cappella, focusing on subdividing the time between each line. Eventually, as the young girl started to nod more assertively, he gestured to the group and waved toward the sound booth at the back of the auditorium. Her fellow students careened toward the stage as the music restarted, throwing their arms in the air and shouting the last word of each line along with the soloist. By the end, though her shoulders were still hunched forward and she clutched the mic with both hands, the girl was smiling.

All of the students I spoke to had already started singing or rapping on their own before the workshop. Anas targeted hackneyed lyrics and stereotypes about rappers as they arose, arguing these were based on his students' limited exposure to the genre. Hours before the final performance, we were greeted with respectful enthusiasm by Zeph Jo, a student in his late teens sporting a *tcharmil* hairstyle—shaved on both sides, long on the top and back, slicked down with gel—and a red and black baseball jersey. When he bounded out of the room, I noticed his jersey read "CLIQUE" across the back in large white letters outlined with metal studs.[29] As Kanye West's 2012 hit started up in my head, Anas looked after him fondly and shook his head. "That guy is really street," he remarked. "But he's a real rapper."

He was doing really typical stuff, Anas continued. "But I worked with him and I told him about how to write positive things and to give positive messages to people." For Anas, his young charge had the dedication, passion, and temperament of a "real rapper." He just needed to channel his energy away from the vulgarity and irrationality associated with the term "street" into work that, Anas implied, would reach more people and communicate something more valuable.

Anas made these comments in English. I didn't ask whether he was familiar with the disputed idiom opposing the Arab elite to "the Arab street" (Regier and Khalidi 2009), because I interpreted his choice as consistent with his and others' hip hop–inflected English. However, his use of "street" potentially conflates two references: the "Arab street" as a condescending term for public opinion that implies Arabs to be "volatile," "chaotic," and uneducated (Khalil 2009: 48), and the invocation of "the streets" in Anglophone hip hop discourse as the genre's authentic home.

During the culminating performance that evening, Zeph Jo's solo was the first of the night. Anas bookended his piece by evoking the multiple meanings of street, framing hip hop arts and culture in ways that resonated with sha'abiyya discourse. In his opening remarks to the audience, Anas described Positive School's goals in a mixture of Derija, French, and English, starting with the official English name for the program:

> Before we begin, here's a little for you about Positive School. In Arabic, it means *al-madrasa al-ijabiya.* . . . This training program educates the children about the history of hip hop, in general, from its first day in the 1970s in America, in New York, in the Bronx exactly, until 2016. . . . Rap is still, as you know, an art of the street [*fann dyal sh'aria*]. You don't go to your mother, and she says, "Yes, I want the truth about your life." She describes herself—this is the art, excuse me—as *peace, love, unity and having fun. Donc,* today, you're going to listen to some rap, to nine songs that speak on positive topics, and we're going to show you the beautiful side of this art that comes from the street.[30]

FIGURE 7. A poster advertising the first Positive School's closing concert is taped to a column in the atrium of Noujoum Sidi Moumen, 2016. Photo by author.

As Anas suggested, he and others claim that rap is still located close to its roots in the street. In a Moroccan context, the street connotes a public, male site opposed to one's home, a private site where one's mother presides over both what is said and how it is said. Yet Anas instructed his audience that hip hop itself claims values anyone can appreciate, citing the Zulu Nation creed of "peace, love, unity, and having fun." "The beautiful side" of this street art, then, simply needs to be uncovered and revealed. These opposing characterizations mirror the ambiguities of shaʿabiyya discourse, in which the oulad shaʿab are othered yet authentic, uneducated yet honest, pitied yet celebrated.

Anas then left the stage to perform the compilation album's introduction. In twelve brief bars, he resignified much of his previous statement offstage while the audience focused on a group photo projected on the stage's back wall. The lights faded to black, coming up again on the opening measures of "Fahmni (Understand Me)." Zeph Jo strode out to center stage, his "CLIQUE" jersey hanging from one shoulder. With angular gestures and outstretched fingers, his grip on the mic, restless pacing, and frequent vocal breaks radiated urgency. In a sign of how much he had practiced, the young man stayed on or just slightly ahead of the beat throughout his performance. "Understand Me" also communicated intensity through its lack of a chorus. Instead, the sixteen-bar loop continued unbroken throughout the song. By the end of his three verses, he was panting as he pumped his fist in the air.

Anas met Zeph Jo at the edge of the stage, gently steering him back toward the audience while taking up the microphone. "Okay," began Anas, arm across his student's shoulder, as the stage lights came up.

> This first song was performed for you by Youssef, aka Zeph Jo. In this song, Zeph Jo tries to present to you all [about] women, his life, and everything that he's seen. He put everything into one song in order to say . . . that the neighborhood, you all who speak with [him] every day, this is rap. *Donc*, it's speech about everything negative and ugly in his life and sends a direct message to anyone [*ay sha'ab*]. This is for you if you've left school. This is to any ugly thing, any difficult thing in his life.

Anas stressed the aesthetic and moral relevance of Zeph Jo's text. If "this is rap," then rap can discuss anything, and it can have therapeutic value for performers and listeners. While Anas introduced performers throughout the evening, this was the only time he interpreted student text for his audience. Starting the set with "Fahmni" allowed Anas, as the teacher and director, to navigate both his students' needs and his audiences' potential concerns. Zeph Jo was able to perform a deeply felt piece that was, of the evening's songs, closest in topics and rhetorics to recorded Moroccan hip hop. Yet by the end of the concert, family and friends in the live audience heard a series of songs on more lighthearted themes, ensuring they came away with an understanding of what Anas characterized as "the beautiful side" of the art form. Facing "reality" through Zeph Jo's rap, often cited as a key value of the transnational hip hop tradition, was followed by explicit statements of empowerment. The evening moved from the most vulnerable and angry expressions to celebrations of children's enthusiasm, creativity, and resilience.

FROM VULNERABLE TO RESILIENT

Since 2016, Positive School trainings have expanded with Noujoum to locations in Tangier, Agadir, and Fes. According to their advertisements, Positive School is accepted by the country's traditional sources of arts funding, including several municipal agencies, postcolonial NGOs such as the Institut Français, and the US Embassy. Positive School pioneered the Moroccan institutionalization of hip hop as both an art form and a form of entrepreneurship. Crucially, this adaptation was not simply imposed by locally powerful institutions leveraging hip hop for existing educational goals, but enthusiastically embraced by artists who pioneered the self-entrepreneurship narrative among themselves in the 1990s. Today's emcees, deejays, dancers, and graffiti artists share common themes of grit and initiative, of adversity and overcoming, that frame their personal narratives of learning and becoming hip hop culture. At Positive School, these frames are the lesson of Anas's history lectures, the model for the students' first rhymes, the currency that helps the organization find actual currency to fund its classes and workshops.

Through my visit to Noujoum, I came to understand the enterprise as grounded in the vulnerability narrative. A foundational, and seemingly unexamined, assumption of this narrative is that impoverished people equate their lack of capital with a lack of personal or inherent value. In other words, the narrative assumes that they see themselves as socioeconomic elites see them, and that this lack of self-worth is among the deepest and most intransigent of the problems caused by poverty.[31] Thus, the response is not only or first to eradicate poverty, but to offer activities that elites believe will allow participants to recognize and express their value to themselves.

During our conversation, Sophia Akhmisse described bringing guest hip hop artists from Boultek, the offices of the Boulevard Festival described in chapter 3, to Noujoum. At the time, she hoped a partnership would provide a well-traveled path for established emcees to volunteer at Noujoum. For her, guest artists drew enthusiastic audiences and could also communicate that Sidi Moumen youths were in turn welcome at Boultek and similar creative hubs in the city. Hip hop arts training was not an end in itself, but a medium through which to convince students of their own capacities and to connect them to people, practices, and places that the staff valued.

This reminded me of Fondation Ali Zaoua's website, where Noujoum's copresident, Mahi Binebine, described the center's goal as helping youths "rediscover a reason to never let themselves be indoctrinated."[32] This "reason," a sense of one's own value, would allow young people to understand influential discourses like those absorbed by the May 16 bombers as "indoctrination" rather than in other ways—as moral suasion, as rational argument, as a way to belong, or even as something to endure in exchange for social services. Binebine frames this as "rediscovering" young peoples' intrinsic worth, suggesting that to him, Sidi Moumen residents' recognition of how little they are valued by elite Moroccans undermines their own estimation of themselves.

In their introduction to Noujoum's press book, Binebine and Ayouch state:

> After having passed two years on this terrain preparing to make *Horses of God* and the writing of *The Stars of Sidi Moumen*, we could see how abandoned they feel, how the tie of identity with the rest of the population has been severed. The reason is simple: in its desire to replace the bidonvilles with apartment blocks, the state has forgotten a major parameter: local culture [*la culture de proximité*]. The departments concerned and the local politicians have made the same errors as the European states in the 1950s and '60s in creating ghettos at the doors of big cities, zones without rights where violence becomes the only form of expression. However, there is a way to reverse this trend. And culture, the arts, has a fundamental role to play in that equation.

Today, we are convinced that one can help the youths of Sidi Moumen by offering them access to culture. Not an elitist culture. No, an accessible culture [*de proximité*] that they create, which tells their story, their daily lives, and which permits them to display their talents. Because talent, there is a lot of it in these neighborhoods. And we believe strongly that thanks to centers such as this one, vocations will emerge in the years to come and genuine stars will come from these neighborhoods, in the manner of France's banlieues.[33]

In Ayouch's and Binebine's statements here and elsewhere, the state has failed to offer people ways to form a sense of belonging in and beyond Sidi Moumen. Nonprofits, funded by private donations, corporate foundations, and government agencies with postcolonial ties to Morocco, must fill that gap. With the exception of a point Ayouch makes frequently—that Morocco's Villes Sans Bidonvilles project repeats mistakes from mid-twentieth-century French housing policy—there is no argument that the state must return to an earlier, broader model of provisioning or create a better one. Instead, Fondation Ali Zaoua raises funds to do the work they believe needs to be done.

Ayouch described the model for his approach in a conversation with my students when he retold the story of his youth in Sarcelles, a suburb north of Paris.

In the banlieue . . . actually one place saved my life and made me become a director, it was the MJC. The *Maison des Jeunes et de la Culture*. And that's where I learned how to tap dance, to sing, to do theater, to write some books, and to change my life. . . . I observed at that time how this place, a place like that, this kind of island in the middle of the buildings, could change the destiny of many of my fellows. And the differences between those who had been in that place and those who had never been in that place and how they finally ended. And so, for me it was really obvious that's exactly what the youngsters [of Sidi Moumen] needed. So I was happy to be of service . . . so I decided that on the ground, on the ugly, I would build something beautiful (April 2023).

In practice, building skills that would help enculturate young people seemed to be less about professionalization, or training for vocations that will allow "stars" to emerge, than about building a sense of self-worth that would prepare motivated students to leave their neighborhood. Noujoum's founders and staff suggested that Sidi Moumen youths lacked that sense of self-worth, but they also assumed that the way Sidi Moumen and other karians had been denied services resulted in residents' ignorance or naïveté. As Akhmisse noted in our conversation, "self-confidence" and the support of Noujoum staff themselves were just as valuable as experience in their hip hop music-making.

In interviews, Noujoum founders and staff speak of *désenclavement*, the un-enclosing and reconnecting of the neighborhood (Derville 2016; Bouithy 2014). Ayouch defines Noujoum as a tool for social mobility: "De-ghetto-ize the neighborhood. Cultivate mixing. Offer to the children transmission, knowledge, relationships" (Derville 2016). The aims of désenclavement, and their primacy over more immediate, material redress, rest on a belief that the informal housing that dominated Sidi Moumen in 2003 imprisoned its residents in both space and time.[34]

As we have seen, expectations that karian residents will fail in Casablanca's regularized urban spaces existed before the 2003 bombings and continue to be reinforced by national and regional media, municipal officials, and socioeconomic elites. However, residents of past and present karians connect to the rest of the city as workers, students, or entrepreneurs, even as their participation is conditioned by their lack of infrastructure. Residents use a variety of tactics to navigate the city and other citizens' expectations of them, including expectations that they will passively accept the City Without Slums relocation program (Atia 2019; Pieprzak 2016: 42–43).

I do not assume that every staff member at Noujoum was from an affluent or elite background, but I can note factors that would incentivize their participation in dominant discourses. The Noujoum staff whom I was able to meet were in a rare position: they did work they were educated for, that took advantage of their artistic and other skills, and they were also paid to help others. Noujoum staff were positioned as entrepreneurial through being youthful cultural workers, but also, for some, being involved in or representative of the hip hop arts (Scharff 2016: 110). Part of the role of the staff and guest teachers who lead emceeing, beatboxing, and dance workshops at the centers is demonstrating the joy and pride they feel as successful entrepreneurs, paid artists in a society where only a few artists in each genre or medium make a living wage. Valuing the determination and work ethic of the students is one way both staff and international journalists situated them as entrepreneurial subjects.

In sum, the Noujoum staff promoted students' identification with Moroccan society through tools that would help them move across class boundaries. However, those class boundaries were consistently depicted as psychological or symbolic, as located in Sidi Moumen residents' heads or in the meaning given to neighborhood structures. According to the discourse enacted during my visit, traversing such boundaries by performing practices associated with more affluent classes would in turn raise youths' valuation of themselves and fortify them against "vulnerabilities" to Islamists or other voices understood as opposed to liberal or civil society. It is here that the service Nabil Ayouch offered to Sidi Moumen's youths becomes clear, as he explains above.

Almost none of the art, commentary, or research I have seen on the May 16 bombers explores the possibility that impoverished Sidi Moumen youths might see themselves outside others' expectations of their vulnerability. When artists do push the boundaries of this discourse, the conditions under which that art is received make it difficult to sustain alternative representations. In 2021, Nabil Ayouch released *Casablanca Beats*, the first Moroccan feature film to screen in the main competition at Cannes. The main characters are students and staff from Noujoum's Positive School, who play fictionalized versions of themselves. During one moving scene that combined scripted and improvised speech, the students discuss how others speak about them as residents of Sidi Moumen. In contextualizing this moment for my students, Ayouch explained that from the 1990s to the present, youths in the neighborhood "grew up in the idea that they are somehow a . . . second division of citizenship. . . . Most of them, as they say in the film, were not even born in 2003. But still they carried this heritage of being all considered as suicide bombers or potential suicide bombers" (April 2023).

Throughout the film, the student actors perform their own raps at moments of conflict, pausing the flow of time in sequences designed to enter the characters' inner worlds. At the same time, *Casablanca Beats* incorporates familiar cinematic tropes into the story of Positive School's impact on the community. The film's climax turns on antagonism between devout parents who refuse to let their daughters emcee in public or private; Noujoum staff who seek to protect the institution; and the teacher who encourages his students to speak their minds. In Ayouch's recollection, Anas the real-life teacher entered the school in much the same way as his character: "He came with a kind of personal history, background, saying that he was a former rapper and that he was somehow disgusted by the system, and the way hip hop turned to be year after year was somehow maybe far away from its first goal and objectives. More egocentric, more bling bling, and so on. And that's why he decided to quit hip hop, and that's why he decided, as he said at that time, to give back" (p.c., April 2023).

At the end of the film, after an altercation between Anas and other men that threatens to shut down Noujoum on the day of the school's performance, viewers surmise that the iconoclastic teacher has been asked to leave. As he packs up his car and prepares to journey on, his students thank him with a jubilant farewell song.

It is difficult to avoid reading *Casablanca Beats*'s teacher as a hero with ostensibly universal values who offers multiply disadvantaged students a form of freedom—the liberty to believe in themselves despite the constraints of poverty, marginalization, and religious dogma. Set alongside the ways the real-life Sidi Moumen and the center have been sensationalized in European, American, and Moroccan narratives, *Casablanca Beats* may reinforce framing around "good" and "bad" Muslims (Mamdani 2004) even as it portrays the teens' interiority. When I asked Ayouch how he thought about his films' potential reception in and beyond Morocco, he responded in, perhaps, the only way possible: "I believe that my only duty is to be sincere and to express what I want to express with this sincerity. And not being a representative of Morocco, or the ministry of tourism, or whatever. What is important to me is that people see us as we are. And that they understand . . . what those youngsters express in this film. I mean, wherever they live, and wherever they are . . . they are facing the same topics, you know, the same obstacles" (April 2023). By moving immediately from his desire to portray realistic, everyday Moroccan life to the universality of adolescent struggles, Ayouch suggests that seeing Moroccans as they are requires seeing versions of ourselves.

The implication that viewers unfamiliar with Morocco may see what Ayouch sees, rather than their own frames of reference, strikes me as both a generous, hopeful statement and an economically necessary belief.

Outreach from any source is inevitably accompanied by ideologies about who is being helped and why. Rather than negating the sincerity of outreach efforts, ideologies about poverty, social models, or success help shape the effects of that sincerity. In their statements about the real-life Noujoum, Ayouch and Binebine imagine that a successful future for the neighborhood is powered by individuals—the few who might, somehow, transcend the limits of their environment, perhaps competing in the rarefied world of international film, music, or television. Once such talents understand their own value, they can develop their human capital and pursue economic value for themselves and others.

Anas Basbousi, the real-life emcee turned teacher turned actor, did not grow up in Sidi Moumen, but he nonetheless exemplifies this trajectory. After his successful debut in *Casablanca Beats*, he has taken roles in Moroccan and international projects (p.c. with Ayouch [April 2023] and Basbousi [March 2023]). It is not surprising that economic value is here framed as expressive of internal value. What is critical to note is how this belief feels to some, and how it is constructed for others, as right, just, and natural, so that assisting young people to develop within the frame of this belief is widely accepted as a good and meaningful act.

Though I did not record anyone using the term "resilience," the values and practices I observed at Noujoum correspond to that idea. A core term in the interrelated domains of counterterrorism, security, and state-building, resilience was initially adapted from ecological studies to describe the ability to withstand intended and unintended harms (Neocleous 2013: 3). It quickly became "an operational strategy of risk management" (Walker and Cooper 2011: 143) and, like other techniques of neoliberal governmentality, was soon applied to oversight of individuals who in turn adopted the concept for their own self-management. Resilient individuals are considered to have "autonomy, self-efficacy, and self-esteem . . . along with environmental factors such as socioeconomic advantage" (Hutcheon and Lashewicz 2014: 1384). The characteristics and values of resilient people track neatly with those identified by critics of neoliberal governmentality as the means of individualizing risk and failure, minimizing belief in the efficacy of collective actions, and investing entrepreneurship and responsibility with moral worth (e.g., Brown 2015; Gershon 2011; McNay 2009).

Not surprisingly, the relationship between the positively valued notion of resilience and the negatively valued notion of vulnerability has drawn critique from a variety of voices, all of whom note that resilience reinscribes value on normative bodies and obscures structural factors that preclude it. Writing from within Disability Studies, Hutcheon and Lashewicz argue that "notions of vulnerability portray diversity as pathological to self and society . . . while equating an individual's value with their usefulness or utility" (2014: 1391). Jan Grue identifies the underlying dynamic as "inspiration porn": "the representation of disability as a form of disadvantage that can be overcome for the titillation of other people/observers" (2016: 838).

William Cheng and Robin James separately address this dynamic within US popular musics. Cheng focuses on the work that insisting upon resilience for non-normative bodies does in popular culture. While musical competitions like *American Idol* or *The Voice* often highlight perceived disabilities to highlight their participants' "overcoming" (2017), the same characteristics—a superhuman ability to absorb pain and suffering and to keep achieving—were and are routinely evoked to dehumanize Black Americans and to stereotype their sonic and musical preferences (2018). James argues that women, people of color, and LGBTQIA individuals are encouraged to "overcome" and "recycle" affronts to their humanity in ways that consumers can appreciate: "Resilience is designed to generate human capital, and this capital *circulates*—in the market, as a means of social interaction—*as spectacle*" (James 2015: 106, italics in original).

As a whole, Noujoum appeared to treat poverty like a disability. Recall that sha'abiyya discourse frames recent migrants to the city and their children as afflicted with naïveté, unwilling or unable to outgrow their rural culture and customs to integrate into urban life. This discourse feeds into assumptions about karian residents' abilities to succeed in or out of the karian environment. Songs and performances by young Positive School students made art out of personal experiences. Journalists' narratives and founders' artwork assume trauma, not just from poverty but the psychological and social degradation accompanying it. In the ways Positive School students were encouraged to perform, and the ways discourse around Noujoum expressed simultaneous appreciation for and exoticization of poor youths' desire to make music and dance, I see a valuation of difference similar to those discussed by James and Cheng. In this case, stories told of Sidi Moumen maintain the assumption that young people are always-already potential Islamists—and potential Islamists are "potential terrorists," as Moroccan sociologist Abdessamad Dialmy concludes (2005: 68). In turn, cultivating youths' artistic potential is not only a way to support individual self-worth and self-expression, but to offer pathways out of poverty that are, by definition, for exceptional individuals rather than a whole group.

The children and youths who thrive in Noujoum's classes inspire deep appreciation, including a desire to serve, among those whose beliefs support the conditions that the students must transcend. In turn, staff and students at Noujoum accept and work toward a capability central to both neoliberal subjects and citizens of authoritarian regimes: the resilience to not only live in but "exploit . . . situations of radical uncertainty" (Joseph 2013: 40). Like subjects of neoliberal governance more broadly, resilient subjects accept the "idea that debasement, destitution, and poverty are not the collective responsibility of states and political institutions, but the responsibility of deficient subjects" (Mavelli 2019: 2). The touchstone concepts powering all the discourses at work in this chapter—including narratives about personal responsibility, the oulad sha'ab, vulnerability, and resilience—relate them to one another in a complex that serves many projects, assigning value to diverse forms of financial, social, and human capital.

HIP HOP: A *MISSION CIVILISATRICE?*

The universal condemnation of the 2003 suicide bombings among hip hop artists, including several songs rejecting violence and the perpetrators, helped legitimize the genre at a moment in the mid-2000s when it was just reaching bigger audiences. As prior chapters note, Moroccan hip hop music and dance were never exclusively performed by the urban poor, but they were associated with stereotypes of Black American criminality. Artists' responses to the 2003 attacks helped to demonstrate to a skeptical public that hip hop practitioners shared core values with most Moroccans. They also differentiated hip hop practitioners from the very poor, and especially from karian residents, who generally did not have the resources to participate in the formation of Moroccan hip hop in its first twenty years. Additionally, they provided a way of agreeing with elite narratives that people who did not identify with elites could still accept.

Under terrorism discourse in Morocco as elsewhere, "radical" serves less as a descriptor of culture (like "radical art") and more as a discursive link to or eventual stand-in for "terrorist" (Bartolucci 2010: 126). As hip hop became more mainstream—not just by appearing on state-sponsored stages, but by stating consensus positions on major political concerns—it was perceived to shed its "radical" potential in both senses of the term. However, there was still a long distance from artists' own small-scale volunteer efforts to the hip hop arts appearing at a prestigious NGO with the explicit mission of bringing cultural and employment opportunities to Sidi Moumen youths. Hip hop's use at Noujoum signified more than the acceptance of individual artists into the slice of Casablanca's artistic sector that benefited from state patronage; that had been happening for over a decade. Instead, it signified acceptance that the multimedia art form had value as a vehicle of self-improvement, beyond the messages and fan bases of exceptional individual artists.

In 2019, 'Ayoun al-Ḥak returned to earlier narrative terrain with a song titled after his nickname from his 2013 hit—"Mr. Boulevard." This piece tells a different angle of the same story: young people trapped in a preprotectorate *medina*, with no opportunities to make a living, who feel forced to attempt migration. The visuals toggle between hopeful children crowded into a one-room, cinder-block classroom and shots of listless and traumatized young adults. The chorus compresses the hopelessness of poverty and the danger of the Gibraltar crossing into a few lines, and like SiSimo's "'Eid al-Faqr," features closely cropped shots of young men mouthing the words:

> The train has left and I'm just watching
> People are dying, you know the Lord sees [them]
> [They take a] bullet or they trouble the fish
> Oulad sha'ab risking death on the boat[35]

In conjunction with his 2013 song, "Mr. Boulevard" perhaps depicts the cyclical failures and immobility of poverty. One imagines this piece as a prequel to "Boulevard," and the video's subjects as the same people who were unable to avoid homelessness in the future. Six years after the release of that song, the needs and challenges 'Ayoun al-Ḥak describes, the imagery and musical semiotics he uses, have not changed. Neither have the reactions of fans, hundreds of whom celebrated his return to form with YouTube comments like "God, 'Ayoun returns to his own style" and "that's the 'Ayoun that we know."[36]

This chapter has explored hip hop artists' embrace of dominant discourses about the urban poor, treating finished songs, professional performances, and student workshops as processes that confirm and recirculate those discourses. "Mr. Boulevard" and the many songs like it do not simply sensationalize mundane contours of urban poverty. Instead, artists promote identification with the poor by simultaneously reproducing and flipping commonplace representations of them.[37] The expectation of sincerity makes possible an unironic identification with the poor that nonetheless distances the emcee precisely because (usually) he can exert the power of choosing to identify, choosing to speak.[38]

The structural inequalities between different actors in this chapter are vital to understanding the continuing power of sha'abiyya discourse and its relationship to the vulnerability narrative underpinning international counterterrorist efforts. Pursuing the shared values and beliefs that powered post-2003 actions toward Sidi Moumen and its residents reveals how coming to share a discourse can itself be an aspirational act. While Anas and other staff, as well as many of their guest teachers, were generally better off socioeconomically than their students, I have avoided flatly characterizing anyone in this discussion as affluent. Such labels can occlude the ways particular individuals, knowingly or unknowingly, wield their class status. Yet the staff of Noujoum, its founders, and the journalists who covered it between 2013–20 do appear to share a perspective that centers elite frames of reference and does not acknowledge the possibility of alternate discourses on Moroccan poverty, including any generated by impoverished Moroccans themselves. In the absence of the political will to accept poverty and disenfranchisement as a structural problem with known solutions, they become something to individually transcend. But transcending something is not the same as exiting it—the underlying state itself may, in fact must, continue so that individuals may continue to be exceptions to social, political, and economic limits.

Songs and interventions in this chapter do not give targets of sha'abiyya discourse the tools to combat it, no matter how explicitly they address the discourse and its material outcomes in state policies and nonprofit projects. Of course,

Moroccan hip hop artists can and do recognize the immaterial richness of poor people's lives. Yet their performances often participate in framing the poor in ways that align with the state's goals, even as they dispute its tactics. Some have the effect of reinforcing discourses that, ultimately, maintain more affluent Moroccans' role in mediating poor citizens' access to resources. Those explored in this chapter can be read as challenging the discourse from within it rather than undermining its core assumptions by successfully delinking personal and economic value. As in other examples throughout this book, such interventions accomplish this reinforcement precisely because the practitioners believe in their work.

Expectations of Feminism

The sun had barely begun to set at 9 p.m. on an August Saturday in Alby, a sub-urban neighborhood about forty-five minutes from central Stockholm.[1] Soultana, her male co-emcee Bawss, and their Danish deejay That Fucking Sara had finished their set an hour earlier. After seemingly endless miscommunications, they were polite following their performance: watching the next act from the sidelines, taking photos with Swedish teens, finding room in the adjacent youth center for an impromptu interview with someone from a world music nonprofit. But now they were tired, and ready to go back to the hotel.

Soultana sent me to ask whether the festival had the meal vouchers she expected for the next day. Our point person forced a smile when she saw me coming. "I'm so sorry," she said. "All of tonight's artists are free tomorrow. We have nothing planned for you." Though Soultana and Bawss were at the hotel until Monday morning in order to attend the second day of the festival, no further meals were provided.

The staff member called the shuttle driver, and I relayed the news on the side-walk in front of the youth center. Sara and I looked at each other, then at our friends. Both of us knew they had no more money. As the shuttle pulled up, Soultana ground her cigarette into the pavement and stomped over to the back door. "Shouldn't we say goodbye?" I said to no one in particular.

"I don't care," shouted Soultana in English over her shoulder, in a voice piercing enough to reach the staff's office on the second floor. "This is the worst festival I've ever been part of. Worse than Morocco," she yelled. "I'm never coming back here."

Soultana had performed at other international festivals before this 2015 trip, but this case highlights how little control she has over her labor conditions and representation before and during events. While she had previously told stories of confusion or disorganization at other performances, this event was exceptional.

Soultana's and Bawss's expectations of Sweden and Swedish culture made it even more disappointing. As Soultana noted years later, Sweden "is like the Moroccan dream" (personal communication [p.c.], July 2018), imagined as one of the best places to go precisely because it seemed so unlike Morocco. Like many Moroccans, both musicians strongly desired to experience the cleanliness, calmness, and affluence that people so frequently mentioned when chatting idly of emigration. Instead, the disorganization and claims of low funding that Soultana and Bawss encountered throughout the planning and execution of the festival named This Is Alby felt similar to Moroccan events. For years, Soultana had argued that sometimes one must sacrifice for a collective goal, performing for low or no pay at events that fell short of her ideals. After all that work, to go to a place so often imagined as a site of fairness, equality, and abundance and have it fail in all the same ways—it was deeply demoralizing.

Her refusal to say goodbye told me she was not only angry, but hurt. For my Moroccan interlocutors, even the most trivial social interactions ideally begin and end by greeting everyone present. I had absorbed this expectation so thoroughly that I experienced the dissonance of a norm being trampled as she yanked the shuttle van's door open. Without realizing it, I was also voicing another unexamined expectation: knowing we would not return the next day, I was suggesting we check on the organizers' feelings and make sure everyone felt appreciated before we left the festival grounds. Soultana was also refusing to perform the caring labor that, as women, she and I would routinely do in our home contexts. ("Shouldn't we?" I had asked.)[2] After all, "saying goodbye" would doubtlessly have included thanking our hosts and appearing grateful for the opportunity to perform.

This chapter discusses Soultana's reactions to both her unmet expectations and her instrumentalization. This Is Alby featured Swedish and foreign performers of African, North African, and Latin American descent to reflect the backgrounds of first- and second- generation immigrants in the neighborhood. While this made Moroccans an attractive choice, the way the festival was advertised, how its volunteers communicated, and how it did and did not anticipate or respond to their musical and personal needs gave Soultana and Bawss the impression that it was their difference that mattered, not their performance. As Soultana remarked when comparing This Is Alby to a previous event, "[The organizers in Copenhagen] were so professional, and my program was not just the show . . . I did a lot of workshops too. It was so good, for real. And I felt [that] I'm an artist" (p.c., August 10, 2018).

This chapter explores such events as part of a transnational market for representations of female Muslim resistance to patriarchy or, less often, Islamophobia. I argue that Soultana and other artists are trapped within interlocking expectations, facing assumptions that mirror and reinforce each other. Like many artists from the SWANA region, Soultana's international appearances are often valued not for their quality, but for the layers of difference her performances index for her audiences. Soultana and other female Muslim artists alternately contend with and benefit from the widespread assumption that Muslim women are more oppressed than non-Muslim women. In addition to her observation that she is seen, as she puts it, "as a case"—as standing in for Muslim women—I note that Soultana and her female collaborators are expected, and sometimes expect themselves, to deal with different treatment, conditions, or wages than their male colleagues. They are called upon to perform caring labor not only for their audiences, who desire to see Muslim women of color refute their own clichés, but for each other when they are frustrated by their work experiences. Like a hall of funhouse mirrors, Soultana must navigate a career generated through and enclosed within this dynamic.

This chapter traces Soultana's path in relationship to this market for Muslim women's resistance since 2010, when her career-defining song "Sawt Nssa (Voice of a Woman)" was released. I discuss two events among several past and current projects to describe how this market leads well-intentioned individuals to reproduce assumptions about Muslim women. In both events, the participants identify encouraging interactions between different groups as an important political and cultural goal. Yet in both cases, stereotypes are tolerated or evoked to battle the perceived presence of other stereotypes.

In one example, as noted above, Soultana grappled with her own expectations of a performance and the opportunities it might afford. In the second, she joined a team of women musicians in a trans-Saharan initiative designed to leverage the goals and beliefs of international funders. Together, these examples demonstrate how demand for products of this market stretches across diplomatic, nonprofit, and commercial domains. In both cases, artists cope with the pressures and contradictions of a global north–centered culture industry through sound during rehearsal and performance.

In support of this argument, I convey ways Soultana and I have benefited each other's careers by making myself quite visible throughout this chapter. Reflecting on the familiar dance of long-term ethnographers with our subjects, in which we wonder how our interlocutors' perceptions of us shape the information we receive and how our presence shapes their thoughts in turn, has attuned me to that same dynamic in these examples. Soultana has been more than my most involved research participant. Her role has taught me what ethnographers hope to express when they replace "informant" with "interlocutor." She has listened to, riffed on, and challenged many of the arguments in this book and this chapter. Like a concerned parent, she assumes responsibility for me even when she gains nothing by doing so. Over time she has been a host, a guide, a negotiator, an advisor, a translator of meaning as well as language, a co-author, a co-presenter. I have been these for her as well, sometimes at the same moment. At the same time, whether I like it or not, my research contributes to the market in which her public persona is valued. While summarizing this as "friends" would obscure more than it reveals about her support for my research, she is nonetheless a dear friend.

THE MAKING OF A "FEMCEE"

As a member of Casablanca's first wave, Soultana has shaped and been shaped by the ideals described in previous chapters. Like other emcees, her work expresses practitioners' desired relationship between citizens' mentalities ('aqliyyat) and the state's policies by critiquing each, often in the same song. In late 2009, she released her most influential song, "Sawt Nssa (Voice of a Woman)." A daring first-person characterization of a repentant young woman, "Sawt Nssa" simultaneously critiques the conditions driving women to prostitution and the hypocrisy of men who judge them (Salois 2014a).

In Morocco, the song reached an unprecedented level of success for its subject matter, catapulting Soultana into international networks that shared an interest in discovering, promoting, and exhibiting expressions of Arab female resistance. With each new opportunity, she attempted to foreground women's experiences as one expression of the economic and political challenges facing all nonelite Moroccans, just as the song itself had done. Over time, largely without her knowledge or consent, she was depicted as fighting for women's rights rather than for Moroccans'. She was also valued more for her ascribed activist identity—which rested on being a woman in two patriarchies, Morocco and hip hop—than as a musician. The more people celebrated this reputation, the less performance organizers and media personnel attended to her and her music.

"Sawt Nssa" has reached more people in more ways than Soultana's previous or subsequent work. It attracted the attention of the US Embassy in Rabat almost immediately after its debut on Morocco's privately owned Hit Radio. In spring 2010, I accompanied Soultana to an interview with the cultural affairs officer at the embassy. As we chatted about her family, her introduction to hip hop, and her love of Aretha Franklin and Tupac Shakur, neither she nor I realized the cultural affairs department was considering nominating her for the International Visitors Leadership Program (IVLP) that year.

In April and May 2011, she visited Atlanta, Los Angeles, and New York alongside SWANA musicians and radio hosts on the IVLP. Her trip ended with a performance at Joe's Pub in New York as part of the French Institute and Alliance Française's World Nomads festival. The festival's press booklet neatly summarized Soultana's appeal: "Soultana is 'old school,' in that she is particularly known for rapping about social issues rather than material acquisition and fame. Her songs focus on women's issues and the challenges faced by her generation, particularly poverty, violence, and cultural matters" (FI:AF 2011: 6). Audiences uninterested in hip hop music, or who assumed all hip hop was about material acquisition, could find justification for their attendance in this description. Surrounded on the World Nomads program by some of Morocco's best-known artists and cultural brokers, including Mahi Binebine, Mahmoud Guinia, Abdellah Taïa, André Azoulay, and Faouzi Skali, Soultana was one of a handful of women and the only musician performing "Western" popular music in the monthlong festival.

In New York, the show *MTV Iggy* shot a video for "Sawt Nssa" during the World Nomads festival. It was released in August 2011, shortly after *Afropop Worldwide* broadcast its interview with Soultana from the same trip (Baird 2011). *Afropop's* interview focused on Soultana's self-described struggles to gain acceptance as a female performer. In the next few years, as more Anglophone outlets reported on Soultana and her song—now thematized as representative of her entire output— she performed in several European cities, was profiled on Public Radio International's *The World* (Stuckey 2013), appeared on production company Nomadic Wax's compilation *World Hip Hop Women: From the Sound Up* (2013), and was featured in a 2014 German documentary.

International interest in "Sawt Nssa" was heightened by the Arab Spring and the emergence of Morocco's February 20 reform movement, which organized weekly marches in Moroccan cities every Sunday through the end of 2011 (Bennani-Chraïbi and Jeghllally 2012). The blog *Revolutionary Arab Rap* included her in a list of "female rappers," linking to her Anglophone media coverage and translating "Sawt Nssa."[3] During the same period, Moroccan festivals that had provided artists' best opportunities for paid performance programmed less or no hip hop.[4]

Both diplomatic practitioners and festival organizers sought Soultana out during this period. Over time, presentations of her narrowed, focusing less on her artistic ability or successes and more on "Sawt Nssa" as activism. Within the United States, public diplomacy practitioners, pundits, and scholars had encouraged the use of hip hop as a tool in Muslim-majority countries since the mid-2000s (Aidi 2014; Salois 2014b). In March 2012, Soultana was invited to reflect on her experiences with the IVLP, alongside Toni Blackman, the first hip hop artist to be a US cultural envoy, at a conference hosted by George Washington University (Jeffers 2012). At Oslo's Mela festival in 2012, the international advocacy group Freemuse quoted her support during a roundtable with their artists of the year, Ramy Essam (from Egypt) and Ferhat Tunç (from Turkey).

The wave of interest in Muslim artists immediately after the early events of the Arab Spring extended to hip hop scholars, who simultaneously critique and participate in discourses presuming hip hop's exceptional capacity to effect change. In 2013, two American Studies scholars hosted a multiday conference in Hanover on the theme of "Hip Hop and Social and Political Empowerment." Funded by the Volkswagen Stiftung, the conference invited twenty-five scholars and five practitioners. The invited artists also spoke during the conference and performed a closing concert at the nearby youth house (*Haus der Jugend*).

Each performer had been suggested by a conference attendee. In discussions with one of the organizers, I made what I thought were persuasive arguments: "If you could take just one artist to represent Morocco or North Africa, I would recommend Soultana . . . she is committed to incorporating a woman's perspective into her critical output, has a strong command of English, and already has experience speaking about her work with scholars and media (and the US State Department)" (email, February 16, 2012). All of the invited performers had similar experiences in overlapping diplomatic and academic domains.

Soultana's conference talk shared stories of striving to be taken seriously by Moroccan gatekeepers both as a woman and as a popular musician. She read from a piece originally published at *World Hip Hop Market*, a home for news on international hip hop artists that was, at the time, promoting the compilation album on which Soultana appeared in 2013:

> A short time before the festival, the organizers said they wanted to confirm the details, asked that I go and see one of them at his house before the festival. It was late at night, around 10 p.m., the night I went over. . . . When I arrived, I realized that the location was remote and far from where I lived. I met the man in question outside and he invited me inside to "see" his place. When I walked in, there were two other girls and two other men—we were three men and three women—and it was at that moment [I realized] what I had walked into. The man wanted me, Soultana, to "play with him" in order to confirm a place as a performer in this festival (Soultana 2012).

As conference-goers, we were, of course, saddened and angered by this story. We sought to contextualize it within our various expertise in gender studies, critical race theory, political economy, or ethnographic experience in music markets across the globe. Soultana's experience confirmed something we already knew: while women artists face specific kinds of violence during their careers, those risks are sometimes heightened by prevailing local attitudes around gender roles and the role of women in public life. By including this anecdote in her public persona, Soultana helped make routine sexual harassment visible and inspired others with her refusal to feel shame for someone else's actions.

Soultana's conference attendance, and scholars' responses to her, help elucidate how this market for representations of resistance works. Without recognizing it this way at the time, I accepted the demand driving that market when I suggested Soultana to one of the conference organizers, Heike Raphael-Hernandez. She and her co-organizer Eva Kimminich, in turn, promoted Soultana to the Volkswagen Stiftung when they sought sponsorship. During her panel, Soultana read aloud an interview she had given several months before, performing a live version of the established narrative about herself. Each of us was sincere in our desires, whether that was to support an independent artist, to share stories of injustice, or to make an impact on hip hop scholarship or the German public. We were already aware of the potential for tokenization: I phrased Soultana's work as "a woman's perspective" within a "critical output," and Raphael-Hernandez emphasized that Soultana's contribution was valuable for her musical experience, not simply because of her gendered trauma. Collectively, we contributed to this market through, not despite, our sincerity, simultaneously disseminating and consuming a true story that had already been packaged as female resistance to gendered Muslim violence.

In 2014, the Danish Center for Research on Women and Gender (known as KVINFO) hosted a weekend event for International Women's Day. Sponsored by the ministry of foreign affairs' Danish-Arab Partnership Program, KVINFO invited Soultana and her male collaborator Bawss to hold workshops with children and to perform at the Royal Library in Copenhagen. KVINFO's press stressed the two emcees' commitment to gender equality, only briefly mentioning other issues discussed in their songs. "Although her lyrics are provocative, she uses her raps to deal with women's lack of rights and the men's moral double standards," an unnamed author summarizes (KVINFO 2014).

Unlike the 2011 World Nomads blurb, which describes Soultana addressing interrelated political issues, here her role as a woman in a man's world is depicted as her only contribution. The piece reinforces expectations that Arab and/or Muslim patriarchy be invoked to justify women's participation: "To have got to where she is today, she has not only had to succeed in breaking into the male-dominated hip hop milieu. She has also had to break away from the traditional role of women in Morocco's conservative, Muslim society, where it is expected that . . . even young women, adopt the role of housewife" (KVINFO 2014). It also calls her, incorrectly, "the only female rapper in Morocco" and avoids mentioning her religious practice, education, reception, or other factors that might complicate presenting her as a presumed secular feminist. These tactics promote reading Soultana as exceptional, Moroccan patriarchy as uniquely virulent, and Danish intervention as appropriate.

Soultana and Bawss respond eloquently throughout the interview. "One of the things I want . . . is to tell women that they are free and that they can do whatever they want with their lives," Soultana is quoted as saying.

Bawss reasons that "women in Morocco do have the right to demonstrate for better rights, but they don't do it. They also have the right to demand their rights, but they don't do this either. Why not? It's because nobody is telling them that they can actually do these things" (KVINFO 2014).

Bawss's quote advocates for precisely the kind of activism the Danish-Arab Partnership Program supports. DAPP grantees' "projects and activities concerning equality" are "specifically aimed to promote the social, economic, and political participation of women, and focus on legislation to prevent child marriages and violence against women."[5] The agency adopts a colonialist perspective as both moral judge and guarantor of market integration, arguing that "the Middle East and North Africa are ranked as . . . farthest away from equality between the sexes, and the absence of equality is . . . a key barrier to human and economic development in the region."[6] Bawss's suggestion, that Moroccan women simply do not yet know that the constitution guarantees them equal rights, aligns with DAPP's construction of the problem as one of participation. His proposed actions, physical protest ("demonstration") or other kinds of calls ("demand"), also suggest three of DAPP's four grantmaking domains (human rights, gender equality, media, and labor markets and labor rights) (KVINFO 2014).

I am not suggesting that Bawss or Soultana were misquoted or that they were familiar with DAPP before the interview. Instead, their speech highlights how well they understood the goals and perspectives of their hosts. As guests and employees, both musicians desired to help meet those goals. "Some women asked [Bawss] and he said I support Soultana for what she's doing and . . . we can talk about the same issues in both female and male side," recalled Soultana when I asked her about this event and article.

According to Soultana, as the more experienced of the two, she counseled him on what to expect from journalists. "So you knew they would ask him what he thought about female hip hop artists and gender and stuff?" I asked.

"Yes for sure. It's the 8th of March [International Women's Day]. So sure they will ask him about how it looks working with a female rapper," she responded (p.c., August 10, 2018).

As DAPP's Copenhagen event demonstrates, after the initial demand for Arab Spring–inspired programming receded, Soultana's international invitations shifted further toward expressing an enduring desire to display women who break global north stereotypes about Muslim gender relations. Live performances by Soultana and women in similar positions meet a demand for counterexamples of outspoken Muslim women while also serving to express event organizers' and audiences' openness and tolerance to each other. Such events perpetuate parallel discourses about Muslim others in Europe, but also about uneducated non-Muslim Europeans who might harbor anti-Muslim views. Responses to the assumptions perceived to be held by non-Muslims about Muslims, and by Muslims about their own religious strictures, tell audiences that these assumptions still exist. By addressing these twin assumptions, events such as KVINFO's or This Is Alby instrumentalize Muslim female musicians in a struggle over what values will be seen as acceptable in the places these women perform.

THIS IS ALBY

Press coverage of high-profile moments in Soultana's international career allows smaller initiatives to reproduce the discourse that solidified around her between 2011 and 2014. The volunteers behind This Is Alby sought to "program artists from the Middle East and Northern Africa and combine that [with] Swedish artists. We came over Soultana[']s name while searching on the internet," recalled her contact

Josefin, a cultural producer in Stockholm who invited the festival's international artists in 2015 (email, Stockholm–DC, August 7, 2018).[7]

In addition to municipal support, funding came from the European Cultural Foundation, a grantmaking office of the European Union, through its program Connected Action for the Commons. An Alby-based nonprofit arts incubator known as Subtopia was a Connected Action "hub" in 2015.[8] Subtopia created This Is Alby as an alternative to festivals like We Are Sthlm, which draw people into the center of Stockholm and promote, as they see it, a unitary Swedish identity (Duregård 2016). Each edition of This Is Alby is collaboratively organized by young volunteers, who not only choose artists to invite, but learn to handle logistics, publicity, and other important jobs.

The 2015 edition was the first held in conjunction with the municipality of Botkyrka and its existing summer festival, Vi är Botkyrka (We Are Botkyrka) (Duregård 2016). The team of mostly young women from ages thirty to twenty, mostly from immigrant families, who volunteered for This Is Alby were encouraged to program artists who reflected their vision of a multicultural Sweden (Josefin email, August 7, 2018). According to the cultural affairs secretary of Botkyrka, Josefin and a handful of other adults were hired by Botkyrka's Culture and Recreation Office to support the fifteen young volunteers (Rynell and Subtopia 2016).

Both the Botkyrka Culture and Recreation Office and Subtopia sought to celebrate Alby's multiethnic community. Alby shares with similar Swedish suburbs a reputation for high concentrations of immigrants and above-average poverty and crime. The apartment towers that shaded the festival stage had been built during the Miljonprogrammet (Million Program), a state affordable housing initiative, in the late 1960s. As Ryan Skinner notes, steadily increasing flows of European and nonwhite migrants arrived in Sweden starting in the 1960s, leading to a robust discourse about "the perceived novelty of an increasingly heterogenous . . . Swedish society" (2019: 3). In Botkyrka municipality, 60.5 percent of residents are considered "with foreign background" (*har utländsk bakgrund*), meaning they were born in a foreign country or were born in Sweden to two foreign-born parents (Botkyrka Kommun and Statistics Sweden).[9]

Alby is best known in European hip hop circles as the home of the Latin Kings, one of the earliest Swedish-language groups in the early 1990s, whose members are of Chilean and Venezuelan descent (DJ Sara, email, October 11, 2018). Benjamin Teitelbaum notes that the separate group Albys Kungar (Kings of Alby), which includes immigrants from the former Yugoslavia, "gained attention in nationalist circles by crudely insulting ethnic Swedes in their songs." In 2007, the "white nationalist" rapper Juice released a diss track aimed at these groups (Teitelbaum 2017: 67). In contrast, the international hip hop artists programmed at the 2015 This Is Alby are presented as activists who avoid glamorizing violence.

The program therefore addressed not only anti-immigrant but anti-hip hop sentiment among Swedish audiences.

The mostly Anglophone narrative about Soultana that the volunteers found online suited This Is Alby's promotional goals. Their Facebook advertisements reproduced it in two sentences: "The rapper MC Soultana . . . is named as Morocco's first female rapper and is one of few women in the hip hop scene in Morocco. Her texts focus on women's rights and the challenges facing women in North African countries."[10] The week before the festival, the English-language website Stocktown highlighted the international artists who would perform that year—Soultana, the Sudanese emcee Emmanuel Jal, and Palestinian British emcee Shadia Mansour. The author opened with the national stakes of the suburban festival: "By inviting artists that have fought for people's freedom of speech and expression, Botkyrka is showing Sweden—and the artists' native countries—that they support the fight that these people have had to endure. Furthermore, they stand [as an] example for some of Sweden's other municipalities who need to work on embracing diversity and multiculturalism" (Widman 2015). The article offers a few lines about each artist; Soultana's section links to the 2012 *World Hip Hop Market* interview and asserts that "she's rapping about why she fights to make the female voice heard" (Widman 2015).

The post ends not with an invitation to enjoy the music, but to enjoy a socially appropriate response to the concert: "This is how you celebrate multicultural citizenship. If you are in Sweden on the 22th August, come and get inspired by these awesome brave artists" (Widman 2015). Like most descriptions of Soultana provided by international events, none of the advertising I found for This Is Alby mentioned musical artistry or promised an entertaining evening.

Online narratives about Soultana not only shaped how This Is Alby presented her, but how festival staff interacted with her. Josefin was Soultana's only contact with the organizers, from their first email exchange in early June 2015 to her arrival on August 21. Throughout their preparations for the trip, Soultana and Bawss received information they did not know how to interpret. Josefin's initial email in June 2015 was addressed to Soultana's unnamed manager. It described the festival as "a gig in Stockholm . . . an outdoor festival called Urban Voices with various Swedish and international artists." To help secure Swedish visas, the head of culture at the Botkyrka municipality provided a letter of invitation, writing, "We will also cater for their accommodation in Stockholm, Sweden," for the duration of their stay (Kasapı, email, June 5, 2015). Josefin had also asked for a "technical rider," a document specifying their needs to be appended to their contract. Soultana had never heard the term before and thought it referred to musicians' preferences for microphones and other equipment. When we discussed this after the fact, she mentioned that she found it strange to be given control of decisions she placed in the sound technicians' domain.

During their arrangements, Soultana asked to bring in DJ That Fucking Sara from Berlin. In order for her to accompany them, Soultana, Bawss, and Josefin agreed that Sara's travel would be covered out of the emcees' fee. Sara, in turn, requested turntables and a monitor be provided by the festival (Sara, email, October 10, 2018).

I booked my own flight and arrived separately to Stockholm on August 21, the day before the event.[11] When I reached the hotel in Alby, about forty-five minutes southwest of Stockholm, the musicians were concerned. "This hotel is so far," Soultana kept repeating. Until they were picked up at the airport, they had not realized that Alby was a suburb rather than a neighborhood within Stockholm.

The afternoon prior to their performance, I started to understand the stakes of the trip. Soultana, Bawss, and Sara planned to rehearse from 1 to 5 p.m. In the morning, we spent several hours at the mall adjacent to the hotel. We flipped through racks of clearance T-shirts and jerseys, scanned caps and jackets for American sports logos, and prowled the aisles of a makeup emporium, scouting for foundation close to Soultana's skin tone that would withstand the heat of stage lighting. Bringing home international fashions was less important than ensuring the right look for the evening. Knowing how much they would be photographed and videotaped, Soultana and Bawss hunted for the most authenticating apparel available on their budgets.

The tension I felt from Soultana in particular increased throughout rehearsal. We gathered around the coffee table in Sara's hotel room to play tracks the two emcees had written over the past year. Many were composed by Soultana's younger brother, a beatmaker known as Mobeezy, and ranged from the ponderous electric piano of "Sawt Nssa" to denser styles inspired by electronic dance music. Some had already been recorded and released on YouTube, but some had not yet been performed live. In each, both emcees supported each other through their respective verses, gesturing on stressed beats and echoing each other's punchlines.

While Sara listened and offered advice on the set list, Bawss focused on rehearsing his entrances, and Soultana expressed her anxiety by joking through the material she knew best. "'Arfti 'Sawt Nssa'? (You know 'Sawt Nssa'?)" she exclaimed to no one in particular as Bawss cued it up, rehearsing her onstage patter. "My solo—it's about one year I haven't . . ." she said to Sara, switching to English and immediately trailing off as she began to listen to the intro.

"You know it," I said from behind my camera.

"I know it because . . . I feel it," she said, with an exaggerated sigh. I suggested they follow this slow track with an upbeat finale. Soultana saw me speak, but did not listen, focused in on her cue. It was Bawss who nailed the pickup to the downbeat, reciting the first line perfectly in time.

By the first chorus, Soultana was trying to lighten her own mood. "Sawt nssa, li 'aliha rani nadi (Voice of a woman, it's to her that I'm calling)," she shouted over her own voice on the chorus. "Sawt lbnat, yda' yfuq ar-rasi (Voice of girls, pretend my head is awake)," she rapped over the second line, rewriting the original to comment on her forgetfulness. I laughed, and she fell toward me across the hotel bed, reaching out to slap my hand the way Moroccans often do when they delight in their own joke. Throughout the verses, I watched her rely on muscle memory rather than think about her text. Each time she missed the second half of a couplet, Bawss seamlessly filled in, prompting her to recover the end of the line.

During the second chorus, Soultana launched into a fake ballad. Shoulders lifted, palm upturned, eyes squinting in feigned passion, she parodied contemporary Arabic singers, dragging a nasal tone through soupy slides up to each pitch. She abandoned the rest of the chorus as we all giggled, telling Sara in English, "One day I had a performance, and a girl from the organization told me 'I really love this song, and I want to sing R & B on the chorus.' And she was singing like this and I really hate myself," she said with a weary smile. She ran through the last verse, missing the final line, then aped the terrible R & B vocalist again. Sara burst out laughing, while Bawss gave his partner a tepid look. "She was singing like this and I had to stop her, but I couldn't," Soultana protested, shrugging theatrically.

I tried not to laugh along as I filmed. While everyone found the jokes funny, we also knew we were in this hotel room because of "Sawt Nssa." The day before we flew to Stockholm, Soultana and I had discussed her aging parents. Her father's diabetes was causing painful complications, but they could not afford his insulin prescription on a retired police officer's pension. International performances seemed prestigious to her Moroccan colleagues, but the fees varied widely, and one or two a year could hardly support both her and her parents. Sometimes she considered abandoning hip hop and collaborating on pop songs with Mobeezy. They could at least perform for rich kids a few times a year, maybe write for TV commercials. Many encouraged her to emigrate and send money home; unlike other Moroccans, she could give a concert and simply not show up for her return flight. But she felt that critiquing Moroccan society from abroad would make no impact. "If in a few years you see me and I have given up all my *principes* and I am just getting money, you will know it's because of my parents," she said that day, staring into her milky coffee.

The undercurrent of long-term stress seemed to compound the anxiety of preparing for performance, of meeting expectations while hoping for an artistically rewarding experience. "Sawt Nssa" was not just her best-known song; it was her career. I had no fear she would forget the lyrics at the concert. Instead, I heard her coping with the gulf between how she felt and how she was expected to feel on stage.

If Soultana and Bawss felt they had to represent Moroccans in the best possible light, they also had high expectations for their first Swedish event. Picked up at promptly 5:30 p.m. in the hotel lobby, we arrived twenty minutes later at the youth center that would serve as the artists' green room.

The cheery, orange-accented lobby offered bowls of pretzel sticks and bottles of water. For dinner, volunteers pointed us to the local booths selling food on the other side of the stage. Sara and I shrugged this off, but the emcees found it surprising. Many Moroccan events paid little or nothing, but they included sandwiches or substantial meals for their performers. Soultana claimed that organizers "always" provided hospitality at her other international gigs. The lack of food exacerbated worries that This Is Alby might be smaller, and less well-funded, than they had assumed.

The youth center and its surrounding park were just a few meters from the stage, which was set up in the plaza of the Alby Centrum T-bana subway stop. Josefin and volunteers met us in the lobby and escorted us down to the stage for sound check. Soultana, Bawss, and Sara trooped up the steps to the stage while I lingered in front of it. In a moment, Josefin came to find me. "Can you please talk to Soultana?" she asked, steering my elbow toward the stage entrance.

I followed her behind the stage to where the musicians were clustered. There was no equipment at the deejay's deck, and Soultana was demanding to know why the vinyl turntables Sara had requested were not there. Josefin explained, gently, that she had never received a technical rider with a list of requirements like these. In any case, anyone who wanted to perform with turntables had to bring their own. Sara responded that she rarely traveled with her own turntables, as they were likely to be damaged in transit, and that professionals expected to perform on house equipment at most events. "I'm sorry. It is a very small festival," repeated Josefin.

Back at the youth center, cradling plastic cups of coffee, the artists discussed how to change their set. In rehearsal, they had planned out how Sara would interact with the emcees. Most of the songs include pre-chorus sections before the final chorus and outro. These moments had little or no new musical material; they were designed for a deejay to show off her technique and energize the crowd. Now, not only would those be empty, but Sara would not even be able to mix from one song into the next. This would force unexpected pauses within and between each song and slow down the energy of the set. Soultana and Bawss sketched out who would address the crowd after each song, glossing the topic of the next piece or asking for audience participation.

Later, we returned to the front of the plaza, facing the stage. I turned away from filming the gathering crowd, filled with clusters of teens and parents with small children, to find Soultana staring at the event posters lining the security fence in front of the stage. "Why is my name not there?" she said, pointing to the list of performers on the poster. "Can you take a picture of that?" said Bawss, gesturing to my camera. Again Josefin apologized, noting that the poster was designed by youth volunteers and pointing out another version that did include Soultana.

In their hours at the festival that evening, the three musicians spent much of their energy encouraging each other. Soultana in particular poured energy into conveying a joyous atmosphere during the performance. As the more experienced emcee, she had evolved strategies to engage unfamiliar listeners that she rarely used with Moroccan audiences. Over the intro to "LBareh O LYoum (Yesterday and Today)," she asked the crowd, "Do you know how to dance?" She did a little two-step across the stage, bending her knees but keeping her hips and upper body straight, swinging her arms and snapping her fingers in the air. "Just a little bit, just move," she coaxed, eyebrows raised, looking toward some stone-faced teenagers behind me.

During the second verse, the emcees traded couplets, one describing Morocco "yesterday" followed by the other's comparison with "today." Bawss planted his feet and pointed forward, emphasizing stressed syllables with his outstretched hand, but Soultana was constantly in motion. She stepped forward with each of her lines, bending at the waist as if to get closer to her listeners. She also gave focus to Bawss throughout, gesturing to him in time with his entrances while still making eye contact with the audience. During the final verse, Soultana walked up to Bawss and stood eye to eye, visibly encouraging him by smiling and filling in the silences after each of his lines.

The end of "LBareh O LYoum" was constructed to allow for seamless transition into another song, with eight "empty" pre-chorus measures followed by two repetitions of the chorus. After reciting one chorus along with the recording, Soultana stepped beyond the stage monitors for the final eight measures. Surrounded by an attentive but immobile audience, grinning from ear to ear, she shouted, "Dance with me!" Waving her free arm over her head, she chanted, "To the right, to the left! To the right, to the left!" to the beat. Behind her laptop, Sara waved in time, laughing aloud when she caught Soultana's eye.

Dancing, smiling, and standing shoulder to shoulder with Bawss all displayed a physicality that Soultana would avoid in front of a Moroccan audience. Home hip hop audiences might read these moves as insufficiently focused on her narrative, while some Moroccans would see them as overly feminine, even sexualized. However, in a context where few listeners would understand her lyrics, Soultana sought to engage audiences musically through her own body. Instead of explaining the text of "LBareh O LYoum," she began by drawing attention to its danceability—the sung chorus, the moderate tempo, and the handclaps on every beat. Even this restrained physical vocabulary departed from her habitual expressions, grounded in masculine comportment from her favorite '90s hip hop and her ingrained discomfort with appearing to emphasize her femininity in public. By contrast, Bawss made no similar attempts to physically engage the audience.

After the set, Soultana's caring labor intensified as she met with fans. The group walked offstage into a small crowd of excited audience members waiting at the security fence. The adult women and teenage volunteers included Bawss in their photos, but they shared personal stories and words of encouragement with Soultana. After all of the other audience members had spoken to the musicians, a blond woman with an Australian accent introduced herself, saying she produced videos for a nonprofit. Would Soultana do a short interview? Yes, of course. As a group, we walked back toward the youth center and found an empty room.

We sat on the floor. Sara and Bawss settled on either side of Soultana while the interviewer tested her camera. All three stared straight ahead in silence for a moment. It was the first time they had rested since leaving the hotel that afternoon.

The interviewer introduced Soultana to her work. "I make videos of small grassroots activists who lift up their voices, and uh, I wanted an interview with you, because you represent women in Morocco." She gave a short laugh, as if to note how self-evident that was. "So if you start off, just, who you are, where you come from . . . your ensemble when you first started, was the first all-women—?"

Soultana had begun to sniffle. "Yeah. It was the first group, Tigresse Flow."

"Okay, if you start with that, just as an introduction."

Soultana looked over at me, filming from the corner, and rubbed at her nose. She murmured "'Andk l-barid (I have a cold)" as the interviewer framed the shot. Sara and I made noises of concern. "Yeah," responded Soultana.

"Okay," said the interviewer into her viewfinder, as if she was about to say more. We all fell silent.

When the woman was ready, Soultana began: "Hi, I'm Youssra Oukaf, my artistic name is Soultana. Uh, this is Bawss, and here is DJ Sara. Uh, I'm the first female rapper in Morocco, and uh—I got a . . ."

"And she has a cold," Sara jumped in with a grin, as Soultana sniffed and pointed at her nose.

"So I'm the first female rapper in Morocco, and I started by creating the first female group, Tigresse Flow. We won a lot of prizes of national competitions. And uh, after that I became solo, a solo artist. And uh, I released a song . . . It was 'Sawt Nssa,' 'Women's Voice.' And now I'm working with Bawss in the first female and male album about the politic [*sic*] and social issues in Morocco. That's it." She smiled, followed by another sniff.

The interviewer looked up from her viewfinder and smiled. "So, being a voice of women in Morocco, what is the response that you get?"

Soultana displayed a practiced ease with such questions. Listening to the follow-up, it occurred to me that when Soultana translated the title of "Sawt Nssa," people might assume she was describing herself as the "women's voice." But during the chorus, instead of claiming that voice for herself, she tries to speak it into being: "Women's voice, I'm calling to it / The girls' voices which are lost in my country / The voice of she who wants to speak / The voice of everyone who wants a sign, a door to repentance."[12]

By combining the singular woman in one line with many women in the next, Soultana moves from personal realization to potentially political action. Her text, and her typical live performance, implicate comprehending listeners as a responsive and responsible public. Without this experience of the song, or this knowledge of the text, interviews like this one placed Soultana back at the center of the narrative she tried to construct with "Sawt Nssa," replacing her analysis of the problem and its victims with an image of the courageous analyst.

The woman's additional questions did offer Soultana the opportunity to discuss other issues. But only she was asked questions, and only about hip hop "as a vehicle of social change." At no point did she offer to pause the interview so that Soultana could blow her nose, or simply rest. While she came away with her interviewer's contact information, as in many similar interactions, Soultana never learned whether or how this interview was used.

After the interview, the musicians returned to the plaza with me to watch Shadia Mansour perform. A steady stream of young people greeted them at the edge of the audience. In my last photos of the night, Soultana is chatting with a young woman wearing a pink volunteer's hoodie and matching badge. She tells Soultana that one of her parents is Moroccan, and she speaks a few words of Derija. Someone gives Soultana a T-shirt with the festival logo, and she puts it on over her jersey and wraps her arm around the volunteer's shoulders for photos. As we walked away, Soultana relayed what her new fan said: she was so excited for this performance, because before discovering Soultana she had no idea women in Morocco were allowed to rap.

By themselves, each of these interactions was small. Collectively, they seemed to contradict the festival's mission. Back at the hotel that night, Soultana did not accept my argument that a small-town festival simply did not have the resources to do everything she expected. If they weren't going to treat artists appropriately, she responded, why bring them at all? In English, she struggled to explain that although individuals might not mean to offend, their attitudes toward her and Bawss were clear. "Those things are like—each thing, it's *there*," she said, landing on the word as if dropping a weight into her lap. "There is no mistake. Do you see?"

Festivals like This Is Alby, designed to counter existing narratives about immigrants for both residents and other Swedes, are increasingly common in the suburbs of Sweden's largest cities.[13] I have no reason to believe this event was anything but effective at promoting local progressive politics. Both the adult and teenage organizers were excited about showcasing what they believed Soultana stood for. Like the young volunteer excited to meet Soultana after the performance, several audience members were clear about how meaningful it was that a local festival reflected parts of their backgrounds as racialized residents in Sweden.

At the same time, Soultana's instrumentalization is central to that programming's effectiveness. Demand for performances like hers exists precisely because discourses on patriarchy and censorship in Arabo-Muslim culture are already so persuasive. She may be reduced to her music, which is reduced again to activism,

FIGURE 8. Soultana posing with a festival volunteer and fan after her performance, Alby, Botkyrka, Sweden, 2015. Photo by author.

but her live performance cannot be reduced to those discourses. Instead, Soultana's work and, eventually, her person are metonyms for the coming victory of "Western" values in places seen as illiberal. Her work must continue to be seen as rare, and as synonymous with her person, for her to be worth bringing to perform, for her position to be worth celebrating. Though she is asked to rap wherever she appears, she continues to be inaudible, because her texts and contexts are rarely understood outside of her home hip hop community. As both a musician trying to make a living through performance and someone willing to identify as an activist, Soultana is not inherently opposed to being understood as a symbol or a model. However, this event accidentally dehumanized her as it leveraged her reputation.

In retrospect, all parties had assumed we understood each other and that nothing needed to be questioned or made explicit. Instead, Soultana and Bawss were expected to know the customs and competencies of the festival rather than the other way around. The festival celebrated Alby's self-identification as welcoming and multicultural yet it did not consider whether international artists had different needs or norms. Soultana's expectations about food were particularly revealing. The language of their invitation from Botkyrka municipality, as well as Soultana's prior experiences, left her confident they would not pay for their own meals.[14] The Moroccan musicians perceived that the organizers did not realize how expensive Swedish goods were for them—an ignorance that expressed their immense privilege. Beyond this, Moroccan hosts of every socioeconomic level often expend significant money, time, and energy on hospitality. Since their physical well-being was not ensured, it seemed Soultana and Bawss were not welcome as guests.[15]

In addition, whether turntables had been agreed upon or not was more important than it might appear. The trio turned the loss of the momentum Sara's deejaying would have provided into further opportunities to interact with their audience. Building a successful performance despite this issue was vital, because audience members could not be expected to know why Soultana lacked turntables while other musicians did not. Appearing poor and amateurish could feed the exoticism they constantly sought to transcend, especially when they could not control the potentially endless recirculation of photos and videos from the concert.

Moments before they took the stage that night, Sara gave the two emcees a pep talk. She reminded them of all the children gathered in front of the stage and encouraged them to focus on giving those kids a great show. *They look like us*, she did not add. Years later, Soultana described the experience to Yoriyas, a dancer and photographer whose accolades frequently take him to Europe. "I saw that all the immigrants lived in just one neighborhood. And the festival [performers were] just people who looked like them. They didn't bring them to the center of Stockholm. They brought them to a suburb," she explained (p.c., July 5, 2018). Her experience at This Is Alby shaped her understanding of her audience as victims of reduced integration and mobility, irrevocably changing her vision of Sweden as a welcoming destination for migrants.

JOKKO FAM

The choices Soultana, Sara, and Bawss were left to make during This Is Alby required a great deal of caring labor toward themselves, their audiences, and each other. The following example demonstrates how demand for expressions of female Muslim resistance shapes decision-making in communities reliant on global north funding. In 2016 and 2017, Soultana took part in Jokko Fam, an artistic residency and tour organized by the leaders of four music festivals in North and West Africa. Festival organizers' experience with funding from national and international nonprofit, governmental, and corporate sources had led them to change the Jokko project from an unmarked male to an all-women residency, reshaping the organizers' expectations of the artists and their financial and artistic investment in the process. All of the artists who have participated in the Jokko project did similar kinds of work to create new songs together across different languages, cultures, styles, and personalities. In addition, the all-female 2017 edition was tasked with composing, directing, and finally recovering from its own instrumentalization as Muslim women of color.

According to the organizers, the Jokko project originated in conversations held at a workshop for African arts professionals in Burkina Faso in the late 2000s.[16] Hicham Bahou, who cofounded the Boulevard festival and today directs EAC-L'Boulvart, recalled meeting Senegalese and Mauritanian counterparts in 2008 or 2009 at the Waga Hip Hop Festival in Ouagadougou. "In parallel there was a seminar bringing together independent African festivals . . . that was the first connection" (interview, Casablanca, August 18, 2015).[17] Recognizing that they shared similar funding sources, challenges, and interests, Bahou, Amadou Fall Ba of Festa2H in Dakar, and Monza of Assalamalekoum Festival in Nouakchott designed a trans-Saharan initiative that would promote unity and counter prejudice across North and West African audiences.

Each year of the Jokko project, deejays, emcees, and beatmakers were chosen by the organizers to collaborate on new songs and performances of their individual repertoires. After one or two weeks in residency early in the year, the group performed at each festival over the summer, fall, and following spring. Between 2014 and 2018, the residency rotated between Casablanca, Nouakchott, and Dakar, and ranged from three to six onstage members. Members were invited by festival organizers based on name recognition, previous collaborative experiences, interest in the projects' stated goals, and organizers' expectations for their abilities to work together. The first edition of Jokko launched in 2014 with two male musicians from each country. In 2016, the project included all female artists for the first time.

The Jokko project reflects both progressive Moroccans' and the state's goals for trans-Saharan relationships. The Moroccan state has responded to recent increases in sub-Saharan migration, and a parallel rise in anti-immigrant behavior, with attempts to better integrate migrants (Berrada 2016: 251). In 2013, King Mohamed VI "regularized" some undocumented migrants. The party closest to the monarchy, the Party of Authenticity and Modernity (PAM), proposed a law punishing expressions of anti-Black racism (Harit 2013a and 2013b). PAM spokesperson Mehdi Bensaid explicitly addressed common attitudes: "Racism against sub-Saharans must be fought. We also want to fight against racist expressions encountered by Moroccans of black skin. Morocco is an African country, no?" (quoted in Harit 2013a). This bill was "roundly rejected in Parliament," though regularization efforts continued (Aïdi 2020: 66–67).

While Bensaid's phrasing presents Morocco's Africanity as an unremarkable fact, the proposed law represents a distinct shift from state-sanctioned patterns of discrimination that date back to at least the 1670s, when sub-Saharan slaves and dark-skinned Moroccans were conscripted into Sultan Moulay Ismail's standing army (El Hamel 2013). At the same time, the state has pushed since the early 2010s to open West African markets to its products and to exert political, cultural, and religious leadership in the region.[18]

The Jokko project takes a short-term international collaboration model, seen locally across genres at major festivals, and applies it to a centuries-old transregional relationship. Both Moroccan and foreign participants close to the project believe performing transcultural unity on stage can help Moroccan audiences reflect on their own prejudices about sub-Saharans, Moroccans of sub-Saharan descent, or simply Moroccans with darker skin. "In the diaspora, Afro-Americans [say], 'I'm going to Africa.' The Moroccans say '*Africa*-Africa' [when] they are a part of Africa," observed Amadou Fall Ba, then the head of Dakar's hip hop nonprofit Africulturban. "I think this kind of project can be helpful to show them 'no no, you are part . . . [you are] on the continent'" (interview, Pikine, June 2015).

Ghita Khaldi founded and directs the Moroccan nonprofit Afrikayna, which co-organized the Jokko project. In Moroccan Arabic, "kayn/a" indicates that the subject of the sentence is present; "Afrikayna" thus argues for its own mission statement through a clever portmanteau that translates to "Africa is here [in Morocco]." Khaldi was inspired to create Afrikayna "when I read the first article about [Moroccan] racism. . . . I have some people in my family from these other countries, so . . . I never expected this." For her, artistic collaboration could spur audiences to examine their own ignorance: "When you see your idol on stage with somebody from another country and you like it . . . you're gonna start to know a little about this country" (interview, Casablanca, August 10 2016).

Transporting musicians within Africa is often more expensive than flights to and from Europe. Jokko musicians' flights are paid for by Africa Art Lines, a foundation within Afrikayna designed to facilitate meetings between Moroccan and West African artists. Africa Art Lines is itself funded by the British Council; the Moroccan Ministry of Foreign Affairs, African Cooperation and Moroccan Expatriates; the philanthropic arm of the Sharifian Office of Phosphates (OCP), Morocco's partially private phosphates mining company; and other organizations (Khaldi, interview, August 10, 2016).

While Moroccan public and private funding generally covers Jokko's transportation needs, organizers obtain the remaining funding from a range of locations and institutions. Some has come from the philanthropic arms of transnational corporations. Partner nonprofits, often ultimately funded by the same national and international sources, help with in-kind donations of space and equipment. The bulk, however, comes from European NGOs such as the Institut Français, which plays a vital role in the cultural sector of each postcolony, and the Organization de la Francophonie. Fall Ba and Bahou each stressed that obtaining funds from their local municipalities is more difficult than from other sources, while the Institut Français has been a reliable partner in all four participating countries for years.

The original Jokko project was explicitly described as a model collaboration that would promote a transregional musical market and demonstrate successful North African and West African collaborations to diverse audiences despite differences in language, culture, and preconceptions. Since 2016, the project relied on expectations of women's caring labor to express this model and to make up for a complementary disinvestment from the male festival leaders and artistic directors. This can be seen in the 2017 edition's organization, rehearsals, and performances.

The 2017 project was renamed Jokko Fam (short for "famille," but pronounced "femme," double entendre intended). That year, Jokko Fam also expanded to include the Festival sur le Niger in Ségou, Mali. For the first time a Malian emcee, Ami Yerewolo, joined the residency. Four of the musicians from the all-female 2016 edition (hereafter Jokko No. 3) stayed on the project for Jokko Fam.

Like the all-male 2014 and 2015 editions, Jokko No. 3 brought together five musicians to collaborate on a new song and integrate each other into existing songs. The set list created in residency included a well-known solo song from each musician, a few collaborations (or "featurings"), and a group finale of a newly written song. According to musicians from the 2014–16 editions, this set was then performed at each of the three festivals with only slight alterations (interview, H-Name, Casablanca, August 2015; interview, DJ Gee-Bayss, Dakar, June 2015).

Jokko No. 3 was the first edition to record their group song. The team created a video for their song, also titled "Jokko," during their summer 2016 residency in Casablanca. Instead of reflecting the lyrical content, the documentary-style video tells the story of the group's work together against a backdrop of iconic Moroccan sites. Shots of each emcee recording their verses, singing together in the studio, and performing at Boultek are intercut with their travels in Casablanca and Rabat. Each emphasizes moments of friendship and support between the onstage musicians and the 2016 edition's musical producers, Casablancan emcee and beatmaker Masta Flow and Senegalese veteran DJ Gee-Bayss. The original chorus of "Jokko" reinforces the notion of a successful collaboration in which each plays her role to best overall effect: Eben of Mauritania sings a mix of English and French; Soultana double-tracks Eben's vocals and yells "Jokko!"; Fatim Sy echoes the last word of each phrase on the pickup to the next and provides the punchline in Wolof.

> We are shining bright like fire (fire!)
> Gonna fight like a lion (like a lion!)
> *L'Unité* go for higher (Jokko, jokko!)
> We are shining bright like fire (fire!)
> Shinin' bright like fire
> [Fatim Sy, spoken:]
> Djiguén bou mane door thi kaw beat man door
> boy sopé yokhoul ney "Jokko!"[19]

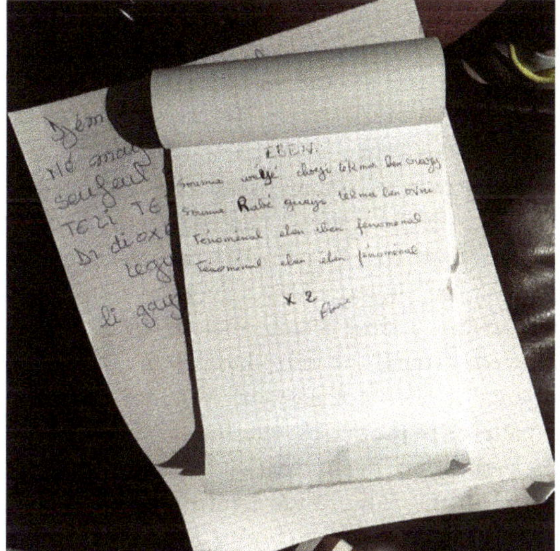

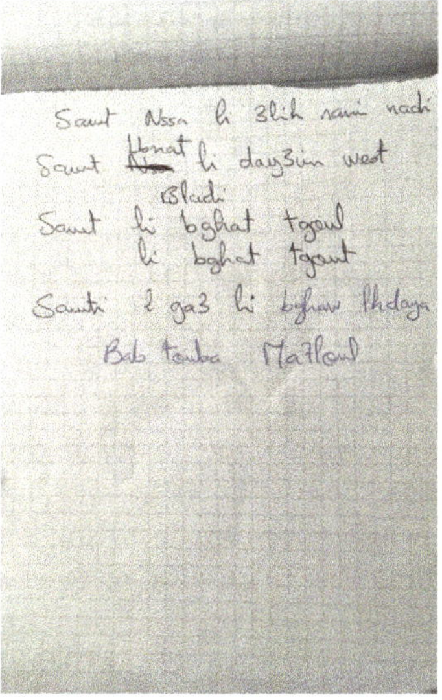

FIGURE 9. Soultana used transcriptions of her collaborators' songs to follow along with the set. Photo by author.

FIGURE 10. Soultana wrote out the lyrics to "Sawt Nssa" for her collaborators. Photo by author.

Watching the women of Jokko Fam rehearse "Jokko," I learned that as in many of their songs, the emcees have only a general idea of the idea behind each woman's verse, composed in her first language. Yet they turned this into a way to promote solidarity. Only Soultana could render a full translation of her verse on "Jokko." But they all heard its energy crest in measures nine and ten, when she called out diverse women audiences: "The voice of she who stays home, she who spends her time on the streets / she who lives in the village and she who raps at Boulevard."[20] In practice, the emcees made a game of shouting "Boulevard!" together at the peak of the verse. Similarly, Fatim Sy's English-studded Wolof verse flips a classic ego-trip by celebrating the other emcees' and deejays' skills in the first half, before boasting about herself in the second.

According to the musicians, the 2017 edition had several structural changes, resulting in new and different demands. DJ Gee-Bayss, who had performed with the first two editions of Jokko, provided artistic guidance in the third edition. In the 2017 edition, he was replaced as artistic director by Monza and Amadou Fall Ba. Starting in spring 2017, musicians told me, the collaboration proceeded with less attention to detail than in the previous editions. Soultana described the apartment rented for the women during their residency in Dakar as far from their rehearsal space and food options, resulting in the visiting musicians spending much of their fees on takeout and transportation. Posters for Jokko Fam on each festival's website and Facebook pages used the press photos taken for Jokko No. 3, which out left Malian emcee Ami Yerewolo. In addition, Yerewolo's legal name, rather than her stage name, was used in the text of the posters. The musicians cited these and other items as evidence of a general pattern of carelessness.

During their Dakar residency, the Jokko Fam team were encouraged to use studio and rehearsal time to record their own solo songs. They also continued to perform "Jokko."[21] For the first time in 2017, the team was asked to write about a specific idea: domestic violence against women as a pan-African problem. This directive resulted in the group composition "Violence."

Built in minor on a booming bassline, a slow countermelody in electronic woodwinds, and increasingly frenzied strings, the introduction to "Violence" quickly establishes a sense of urgency it does not sustain. A skittering hi-hat switches between duple and triple patterns in the verses, offering the emcees multiple ways to rap with or against the percussion. In a move that increases the emotional pace of the song even further, Ami and Fatim trade eight-measure sections over the first two verses. After the first iteration of the chorus, Eben sings rather than raps in the third verse, while Soultana makes the greatest use of silence and the least use of syncopation in the fourth. As a result, the song gradually decreases in intensity after the first two verses.

The structure of "Violence" also minimized the women's individual contributions in favor of chorus repetitions. With just two lines in French, the language shared by all four emcees and most of their audiences, the chorus aimed to maximize audience participation:

> We say "no" to violence against women (No!)
> We say "yes" to everything that women claim (Yes!)
> We say no (No!)
> We say no (No!)
> We say "no" to violence against women[22]

After Soultana's verse, the song concludes with six repetitions of the chorus—two over verse material, two over chorus material, and two over a repetition of the percussion-free introduction. Success in live performance thus depended on audiences staying interested through each chorus, ideally shouting "Non!" and "Oui!" with the artists.

Each time the women of Jokko Fam discussed or performed "Violence," the tenor of the room would change. On the first day of their rehearsal week in Casablanca, the women ran through the set they had performed at their previous two concerts. As unidentified cameramen drifted in and out of their tiny green-painted rehearsal room, they finished an uproarious version of "Jokko" by joyfully shouting its chorus together. Everyone took a break, falling into chairs and joking, as DJ Zeyna started scratching over high-pitched squeals. The women paused to listen as the squeals slowed into tinny string samples. "La 'Violence'?" asked Ami, holding up her microphone like an invitation.

"Contre les armes [Against [all] weapons]," groaned Soultana, prompting grins.

"Oui, pas du tout! On ne parle pas de violence ici [Yes, absolutely not! We don't speak of violence here]," claimed Fatim in mock-affronted tones.

Ami walked among the seated women as if preening across the stage, exaggerating her diction as she belted the chorus. Each musician climbed to her feet, slower than before, as Zeyna launched the backing track. Bouncing on the balls of her feet, gripping her notebook and mic in the same hand, Ami rehearsed her energizing stage movements as well as her couplets. Soultana opened the notes app on her phone and scrolled to her lyrics. Fatim pulled a folded piece of paper out of her pocket just in time to deliver her verse. As soon as the last videographer left the room, Soultana looked over at me in the corner and rolled her eyes as she sang along with the chorus a third time. During one of several chorus repetitions, Fatim ducked out, and Soultana sank into a chair. Even the normally taciturn Zeyna smiled as Eben and Ami alone ran through the final two iterations of the chorus. The rest of us gave them a round of applause for staying the course.

Each of the Jokko Fam artists was already well known in her home hip hop community, and each had experience on national or international stages. Like Soultana, each was accustomed to journalists stressing their uniqueness. When a freelance journalist asked to record a group interview, they focused on highlighting the Jokko message by emphasizing their successful musical and personal collaboration, citing what they had learned from each other and complimenting each other's abilities (Doublier 2017).[23]

As they gathered in a circle on the rehearsal room floor, the journalist checked her recording's levels while asking each artist to introduce herself and explain how she knew the other musicians. "And artistically, what do you learn [savez-vous importe quoi]? Who wants to respond?" asked the journalist, waving the microphone in Soultana's direction. Instead of answering, Soultana mumbled to Fatim, "Lots of things, eh?"

"Lots of things," affirmed Fatim, leaning forward. "When Soultana raps in Arabic, it takes me back to school [j'essaye prendre le bac]. And . . . with Ami, it's the same thing. Together it permits us truly to exchange our cultures, to break stereotypes, to break the chains."

After a few more questions, the journalist stated, "You are female rappers in Africa. The problems you face are the same." Ami responded by comparing what she had learned about women's roles in Morocco to Mali, then transitioning to her own experience: "It's a so-called Muslim country. So sometimes the society puts pressure on you. And also the family . . . they expect her to get married, to have children. And we, we say that music, and above all rap, it's a career of the future.

It has taken years and years to make a place, and after to enjoy this. And we need time for this, if the family is going to understand [our careers]."

Eben added, "Mauritania is considered an Islamic country, therefore the women cover everything. . . . It was not easy, I encountered many problems, but I continued because I love rap, I love the music."

"And working with other women, it gives you courage?" asked Sara.

"Yes," said everyone at once.

"For me, Jokko is a family . . . we understand each other," continued Eben. To my left, Zeyna nodded vigorously.

Over the weeks they spent together in 2017, the women of Jokko Fam cultivated solidarity through both positive and negative experiences. The artistic directors did not appear during the women's rehearsals in Casablanca that week. However, they had told Fatim that the group should rework its set list. Instead of the previous set's solos and duets, they wanted this performance to include at least three musicians on each song. As a result, the group spent three of their four days of rehearsal integrating each other into solo songs. Integration ranged from teaching foreign chorus lyrics phonetically, to swapping someone in for a verse, to an entirely new piece on shared postcolonial trauma. Throughout the week, the musicians sought to create leading and supporting roles for everyone.

At 4 p.m. on Wednesday of rehearsal week, Mauritanian festival organizer Monza was scheduled to watch a run-through of the set. Instead, he messaged Fatim. He was unable to leave a prior meeting, but the musicians would have to cut their forty-five-minute set to thirty minutes.

This surprise put the group in a doubly difficult position. First, reshaping their set again without disadvantaging anyone was put on their shoulders, while the directors retained final say over the performance. Second, they were scheduled to spend the following day videotaping, so they would have to drop material without additional rehearsal time. After several hours of shooting Thursday afternoon, the group held a tense discussion, eventually cutting three songs and a showcase for DJ Zeyna out of the set. The result satisfied no one. However, everyone agreed to include "Violence" as their penultimate song, followed by an upbeat conclusion with "Jokko."

By the day of the concert, shared discontent culminated in an argument. The lack of communication from the organizers had exacerbated in-group dynamics. Their argument was ostensibly about whether everyone had contributed equally to the difficult decision of what to cut from their performance. At its height, Eben tried to calm tempers by again calling Jokko a family. They may have disagreements, but "we work them out, that's what families do," she said. Yet Ami, who had forcefully argued that she was being left out of decisions made primarily in Wolof, shot back that Jokko Fam "is not a family." We're here to do a job, she continued, contrasting the obligations of work and of family.

That night during their performance at Boulevard, the group's tensions were most visible during "Violence." Ami led during the long intro, asking the audience to raise their right arms high with their open palms toward the stage in a "stop" gesture. The other emcees joined in, facing the audience in a row as they launched into the first verse. While Ami directed the audience's attention by watching and interacting with each soloist in turn, Soultana and Fatim sought to connect to the audience throughout, even when silent. Eben interacted the least, standing behind the other emcees and moving center stage only for the chorus.

By the last four choruses, no one was looking at each other. At times, Ami lined up next to another emcee; they would face the audience together, sometimes mimicking each other's movements and gestures. But each emcee also strode her patch of the stage separately. Each held up the open palm gesture at a different time rather than in unison as they had practiced. And downstage from their colleagues, Soultana and Fatim, holding out their microphones to elicit "non" and "oui" throughout the chorus, smiled and laughed at the mix of earnest and mocking responses they received from the young men nearest the stage.

By the time I joined the Jokko Fam team in Casablanca in September 2017, their prior experiences had led the musicians to interpret any changes to their work agreements or creative autonomy as part of a larger pattern of disinvestment. Because last-minute changes were communicated partially or not at all, the musicians often filled in their understanding of the situation by reasoning from their own experiences. Team conversations that might be read as gossip worked to place the organizers' actions in an existing narrative about their motivations and intentions and to ensure that all five musicians agreed among themselves on the truthfulness of that narrative. In other words, the musicians were caring for each others' responses in ways that would enhance the group's performance of solidarity, even as the organizers' actions or lack of actions undermined that solidarity.

Gossip, in this situation, functioned both as a rejection of the team's working conditions and as caring labor within the group. I focus on caring labor here not because female labor is coded as more emotive than male labor on themselves, with, or for others.[24] Instead, caring labor is central to my analysis because the Jokko Fam team took its task so seriously. Charged with depicting to their audiences sincere bonds across difference, they built those bonds by validating each other in the face of others' invalidation. As their group interview and countless rehearsal moments demonstrated, each took pleasure in supporting her colleagues, even as they navigated spoken and unspoken scripts.

The 2016 video for "Jokko," which showcased for an international audience the women's joy and pride at working together, underscores the entire team's learned expectation that displays of feeling and solidarity would satisfy viewers as much as, if not more than, the musical products. When Ami asserted, the afternoon of the concert, that Jokko Fam was not a family, her colleagues appeared shocked by her vehemence. The idea of "family" was not only important because it implied support as the artists took creative risks together. It also made the inequity of their work more bearable. At the same time, the more closely connected the musicians became, the more effectively they could do their job of performing that connection. Building family-like ties was then important labor in its own right.

As organizers and artists explained, the Jokko project demonstrates connection across difference both as a genuine invitation to individual audience members and as a metaphor for regional political relations. Funders, organizers, and artists themselves understood women as better vessels for this message than previous all-male teams; all of these actors considered women more empathetic than their male counterparts.

Organizers also recognized the demand for representations of resistant Muslim women via their long familiarity with the rhetorics and assumptions of development-style funding. In interviews and conversations, Fall Ba repeatedly noted that the female editions of Jokko brought in more funding than in earlier years. Monza, the Mauritanian organizer, commented that "for us, the women respond to a challenge: 'hip hop is too macho, hip hop has too many men,' etc." (interview, Casablanca, September 21, 2017).

Yet while Jokko Fam, as proposed, leveraged global north assumptions about Muslim and African women's unfreedom for better support, it denied its artists the same creative control their male counterparts had enjoyed. In part, this reflected the fact that several participants in former editions were not only emcees, but producers, deejays, studio owners, and artist managers. Collectively, the women chosen for the 2016 and 2017 editions had fewer of those experiences for the same reasons their presence in Jokko was valued in the first place. While each woman had different goals for her participation in the group, the expectation—reinforced among themselves as well as externally—that they would place solidarity and social cohesion above their own needs kept the collaboration going, but it hindered the gender equality they were funded to promote.

THE DOUBLE BIND:
SOLIDARITY, COMPLICITY, AND CARING LABOR

Both of the events in this chapter appeared, according to both organizers and artists, to successfully advance their priorities with their audiences. In both examples, female performers bear the burden of embodying properly international, Westernized, liberal orientations to their audiences, who some of the actors consider not yet sufficiently liberal. Each musician in this chapter has experienced sexism, racism, or other kinds of discrimination. Indeed, Soultana has highlighted the double standards of the Moroccan government and her fellow citizens throughout her career. But the market for representations of resistance depends on the reification of women's, especially Muslim women's, unfreedom so that consumers find resistance meaningful. In that sense, the artists in this chapter must choose between trading one kind of devaluation for another, or losing vital work opportunities. In turn, as Jokko in particular demonstrates, global north demand for portrayals of "good Muslims" feeds state-sponsored and private representations of the ideal citizen nationally and internationally. As I argued in the previous chapters, musicians' sincerely held values thus overlap with those encouraged by the state in its cultural neoliberalization, even when individual practitioners oppose some or all of the state's policies.

Valued for the potential to represent themselves to others as resistant Muslim women, Soultana and others participate in one aspect of a global north market for "culture"—which can amount to an uneven transnational market for women and people of color's caring labor. World music scholars have been making this point, with different conceptual language, since the 1990s. It is often, though not always, women performers who "teach" global north listeners, inheritors of the benefits of colonial capitalism, what we wish to be true about human connection across difference.

Women in all of the cultures discussed here—including my own white American culture—are expected to perform certain kinds of caring labor while men conduct others. For the women of Jokko Fam, representing themselves as a family was a step toward representing themselves as family to each other, with all the expectations for reciprocity associated with that idea in their home contexts. In the vignette that began this chapter, caring labor became visible when Soultana finally refused to do it. In previous chapters, men organize structures through which they can mentor (primarily male) youths, teaching them that musical and entrepreneurial skills are equally important. Caring labor thus captures the vital role sincerity plays in sustaining market orientations: as individuals experience themselves as both a subject hailed by market discourse and an object circulated in that market, as both producer and consumer of themselves, their recognition and support of that duality in each other renders their position coherent.

The circulating and recirculating demand for representations of resistance I describe in this chapter is not a metaphor. In these examples, African Muslim women are most valuable to organizers whose events form the nodes of this market as representations of themselves, and least valuable when they resist their working conditions. They are human capital not only in Gary Becker's sense, in which individuals' skills and knowledge cannot be divorced from their bodies, but also because their presence allows others to celebrate their own moral superiority, thereby increasing viewers' valuation of themselves (Becker 1993: 40).

Yet the artists in this chapter cannot survive by this market alone. Given my insistence on this framework, one might expect Soultana's remuneration to rise and fall according to the demand for representations of resistance, according to her currency with consumers.[25] Instead, this market devalues artists in two ways. First, it perpetuates stereotypes of unfreedom to ensure continuing demand for counter-representations that appear to perform freedom. Equally important, the artists discussed here have few opportunities to "move up" or successfully negotiate more money as their expertise and recognition grow.[26] This is not a metaphor, but a market whose inequalities and constraints are made visible on women's bodies and in their lives.

I have argued that for Muslim artists, the flip side of gaining international attention is being interpellated into "a discourse whose terms she cannot control" (Salois 2012). Reflecting on the role of white researchers like herself in recirculating hip hop's "myths of resistance," Catherine Appert notes, "As [Senegalese emcee] Almamy's wording uncomfortably reminded me, ['another white girl'] was an interchangeable link in an endless cycle of researchers unified not only in our geopolitical and racial privilege, but also in our predictable patterns of . . . data retrieval and disappearance" (2018: 187). I would add to these repetitions the deconstructive move central to this chapter. Highlighting the marketed assumptions at work may have the unintended (not unimagined) effect of further circulating those assumptions. In fact, if, as I am arguing, this market's audience values its ability to transform itself through consumption of the other, then critiques are more valuable than other performances. As I write, I commoditize my own embodied "data retrieval" and the feelingful critiques it engenders. The struggle to decommodify representations of Muslim women artists like Soultana, including the representation you are reading, is readily reincorporated as a preferred version of the commodity.

By detailing women's caring labor in sound, speech, song, and affect throughout this chapter, I participate in the transformation of individual experiences to illustrations of a larger phenomenon while insisting on the uniqueness of each interaction. This essential sleight of hand powers contemporary ethnographic argument, rendering our deeply personal, contextual, and contingent work legible to others. Even if none of the typical kinds of academic currency accrue to me as a result, I am furthering one kind of literal objectification: transforming women's words, musicking, and career paths into a symbol and metonym for my argument that can then continue to circulate in the same markets I have described here.[27] Are my representations of Soultana and her colleagues somehow better than the versions described above, and if so, in what ways? Am I not doing the same work as the volunteers at This Is Alby, attempting to expand the ways Muslim women are understood as agents by certain global north audiences? Can such instrumentalization be avoided if we are to learn anything? If the answer to the latter question is "no," then do we merely learn what we wish to learn? Both Soultana's work and my work are always already woven into historic, recursive relations of complicity with material and intellectual consequences.

As is surely clear by now, this conclusion itself participates in a venerable market for ethnographic virtue. I trained in a moment Bruno Nettl describes as a high point in ethnomusicologists' periodic tradition of internal criticism, in which scholars return to "a sharply evaluative lens" on their collective work (2010: 55).[28] These peaks often amplify interventions from anthropology, musicology, or critical theory, resulting in a transdisciplinary genealogy of humanists' diagnoses of power relations. My appearances in this chapter, as researcher or performer of ethnographic authority, highlight how our knowledge circulates in the same markets we study.

This is both heartening and disappointing if one believes research ought to "do something" with and for research subjects. As Jason Pine puts it, "I too am sometimes intoxicated with hope . . . that ethnography can matter" (2016: 311). There is no reason to think it can matter outside the frameworks through which, as musicians, scholars, and people, we constitute ourselves. In the epilogue, I reflect on how pioneering and current practitioners celebrate their own understanding of themselves as potential capital.

Epilogue

The World the Wave Made, or The Sincerity of Capital

*The international journalists and observers who are interested in our young
musical scene very rarely escape from their Western-centric reflexes.*
(ZINE 2006: 23)

*We believe that all cultures are equal in a world that is not, and that
all artists should be able to tell their stories by themselves.*
(NAAR 2018: HTTP://NAAR.FR/ABOUT/)

*We're like the Bronx in the 1970s. We need ten years to get hip hop
as a confirmed culture.*
(DON BIGG, PERSONAL COMMUNICATION [P.C.]., CASABLANCA,
OCTOBER 21, 2009)

In September 2017, I watched a musical and cultural transition take place backstage
at the Boulevard Festival in Casablanca. The first night of the festival included a
diverse slate of hip hop artists, beginning with the first- and second-prize winners
of the Tremplin. The women of Jokko Fam shared an artist's tent next to Proof G
Killah, a second-generation emcee and former Tremplin laureate who had brought
along 7liwa (pronounced *ḥliwa*) and L'Ferda, two young trap musicians generating
lots of social media chatter. Masta Flow, one of the emcees from first-generation
group Casa Crew, was billed as a solo artist, though he was supported onstage
by other members of his group and a live band. And following their tradition of
bringing internationally recognized headliners to the festival, Boulevard closed
the night with the New York duo M.O.P.

As people circulated through the tents, chatting and doing interviews with local
media, I noticed divisions emerging by musical style, age, and markers of class status. While Masta Flow hosted a stream of musicians through his tent, the youngest

performers politely avoided his bandmates J-Ok and Caprice, sharing deferential nods and hellos before moving on to their own conversations.

As I watched, I considered reasons this might be so. Caprice and J-Ok had released little music since Casa Crew stopped recording together in the early 2010s. As a beatmaker and producer, Masta Flow continued to record new music for himself and others. The younger performers were recognized, by the media, the audiences, and the musicians themselves, as the leading edge present at the festival. In addition, I could not help but notice that the performers receiving intense attention on social media were attired in fashionable clothes, caps, and sneakers, with the most recent bags and cell phones. Caprice, by contrast, wore a plain white polo and a camouflage-printed baseball cap with the pirated logo of a luxury designer.

Once we sat down to catch up, I realized there might be additional reasons Caprice was not at the center of the evening's socializing. Shouting over the sound of that year's Tremplin winners, who were sharing an extended call-and-response with the audience a few yards away, I asked him how things had changed in hip hop since our last interview in 2010. "It's been like a big change all these couple years," he began.[1] "It's like the same thing that happened in the United States. It's like, rap told stories. Now it's like too much loud, now it's like trap music or that kind, you know what I mean? So . . . that thing is not like real hip hop, not like the first rappers . . . it doesn't have anything in the lyrics. The people, they just wanna get high and listen."

I next asked, "Do you think that the young audience is different than the audience in the 2000s?"

> C: Yeah. This is something, like, that you see . . . They don't say "look at them, they are the originators of hip hop, we're gonna respect that guy." Muslim is doing this all for hip hop, Aminoffice.[2] . . . Like J. Cole is saying in his song, I listened to it, he's saying Nas—they say "Tupac is Jesus, and Nas wrote the Bible."[3] So he means, like, there's something bigger. It has nothing to do with religion but I understand his philosophy. . . . You gotta respect older rappers, because they're the ones that started things. You don't have to say "yeah, yeah, that's old rap."
>
> KS: . . . It sounds like you're saying that today's hip hop fans don't know Moroccan hip hop history.
>
> C: Some of them—a lot of them—know about the history of hip hop. But just he doesn't wanna say the truth. Know what I mean? Because the truth [is], somebody, he's, you know, he's like [points to himself].

Caprice's comments fit a discourse I heard with increased frequency in 2017. According to this narrative—shared by some younger artists—young audiences lacked interest in the traditional qualities that Caprice found so important. By comparing trap to "real hip hop" and suggesting both emcees and listeners were uninterested in thoughtful lyrics, Caprice was making an argument about what "real hip hop" did or should do and complaining that others were abandoning what made the art form great. In this discourse, the move to a new style of hip hop also had implications for community ethics, as both artists and audiences either didn't know or didn't care to respect their elders' contributions. Instead, as he intimated by gesture, they preferred to represent themselves as new, unique, or self-made.

Before I left the artists' tents that evening, I asked Masta Flow some of the same questions I had asked Caprice.

> *KS:* For you, what has changed in Moroccan hip hop [since 2010]?[4]
>
> *MF:* Just as [it has in] the whole world, especially like the US. There's classic rap, after that . . . [styles like] bounce, now we got trap music . . . this is the way it is. But I got no problem with this. You understand? I've got to accept it. Because music changes. First there was rap . . . now trap music, in the future, there will be something else. . . . Things change, *kaydour kaydour.*[5]
>
> *KS:* It sounds like you've had this conversation before.
>
> *MF:* Yeah yeah yeah. Just now on the TV, they asked me and I gave them the same answer. Everyone—like, the people who came up with us, we don't like this new generation. [But] you don't say that, you know? Every generation has its own lifestyle and their own things, you know? Us, our lifestyle was the real life . . . in the street, with the people. . . . Them, the new generation, it's more about digital. The digital and, after this, the real life. But us, it was the real life first, then the digital.
>
> *KS:* Not all of the first generation have made a transition to digital. . . . But you have.
>
> *MF:* This is not a choice, you know. It's an obligation. . . . This is the new way of communication with the people. I don't use digital [as well as] the new generation does. I just use it to *be* digital, because if I'm not in the digital, someone else will take my personality . . . and my place.

Masta Flow and Caprice reacted differently to the same trends in transnational hip hop culture. Where Caprice felt something valuable receding into the past, Masta Flow stressed his "obligation," using the English term, to follow the culture into new platforms if not new musical styles.[6] Both understood responsibility to one's audiences to be at the center of one's practice, but they attached different expectations to that understanding. For Caprice, some audiences were no longer doing their part to seek out, absorb, and be sensitized to the lessons emcees delivered through both music and text. When I asked him if audiences were different now than in the early 2000s, his complaints sounded like the familiar concerns of elders from many genres: "Now they just listen to the rhythm. They don't care about the lyrics, about the flow." By contrast, Masta Flow characterized the era as part of a natural cycle. Younger audiences were simply finding their own voice, and in order to connect with "the people"—an artistic and economic necessity—he would have to listen and change as well.

Near the end of our conversation, Caprice explained that he hoped the lyricism and critique he loved would continue to find dedicated listeners. "The public must have knowledge," he said, echoing concerns he and his generation had expressed for over two decades. I had expected elder musicians to critique the new generation's preferences. But beliefs about class positioning, self-fashioning, epistemologies of listening, and music's role as a driver of change were just as divisive as differences in musical style.

In September 2017, "trap" could refer to multiple things. For some, it was a particular style with a distinct history; for others, the term seemed to stand in for any new developments in hip hop. But at the time, one song came up repeatedly: 7liwa's "Haribo." Released in 2015 on his mixtape *Wald Fatima* (Fatima's Son), it circulated much further after the launch of its video in January 2017. 7liwa was among the first Moroccan artists to use trap's signature vocal sounds, styles of delivery, and drum sounds and patterns. For the first-generation musicians with whom I mostly conversed, the musical and sonic aspects were less important than the song's gleeful references to illicit drugs, made explicit in the video, and its insistent lyrical repetition, enhanced by sections of triplet-based flow in the verses. But for those listening carefully, 7liwa was speaking to issues that were vital to any of Moroccan hip hop's most "conscious" artists, including inequality, emigration, and the distance between the nation-state's self-portrayal on the international stage and citizens' experiences of the state at home.

That evening, at the Boulevard Festival, 7liwa was the most controversial exponent of trap on the stage. The festival itself took an active role in the debate around trap; in its press release following the event, it described 7liwa and his fellow emcee L'Ferda as "the new idols of the youth, straight from the internet . . . whose success is counted in clicks" (EAC-L'Boulvart 2017: 2). It also highlighted Masta Flow discussing the new generation, just as he had told me: "We were sniped at by classical musicians back in the day, we won't make the same mistakes" (EAC-L'Boulvart 2017: 2).

For my interlocutors, the questions I asked connected to a conversation already roiling about the practices and mentalities trap encouraged among listeners and, in turn, the future of hip hop. As some of the relatively few first-generation artists who had continued to make music into the late 2010s, Masta Flow, Caprice, and others were understandably concerned about the material and social infrastructure they had left for future musicians. In our conversation at Sbagha Bagha, MC Dalim compared the situation to that which he had studied for his degree. Just as the Harlem Renaissance had paved the way for midcentury intellectuals and activists, he said, first-generation hip hop practitioners should have "laid the road (dar al-triq)" for the next generation—and some, like him, were still trying to do so (Casablanca, July 1, 2018).

This epilogue starts from these discourses to consider how, in the years after the February 20 reform movement of 2011 and 2012 and subsequent changes in the state's support for popular musicians, Moroccan hip hop's oldest performing musicians view the musical world they made. How does the emergence of the "new generation" reveal the "old school's" values?

In the preceding chapters, practitioners insist on their responsibility to educate a national public and on possibilities for change through, not despite, the ways they are naturalized as neoliberal citizens. Trap music and discourses, by contrast, are often considered by both Moroccan artists and music scholars to be post the failed political, economic, and moral nexus of neoliberalization (Burton 2017). Yet the seemingly apolitical stance of some trap musicians is also a political choice, and throughout this epilogue, I suggest that trap's silences on some issues and volume on others show how little the larger political-economic conjuncture has changed since the 1990s. Moreover, while several Moroccan hip hop artists are now signed to major labels or subsidiaries based in Europe or the United States, the discourses within which artists find success continually expect them to reperform their difference.

Throughout this book, I have asked: How are those not currently understood as "subjects of value" (Skeggs 2004, 2014)—that is, those who are valued and work with value, rather than those who are objectified by valuation and evaluation— trying to make themselves into subjects of value? One way is by adopting tools of neoliberal self-making, including discourses and practices of entrepreneurship, resilience, and speculation, a package we might call self-financialization. I have sought to balance discussion of these tools with the fervent commitments practitioners hold in order to show how my interlocutors intertwine the two in everyday life. As recent reconsiderations of neoliberalization have pointed out, reframing studies of neoliberal contexts as "track[ing] a logic of exclusion from the economy rather than total subsumption in it" better foregrounds that "many of the subjects of the present know full well the conditions of the world in which they live" (McClanahan 2019: 123–24). Starting from recognition of their own intersecting forms of exclusion, my interlocutors and the musicians who followed them assert their own unquantifiable value as people by tracking, discussing, and creating economic value for themselves and others. As we have seen, practitioners are well aware that critiques of national and global political-economic systems, when rendered by the global north's postcolonial others, generate multiple kinds of value in markets for racialized music and representations (Hilgers 2013: 75; Rollefson 2017). Informed in part by the transnational hip hop tradition's forms of argument and analysis, practitioners use music, discourse, and action to perform responses to neoliberalization that simultaneously adopt many of its premises and insist on their value within an exclusionary system.

DIR AL-TRIQ

In 2014, Soultana created a nonprofit association named Youth Vision. Inspired by meeting the leaders of Chicago's Kuumba Lynx, she wanted to create similar hip hop–based educational projects for young people. In 2015, I accompanied Soultana as she and Youth Vision worked to create a benefit concert featuring first-, second-, and third-generation hip hop musicians in Meknes. The proceeds from ticket sales and donations would go to school supplies for underprivileged children in the rural areas outside the city. After securing and then losing commitments from performers, struggling to find a venue that would allow a hip hop concert, and finding themselves unable to cover costs through donations or their own money, they eventually gave up on their plan. The association wanted to fill a small but meaningful hole in the safety net, but it found insurmountable roadblocks at individual and institutional levels.

A few years later, Soultana and I were discussing the "new generation" and their attitudes toward older hip hop artists. "It's partly the old generation's fault," said Soultana, that the youngest artists lacked understanding of "the real meaning of hip hop" and of their country's history in the genre. In the late 2000s, when some leaders were receiving relatively large sums from competitions and to perform at national festivals, artists "didn't invest in hip hop," she argued.

I reminded Soultana of Youth Vision and the Meknes benefit concert project. "But what if we had started . . . in 2010 instead of 2014," she responded.

"If you had started in 2010, you might have been shut down in 2011," I suggested.

"2011! Yeah, that's right. As soon as *al-'Adl wa al-Tanmia* came in!" (p.c., January 2018).[7]

Soultana's memory of her own actions, and her reactions to other initiatives, centered on work ethic, intention, and imagination rather than on the surrounding context. She held herself and her colleagues responsible for shaping the aesthetic and social commitments of the new generation, without considering the external factors—from the opaque Meknes bureaucracy to changes in national leadership—that stymied her and others' projects. Like many of the pioneering musicians throughout this book, Soultana embodied aspects of the responsibilization that hip hop artists promoted in the 2000s. Dedicated to articulating and denouncing problems, but also to the possibility of progress, Soultana's meritocratic ideology was both deeply individualized and committed to reproducing generational and familial obligations. Only when frustrated—or when analyzing them in her lyrics—did she consider the systems of governance in which she was embedded.

Like other first- and second-generation musicians with whom I worked, Soultana was convinced the first generation had failed to "lay the road (dir al-triq)" for the next hip hop artists. I often heard this from people actively engaged in laying the road, such as the mentors at Sbagha Bagha (see chapter 4), as well as younger artists who found themselves diagnosing the same issues as their elders had done.

Trap artists explain with acute analysis and poignant repetition the challenges they face as artists and cultural producers. Shayfeen, a duo from the small Atlantic coast town of Safi, first gained wide appreciation among hip hop listeners in Morocco with their mixtape *L'Energie* (2012). In 2015, they won the grand prize in the national Generation Mawazine competition. In 2018, they joined NAAR, a nascent cultural collective based in Paris. In preparation for their first Paris concert, they gave interviews that recapitulated the aesthetic, economic, and political motivations I had heard from first-generation interlocutors since 2008.

Like their predecessors, who heard the Arabic and Moroccan pop that dominated the airwaves in the 1990s as musically and socially empty, Shayfeen experienced a profound impulse to move away from conventions they found stifling. "We really wanted to leave behind this very lyrical rap, we had already proven ourselves [able to do it] before. . . . When we began with trap, we found more pleasure and more artistic freedom" (Simonian 2018). Maha Rhannam notes that Shayfeen "argue that conscious rap is only to be associated with the old-school generations and stated their preferences for rap showcasing the flow and beat features of the rappers" (2019: 59).

Shayfeen also compared their country's media economy and ecosystem to Europe's in exactly the same terms as my first-generation interlocutors. "We have nothing," Shobee, one half of the duo, told the French magazine *Konbini* in a video interview. "No [music] industry, no subventions, nothing at all. But at the same time, we make it happen" (Konbini 2018).

Their success at Morocco's largest and best-funded festival was also framed as evidence of the paucity of opportunity they and others faced. "At one moment, we participated in the Mawazine festival in Salé, but the headliners' stage, it's for foreign stars. If you want more, you must move [out of the country]," Shobee explained to *Jeune Afrique*. In their view, Moroccan institutional support "goes first to that which is classified as world music" (Crétois 2018).

These complaints echo concerns listed to me by everyday aspiring musicians and cultural elites in the late 2000s. Compare Shobee's list, for example, with the things L-Tzack explained that Morocco's popular music infrastructure lacked in 2010 (see chapter 3). Ahmed Benchemsi, then editor-in-chief of the Francophone weekly *TelQuel*, ticked off the consensus in a 2008 editorial: album production "depends on the whims of sponsors"; Morocco as a whole had little recording or performance infrastructure, and Casablanca had "not one concert hall (or even rehearsal space) to its name"; cultural activities were dominated by the Institut Français and Instituto Cervantes instead of Moroccan-led organizations; and the Moroccan Bureau of Author's Rights (BMDA) is an "administrative aberration that no one understands" (Benchemsi 2008).[8]

NAAR co-founder Mohamed Sqalli links what artists see as infrastructural deficiencies, and what I have characterized as underdevelopment, to the larger global north market for representations of Arab identities. Describing his decision to ask American music magazine *The Fader* to premiere "Money Call," a Franco-Moroccan collaboration featuring Shobee of Shayfeen and shot in Meknes, he explained,

> That's what I told you . . . about authenticity and the power of storytelling—by doing this rap project, I knew that it was going to be successful for this kind of media, that is always in research of these kind of projects. And now our objective is not to stick to that. . . . Because all the social things that I can say with NAAR . . . I think it's important in the beginning, but now I know it's important that these [Moroccan] guys

are considered only as what they are, which is like artists who work all the time and who have high ambitions of succeeding in music. I don't want people to think that they are here only because of their stories and the fact that they come from a poor country . . . and it's really hard to prevent the media to focus only on that. (interview, Paris-Washington, DC, May 2018)[9]

With his colleague, photographer Ilyes Griyeb, Sqalli walks through why contemporary ways North Africans are made visible and audible in popular culture continue the colonialist gaze. They argue that "what makes Arab societies interesting is often symptomatic of their social and economical challenges. . . . What we see is . . . something like an offsite moodboarding of their socioeconomical weaknesses" (Sqalli 2017). Taking as axiomatic that "culture is a market," NAAR points out that "Western cultural industries are so powerful that Arab artists can only exist in Europe thanks to public . . . [funding] bodies."[10] In our conversation, Sqalli described this as a pitfall of the governmental support that Moroccan artists so often envied. "Most of the times Moroccan artists are only promoted in public media in France, like France24, or TV5monde, or RFI . . . who are funded by public money to promote different cultures. And Moroccan artists are always there for an audience of old people, you know? . . . It's not representative of the youth and the vitality of the Moroccan scene" (interview, Paris–Washington, DC, May 2018).

Based on their understanding that the discourses of discovery powering world music markets were just as relevant in pop, NAAR highlighted those musicians from so-called exotic places doing perfectly global-north work. In this way, the third-generation artists promoted by NAAR in the late 2010s—including Shayfeen, LeGrande Toto, Madd, and Issam Harris—found themselves in a situation very similar to that of the leading first-generation artists in the mid-2000s. For both generations, after years of work reaching wide recognition within Morocco, artists were pressured to leverage their own exoticization to reach beyond North African audiences in their European performances.

As Sqalli explained, after the success of "Money Call" and his artists' first Parisian concert, "we had a lot of solicitations I didn't answer . . . from media wanting to talk only about, you know, this narrative consisting to say they were poor people with difficult family backgrounds who have only rap music to succeed. And . . . we didn't want to stick to that vision, because, you know, it's bigoted. And Shayfeen are not bigoted" (interview, Paris–Washington, DC, May 2018). Musicians who understood themselves as part of translocal and transnational formations were frequently reminded, whether through discrimination or celebration, that the difference ascribed to them in global north narratives was heard before or in place of their music. That difference is not granted the texture of their own unique lives, but fitted to an existing narrative about the value of the hip hop arts to impoverished urban youths.[11]

From this perspective, authenticity—here as a non-Westerner and Muslim as well as a hip hop artist—is both factual and manufactured, empowering and compelled, desirable and limiting. As Sqalli and Griyeb powerfully pointed out, "By fetishizing misery[,] . . . Western creatives decide to ignore a colonization of ideas that cannot be legitimized by their global freedom of circulation" (2017). Even as NAAR, Shayfeen, and the other members of Shayfeen's collective comment on and react against the strictures of the world music industry, the pop industry insists on confirming its own narrow expectations.[12]

Artists like Shayfeen responded in familiar ways to recurrent challenges. In a documentary produced for the Moroccan television channel 2M, director Fatim Zahra Bencherki captures the frustrations and motivations powering every generation of Moroccan hip hop through statements from Shobee, Small X, and their friends and family. As they discuss issues that returned again and again in the music and narratives of earlier hip hop artists, such as unsupportive family members, the failures of the educational system, mass unemployment and visible poverty, the ways the state surveilled hip hop in the 2000s, or the emptiness of patriotic music, they return to two interrelated themes: first, "whatever you do, concentrate on it until you arrive" at a high level, and second, "rely only on yourself" (Small X in Bencherki 2019).

After two decades in which artists and listeners judged how well hip hop artists analyzed the ineluctable inequities of Moroccan life, Shayfeen "don't want to fall into the 'consciousness-raising' thing. We're not here for that. . . . Music is what saved Abdelssamad [Small X] and me. We want to give people who listen to us . . . even a little hope" (Shobee in Bencherki 2019). Instead of thinking of their performances as sources of education, galvanizing anger, or insights into the lives of the poor, they focused on the opportunity to produce and feel positive affects.

To some, trap artists' rejection of an earlier emphasis on progress reads as lack of a future-facing vision altogether. For these listeners, Shayfeen's and others' statements create a tragic narrative matched by trap's semiotics of woozy timbres, narrowly repetitive melodies, and vocalized sounds enhancing or replacing the expressiveness of lyrics. However, new-generation artists' recognition that they can do little or nothing about the country's ills can crystalize into pointed ambition. As Mohamed Sqalli commented, "Shobee . . . has had this vision for years now. . . . He managed his band . . . just like a label manager. . . . Even if there was no industry, he worked like there was an industry." While first-generation hip hop artists may not recognize its expression, this is one way that they laid a road effectively. Their discourse of self-creation and self-entrepreneurship has been taken up in a way few could have achieved in the 2000s.

Artists' narratives about Morocco's chronic inequality and social and political immobility have changed shape, sound, and emphasis over time. Yet multiple generations, literally and metaphorically, of hip hop practitioners have focused on individualization and responsibilization in a way that responds to their postcolonial country's neocolonial role in the global market economy. Chronic complaints about Morocco's lack of music infrastructure are slowly receding for those with access to newer studios, rehearsal spaces, mixing and mastering services, and venues catering to the affluent. Yet even practitioners without access to these are deeply invested in building a system in which, by definition, only a small percentage of artists would be able to make a living. Simultaneously, practitioners' texts, performances, and actions mitigate against the idea that, in a nation where un- and underemployment is a defining feature of urban life, one's value to the economy should be the only way one is valued. Within the genre that most explicitly validates neoliberal rhetoric of the inexhaustible worker-turned-capitalist, practitioners shape themselves and each other to become deeply motivated human capital as a practice of freedom.

THE SINCERITY OF CAPITAL

N'aich ki bghit, euro euro euro euro
N'aich ki bghit, njibha devise devise devise devise

. . .

Hadi nasiḥa machi chi clash
Tay'arfona kamline men yamat La Cage

GHOST PROJECT X DRAGANOV, *"KI BGHIT"* (2017)

"I live how I want," sings Draganov in the chorus to "Ki Bghit" (2017). Moving so fluidly between Derija and French that they sound like a single language, and relying on trap's conventions of repetition, he creates layers of potential meaning from the pairing of *euro* and *devise* (currency, in French). One might hear the second line as simply underscoring the first statement. Or one could hear "N'aich ki bghit, njibha (I live how I want, I get it)" as the credo (*la devise*) Draganov is declaring he holds.

In the second couplet above, the emcee Hoofer, who has made hip hop since at least the early 2000s, ends his verse with reassurance: "This is advice, not some clash / They've known all of us since the days of La Cage." An iconic site in Moroccan hip hop history, many Casablancans of the first generation credit this club's hip hop nights with introducing them to the newest tracks from the United States in the 1990s "just as soon as they were released in the US" and with allowing them to build networks with other lovers of the genre (p.c., Barry, October 21, 2009; see chapter 1). Hoofer places himself in his city and era with this line, authenticating himself as the right person to give advice.

The song itself enacts this statement in its sounds and its relationships. Opening with the filtered, sluggish, auto-tuned timbre of Draganov's sung chorus, it next proceeds to a verse by M-Doc before arriving at Hoofer. M-Doc's vocal timbre and rhythms strongly recall Dr. Dre, invoking the 1990s West Coast hip hop he has emulated throughout his career and provoking a productive unease against the trap-influenced beat. Hoofer splits the chronological difference, building reoccurring rhythmic patterns and rhyme schemes throughout his verse, dropping a self-referential punchline yet delivering his lines within a restrained melody.

Preceded and followed by Draganov's chorus and verse, embedded in a beat featuring signature sounds of that year's trap, the two emcees' voices are enfolded into a sound from the future of their styles. Ghost Project—a collective including first- and second-generation musicians—joins with a leader of the new generation, Draganov, to simultaneously benefit from their expertise and to bring them credibility with younger listeners. As the styling of their names and the music indicate, this is less a "featuring" and more a strategic partnership.

These juxtaposed rhymes help me recapitulate interrelated themes of this book. As discussed in the introduction, for me these themes take the shape of pairs held together by their constitutive tensions. Just as competition was often (though not always) mediated by solidarity, the inability to avoid one's complicity was often mediated by sincerity. The parallel repetitions of "euro" and "devise" in the chorus of "Ki Bghit" neatly illustrate how hip hop and trap anticipate my argument: once "devise" is heard simultaneously as "currency" and as "credo," the pair may then take on an additional sense in which euros are the credo itself. Put more simply, market structures as well as market actions both express and encourage deeply held values. As I have attempted to show, inclusion into markets for music, for labor, or for representations of otherness allows those who control the terms of inclusion to profit from difference, regardless of whether the included actors also profit or even understand themselves as equal partners in the exchange.

The ability to hold these pairs in tension together, when market structures and interactions so often and so clearly sustain inequality, I call the sincerity of capital. On one level, this is a simple syllogism: if one consciously develops one's human capital, acting as its manager and bearer, then one's sincerely felt expressions are expressions of that capital. On another level, the space my interlocutors crafted with each other, away from their families, homes, lineages, and religious ties, allowed for sincere investments in a different future—one sought through and felt in collective efforts toward commercial success.

Originated by Gary Becker, Foucault reads "human capital" as reorienting economists' understanding away from a quantitative conception of labor as interchangeable units of time and toward skills and practices that were inalienable from the laborer (Foucault 2008: 226). This produces, for Foucault, a reevaluation of *homo oeconomicus* as entrepreneur of himself, a person encouraged to think of themselves as a firm with assets whose purpose was growth. How that self-entrepreneur then relates this identity to other ways of thinking about the self—notably as a being with the same intrinsic value as other beings, perhaps endowed with this value by a higher power—is not typically discussed in the Foucauldian literature on neoliberal subjectification; rather, the emphasis is on how *neoliberalism newly* crowds out or subsumes older forms of self-making (e.g., Brown 2003 and 2015; Donzelot 2008; Read 2009; McNay 2009).[13] Yet the intersection of neoliberal discourses on the self with equally compelling, equally naturalized understandings of selfhood is not only the location from which my interlocutors seek locally valorized freedoms, build solidarity, and make art; it is where all of us live.

Much theorizing from the global north focuses on aspirational discourses of entrepreneurship. Even when these are expressions of cruel optimism (Berlant 2011), tracing the implicit contradiction of "ideologies through which structurally dislocated men reinforce hegemonic norms" helps link massive structures to individual life chances (Matlon 2016: 1017).[14] Like many others, I take quite seriously the narratives of those who frame their actions in a capitalist relation to themselves as simultaneous personal and financial development. However, when attempting to intervene in transnational markets, my interlocutors' opportunities to build enterprises of and for themselves are indistinguishable from self-commodification. The structures they can access value them primarily as salable representations of themselves, in part because they lack other forms of capital with which to pursue other strategies.

Becker understood human capital as inalienable from the subject, but when that capital is difference that is desirable precisely because global north subjects use it as a technology of social and ethical development, the human carrying the capital is more objectified the further they circulate. For my interlocutors, this has occurred across contexts and despite varied socioeconomic locations, whether the form of circulation is in person to a European city, virtually to an unmapped audience, or textually as a representation of a vexed subject position in this book. The global south artist's successful insertion into global markets for difference can be described as neither forced nor unforced, authentic or inauthentic, but a process by which racialized actors experience inclusion without equalization.

One's ability to capitalize oneself, to offer oneself as this form of difference-capital, enables better circulation in markets for commodities like representations of Blackness or Arabness.[15] This may afford incisive critique—as Moten notes, "the commodity whose speech sounds embodies the critique of value, of private property, of the sign" (2003: 12)—while it responds to the desires that produce the market itself. By exercising one's speech to better compete as a silenced object, actors produce moving, polysemic work as they move through and with their complicities.

In this sense, I imagine the sincerity of capital as that which allows practitioners to invest their energy in imagining and building toward ethical circulation, to hold one's selfhood in productive tension with one's self-objectification as a commodity. Speech from within this tension is impossible, or rather unintelligible, without a technology of linkage and repair—the affect of sincerity.[16]

As I've argued throughout, equating entrepreneurship and the embrace of market rationalities with full and natural personhood, as theorists have argued is a hallmark of how neoliberalized subjects imagine themselves, does not negate the passionate attachments and caring labor of those subjects. My interlocutors are perfectly sincere in their attempts to both build and benefit from markets and to care for themselves and others; in fact, the former is conceptualized as a form of the latter. To return to "Ki Bghit," Hoofer's verse, boastful and competitive in classic hip hop style, closes with solidarity with the younger generation. Draganov's insistence, through repetition, on the primacy of cash readily evokes both the urgency and the deadening of poverty. Among transnational hip hop's listeners and detractors, statements like his have been read generously as an indictment of inequality or uncharitably as too materialist. When artists acknowledge themselves as materialist, the position is rendered legible, rational, or even ethical through analysis of that inequality. To survive, one cannot avoid complicity with neoliberalized practices and institutions; to thrive, one must feel sincerely attached to some aspects of neoliberalization.

If humans work on themselves to become better human capital, then working on one's community also generates a form of that capital-in-waiting or capital-in-speculation. In this way, we might theorize my interlocutors' unsparing labor in and for their musical communities as simultaneously productive of material and nonmaterial value, of present and future capital. The community production of individuals with use-value—individuals whose often unpaid nonperformance work is vital to the success of artists—is simultaneously the cultivation of future, latent, exchange value that may reside in another member of the community. Producing oneself and others as noncommodities who love their art forms and believe in their beauty and value simultaneously prepares the ground on which exchange-value might suddenly appear in the future. Actions that may build potential future value are necessarily relational—that is, they afford and are afforded by specific ties. Social reproduction by practitioners of all genders is vital not just to the bonds that sustain the few who perform remunerated labor, but to producing the belief in and possibility of future capital. In this way, solidarity can be simultaneously a source of well-being and an economic imperative (Struch 2022: 75).

Anthropologist Michael Lambek argues that "ethical" and "market" value must be understood as "incommensurable." In his comparison, *Economics chooses between commensurable values operative under a single meta-value while ethics judges among incommensurable values or meta-values*" (2008: 145, italics in original). Lambek's terms describe economics itself as a market that renders values similar via their possibility of exchange, thus using "market" as a synecdoche for "economy" or perhaps capitalism. I have argued that, for my interlocutors, ethics exist under a single meta-value of surviving in a market economy that functions by devaluing the excluded before reincluding them as circulating objects. They cannot afford to understand the economic as outside, rather than as intrinsic to, the cultural or political. My interlocutors demonstrate that, for them, economic expressions of value have acknowledged and profound affective value, not least because creating and participating in translocal and transnational markets helps to delineate one to oneself and others as a proper modern subject.

Finally, I have sought throughout to note when the subjectification framework, as articulated by Wendy Brown and others, illustrates well what my interlocutors have done and are doing, and when their actions exceed it. At the same time, I recognize my own desire to understand practitioners as "inhabit[ing] a certain mode of subjection in order to . . . turn it against its instigators" (Feher 2009: 23), to see and hear a way out of neoliberalization in the insights of Moroccan musicians. Rather than categorize actions within or beyond theoretical models of neoliberal subjectification, I have attempted to dwell on "the ambivalence of subjectification" (Binkley 2011: 85) by introducing complicity as a frame: the historically situated, power-saturated, lived environment in which people strategize among limited options and in which they live continuously, despite generational and economic changes with enormous social, cultural, and political effects.

Throughout, I have argued that relations of complicity render sincerity both necessary to social relations and insufficient to moral life under neoliberalism. This is as true of me as it is of my interlocutors. I apprehend the complicit social world as a web of intersecting, seemingly self-regenerating relationships—a hall of mirrors in which moral reasoning must take place in perpetuity. This applies equally well to work like this book, academy-facing writing that seeks to provoke others' thinking in a way the author wishes would lead, in likely untraceable ways, to more just action.

One of the earliest exchanges I had during fieldwork concerned outside observers' habit of eliding the temporality of non-Western art and artists—one of the "reflexes" that journalist Reda Zine describes in the first epigraph at the beginning of this epilogue. During our initial meeting, I mentioned to Don Bigg the 2007 documentary *I Love Hip Hop in Morocco*. Bigg scoffed at the reference, despite having significant airtime in the film. He was less annoyed about the fact that it had barely screened in Morocco than he was that footage from 2003 and 2004 was only circulating in 2008 and 2009. "It ain't showing us in a professional way," he said in his hip hop–inflected English (p.c., October 21, 2009).

Viewers might reasonably assume, he feared, that Morocco was five years behind the sounds and fashions of transnational hip hop. More broadly, the struggles on which the documentary focused—young artists seeking social, municipal, and financial support for a live concert—recapitulated tropes in which the majority of Arab societies reject Western media and mores, choosing particularity and tradition over transnationalism, modernity, and "professionalism." While Bigg was not suggesting hip hop had reached mainstream acceptance—as he noted in his epigraph at the beginning of this epilogue, few regarded hip hop as "a confirmed culture" in 2009—he was concerned about inadvertently supporting stereotypes of Arab backwardness.[17]

I am lucky to have had that conversation and remain grateful to Bigg and others who articulated this concern in spoken and unspoken ways. If, as David Crawford writes, ethnographers "implicitly convert space to time," ineluctably sharing that outcome with the explicit goals of our colonialist disciplinary ancestors, then our rhetorical and argumentative tactics may bring the simultaneous past closer or push it away (2014: 20). Yet, as Crawford puts it, "a known past is known only because it has been conceived in us presently for our immediate purposes" (2014: 23). The further away I move from the majority of my fieldwork in time, the clearer my own investment in an economy of knowledge-making appears. Like other capitalist markets, academic knowledge-making prizes innovations (or "interventions") and rests on an assumption of limitless accumulation. As in other complicities my interlocutors and I have shared, this book participates in this economy seemingly without the possibility of escape. Writing out the conditions of participation as a form of critique, as this epilogue has done, simply occupies the place of theoretical intervention and functions as a contribution to the intellectual market—regardless of how well that contribution is received. Like NAAR anticipating audiences' desire for difference, like first-generation artists leveraging hip hop's aesthetics of refusal to construct their own way to belong, my attempt to analyze the project in which I participate contests its terms without the ability to meaningfully resist them.

NOTES

INTRODUCTION: THE WAVE

1. This event is officially known as Festival Mawazine Rythmes du Monde. In a musical context, *mawazin* (sing. *wazan*) in Arabic refers to meters or rhythmic patterns.

2. The festival continued to program competition winners and stars of Morocco's hip hop, rock, and fusion scenes before and after this period, but not under the title of L'Mouja.

3. I follow Saba Mahmood here in considering the ethical as well as social weight that emergent actions and relations—"forms" in the broadest sense—take on over the course of hip hop practitioners' socialization and the genre's history. My interlocutors, like Mahmood's, "elaborate the architecture of the self through the immanent form bodily practices take," including their cultivation of dancing, writing graffiti, musicking, and tastes in music and sound (2005: 121).

4. An incomplete list of scholars who address Moroccan authoritarianism in conjunction with neoliberal development includes: Atia 2019, Bergh 2012, Bogaert 2012, Bono et al. 2015, Catusse 2008 and 2009, Cavatorta 2013, Hibou 2015, Hibou and Bono 2016, Kreitmeyr 2019, Rinker 2020, Zemni and Bogaert 2011.

5. The monarchy is "neither the state nor the nation," but it does hold supreme executive power, including the power to dissolve the Parliament (Saghi 2016: 77; Waterbury 1970). As the monarch, King Mohamed VI is head of state and the national head of the Muslim faith. The government exercises control over Muslim doctrine and practice by appointing the national council of 'ulama, or religious scholars, and promoting the monarchy's preferred jurisprudential tradition (Maliki) and Sufi groups.

6. Louise Meintjes writes that aesthetic ambiguities "enable life to go on without closure or fixity or certainty, and they ensure that the capacity to instrumentalize the arts toward political ends can never be contained or complete" (2017: 16).

7. The multiple registers of "value" he invokes are present in the English, French, and Arabic equivalents.

8. I am not suggesting that values themselves, in the sense of unexchangeable personal beliefs, can be commoditized separately from the person who holds them; rather, that they can be and are reconsidered by their holders as assets in an imaginary of personal capital. For reviews of value and exchange theory, see Narotzky and Besnier 2014 and Morcom 2020.

9. Al-Makhzen is the precolonial term for the Moroccan state; in today's usage, it indicates the monarchy and the king's closest circle, and that small group's traditional, supra-governmental hold on political and economic life. For some observers, the Makhzen is the true locus of the "apparatus of state violence and domination" and expropriation that defines the state, rather than elected officials or government ministries (Daadaoui 2011: 41). On the precolonial sultanate's economy and its interactions with European imperial capitalism, see Ben Srhir 2005, Brown 1976, Schroeter 1988. Today, King Mohamed VI and his family control several prominent Moroccan corporations and possess an extensive personal fortune through Al-Mada Holding, formerly known as Omnium Nord-Africain (Greene 2008).

10. Elyachar beautifully encapsulates this process, and the effects of successful ideological spread, from a state perspective: "Within the framework of 'social capital,' the cultural practices of people once condemned as backwards and in need of development became an important terrain for the accumulation of capital and a strategic resource through which new forms of governance could be reproduced at little cost to the downsized, neoliberal state" (2005: 147). Here, I focus on practitioners' theories and strategies for coping with change that seemed both pervasive and inchoate.

11. Deborah Wong observes, "working with or against the assumptions driving music departments means, necessarily, that [ethnomusicologists] have been co-opted before we even begin. . . . We give ourselves over to value systems that dictate we work in permanent states of contradiction and asymmetry" (2014: 347). While my interlocutors "work in permanent states of contradiction," not all had to adopt or perform new values to receive recognition.

12. Marcus describes anthropologists, especially Geertz, as possessing a "calculated and imposed naiveté . . . [that] is potentially the source of greatest strength and special insight of ethnographic analysis, leading to both the 'complex or involved' sense of complicity as well as exposure to complicity's other sense of 'being an accomplice, partnership in an evil action'" (124). The two "senses" here both extend from underlying assumptions of collectivity. These assumptions in turn allow us to position complicity as a place from which to contest the individualization and depoliticization of the neoliberal subject.

13. Feld and Kirkegaard (2010) explicitly critique the actions of their subjects, but these are scholars and industry professionals.

14. However, a recent branch of philosophy grapples with collective responsibility for structural injustices (e.g., Nuti 2019).

15. Like Stein, I understand hip hop practitioners' politics as "complicitous with power, emerging through the marketplace and the commodity form, not in spite of them, in sites made available by state policy" (1998: 92).

16. Moten notes that he is paraphrasing Judith Butler in *The Psychic Life of Power* (1997).

17. This is one of two ways that complicity, as sketched here, departs from a Gramscian framework in which hegemonic logics either induce consent, or provoke nondominant

groups into a "war of position" where they seek to undermine hegemonic forces over time (1992: 219). Productive analysis of subtle forms of political dissent need not address this ethical paradox at the heart of the complicity concept—that is, a belief in human collectivity and therefore human deservingness. In addition, consent is sometimes understood as produced without the consentor's self-awareness, whereas I use complicity to commit to all actors' ability to analyze the structures in which they live.

18. This holds whether one views neoliberalism primarily as a normative economic doctrine and project of class maintenance (Harvey 2005); an era of world history (Slobodian 2018; Mirowski and Plehwe 2015); a political rationality (Brown 2005, 2012); or a technology of the self (Foucault 2008).

19. James Laidlaw critiques "practice theory" for popularizing agency-as-opposition, which, according to him, prizes analysts' preference for examples of opposition to dominant structures over an appreciation of all that people actually do (2014: 182). Diverse musicological calls to expand agency to encompass nonhuman agents include Guilbault 1997, Stanyek and Piekut 2010, Piekut 2014.

20. Interview, Fes, June 6, 2010.

21. In Derija: "Rap dyali thawra, mashi mujarad mouja . . . Rap machi ḥyati, rap ulla mouti." See emcee Muslim, "A.K.A. Moutamarred (A.K.A. Rebel)," *al-Tamarroud Vol. 1* (The Rebellion Vol. 1), 2010.

22. Le Monde 6/6/2018, 6/9/18; Les Eco 3/5/2018. The creator of the leading Facebook image, Aziz Garroud, published his own statistics: after one week, the image had been adopted by 221,000 Facebook users, of which 42 percent were between twenty-three to thirty-seven years old. Sixteen "prominent artistic figures (shaksiyya barza min finaniyat)" had adopted it as their profile picture (Facebook post, April 28, 2018).

23. Complaints about Mawazine are long-standing, numerous, and diverse (Alami 2011). As *Jeune Afrique* summarizes, "For several years, the critiques have come from all sides. Cultural actors point to the tendency to suck up [*vampiriser*] resources and sponsors to the detriment of other events, while Islamists see it as a site of debauchery" (My translation of Youssef Ait Adkim, "Maroc: Touche pas Mawazine!" *Jeune Afrique*, March 12, 2012, https://www.jeuneafrique.com/142546/culture/maroc-touche-pas-mawazine/).

24. https://www.videoclip.site/video/-qJgauY5iSw/-/, uploaded June 29, 2018.

25. I have not been able to recover this social media post. However, this report, which circulated by the following day, became a piece of the media event in its own right and informs my understanding of the video's reception.

26. Fieldnotes, Casablanca, June 30, 2018.

27. In a similar fashion, Bigg was once told by an interviewer that he must "love money a great deal" in order to perform at an event for a political party Bigg did not support. Bigg answered, "It's true, I love money, but no more than most human beings. And the difference is . . . that I say it loudly and strongly" (Ziraoui 2007). Both Bigg and Muslim link entrepreneurship and sincerity, suggesting that entrepreneurship is merely human nature, and honesty about that nature is not only appropriate but moral.

28. A short list of scholarship that draws on Jackson's framework, itself responding to a long-standing distinction between authenticity and sincerity in sociology, includes Bradley 2012, Harrison 2009, Khabeer 2016, Ramirez 2021, Sharma 2010.

29. On sincerity as a key concept underpinning the modern liberal subject, see Haeri 2017a, Keane 2002, Mahmood 2001, Seligman et al. 2008, Trilling 1972.

30. Erik Nielsen et al., "*Amici Curiae* Brief of Erik Nielson, Charis S. Kubrin, Travis L. Gosa, Michael Render (aka 'Killer Mike') and Other Scholars and Artists in Support of Petitioner [Taylor Bell]," Washington, DC, 2015, 6.

31. See Asad (2009 [1986]: 21–23) for a response to similar denials of Muslim interiority.

32. Saba Mahmood responds to such orientalist denigrations of Muslim subjectivity by "revers[ing] the usual routing from interiority to exteriority in which the unconscious manifests itself in somatic forms," showing this reversal is not only an explicit aspect of some Egyptians' religious thought but an effective critique of liberal universalism with its own theoretical applications (2005: 121–22).

33. As with many concepts for which Moroccans integrate different enculturated understandings, there are multiple ways of thinking about *niyya*, influenced by both broadly "liberal" and broadly "Islamic" histories of thought. The influential twelfth-century philosopher Abu Hamid al-Ghazali "maintains that God rewards good intentions even if they are not put into action, suggesting that for him niyya is the ethical core of an individual's actions," a position broadly congruent with liberal Protestantism (Powers 2004: 451n28). Haeri notes that, in contemporary Iran, "there is a great deal of ambivalence and ambiguity" in debates around "the relative importance of intention versus sincerity with regard to acts of worship" (2017: 144). Saba Mahmood notes that individual worshipers consider more than intention: "The attitude with which [prayers and other rituals] are performed is as important as their prescribed form: sincerity (*al-ikhlas*), humility (*khushol*), and feelings of virtuous fear and awe (*khashya* or *taqwa*), are all emotions by which excellence and virtuosity in piety are measured and marked" (2001: 830). Each of these suggests that a concept of sincerity that subsumes intention may be influential in various Muslims' work toward proper orientations. It is possible, but not necessary, that contemporary "liberal" formulations of sincerity come from liberalism's sources.

34. This connects to the concept of ʿaqliyya, "mentality," which conveys "worldview" and also describes an obligation to know and restrain oneself in order to be a prosocial person (Rosen 1984).

35. In H-Kayne's "Ana Ḥor (I Am Free)" (2017), they implore, "Understand . . . and turn around with intention / Moroccans are always brothers and love each other (Fahem . . . wa dayr bi niyya / Magharba daʾiman khout wa ḥbab)". Translation is mine. See "H-KAYNE Ana Hor (EXCLUSIVE MUSIC VIDEO)," posted by H-Kayne, July 28, 2017, YouTube, https://www.youtube.com/watch?v = K4_Z5i_qMYk. In the chorus of Fnaire's "Yed el-Ḥenna (Hand of Ḥenna)" (2007), they sing, "With intention we contribute to [national] development (Bi niyya nsahemou fil tanmiyya)." Translation is mine. See "Yed El Henna" at Genius, https://genius.com/Fnaire-yed-el-henna-lyrics, my translation).

36. See, for example, rock band Hoba Hoba Spirit's 2010 album, *Nafs u Niya* (*Self and Intention*), or lines from Casa Crew's "Bureau" (2007) or Mobydick's "Kaba" (2018).

37. Within Islamic jurisprudence, sincerity (*ikhlas*) is not a quality applied to intention, but a separate orientation one ought to cultivate. "One need not pile layer upon layer of niyya, so that one must not only 'mean it' when one acts but also 'mean to mean it' and so on indefinitely," as Powers remarks (2004: 454).

38. As Thomas Docherty asks via Hannah Arendt: "How, then, to engage the world when we live in a state of affairs where 'every resisting of the evil done in the world necessarily entails some implication in evil'?" (Arendt 2003: 152, as quoted in Docherty 2016: 20).

39. In the 2023 Society for Ethnomusicology Seeger Lecture, the collaborating scholar-performers were Heidi Aklaseaq Senungetuk, Dawn Avery, Sunaina Kale, Haliehana Stepetin, Dylan Robinson, and Trevor Reed.

40. "Transactions" can include many different kinds of interactions, including those in which fieldworkers gain information while research subjects gain less-defined but possibly beneficial experiences. As Jeff Todd Titon explains, applied ethnomusicology in the United States falls broadly into cultural policy interventions, advocacy, and education (2016: 5–8). The first two of these categories can be understood as kinds of completed transactions in which actively addressing and alleviating power relations is a goal. This is not to adopt a procapitalist stance in which "transactions" are a positive way of viewing all interactions, but to theorize from within the poverty of forms and metaphors at my disposal as a neoliberal subject.

41. For Hannah Arendt, solidarity contains the seeds of its own deformation into complicity, because those with greater power are sorely tempted to romanticize their own goodness (1990 [1963]: 88).

42. By "political quietism," I refer to an orientation away from electoral politics or activities understood as overtly "political," in which actors invest in other ways of building the structures and relations they desire (Cavatorta 2020).

1. CRITICAL TRADITIONS: THE POETICS AND POLITICS OF AMBIGUITY

1. A full translation of the original can be found at "Nass El Ghiwane: The Sheepskin (1st stanza)," translated by Mohammed Najmi and Doug Davis, http://d2ssd.com/cybermaroc/ghiwane_lebtana_english.htm.

2. The World Bank estimates that 84 percent of Moroccans used the internet in 2020, compared with 72 percent in Tunisia and Egypt, and 63 percent in Algeria. See World Bank, Data Indicator, https://data.worldbank.org/indicator/IT.NET.USER.ZS?locations=MA.

3. Scholars vary in their estimates of the Years of Lead. Susan Gilson-Miller dates it to 1975, when activists were jailed and tortured on flimsy charges (2013: 170). However, attempts to stifle the Moroccan left began much earlier, such as the state of emergency imposed after student-led riots in 1965 (Gilson-Miller 2013: 169). Brahim el Guabli names 1956—the year of Morocco's independence from France—through the end of Hassan II's regime (2020: 146). Susan Slyomovics ends it in 1990, with the creation of the Advisory Council on Human Rights (2001: 18). Moroccan human rights scholar and victim Fadoua Loudiy dates the end to 1999, when King Mohamed VI opened an "indemnification commission" for victims of state crimes and abuses (2014: 5).

4. Despite general strikes in response to rising costs of living in 1981, the Moroccan government moved from short-term support to a World Bank structural adjustment program in 1983. Over the twenty years, the state "reformed" its economy in exchange for debt rescheduling and continued loans. This included opening capital and consumer markets, increasing foreign direct investment, privatizing state-owned industries, and lowering business taxes, all of which disproportionately benefited the king and his family through their corporate holdings, as well as the nation's land- and business-owning class. The state also shed and added salary caps to public sector jobs, cut consumer and industry subsidies, paid the government's creditors, and deregulated its markets by reducing tariffs and negotiating

free-trade agreements (Cohen and Jaidi 2006; Maghraoui 2001; Pfeifer 1999; Kydd and Thoyer 1992; Catusse 2009).

5. In 1956, most of the country's best land was "concentrated in the hands of 5,900 Europeans and 1,700 Moroccans" (Swearingen 1987: 143). Instead of returning formerly French-owned land to poor Moroccan farmers, the state either controlled parcels outright or allowed the Moroccan elite to profit from them (Gilson-Miller 2013: 173). Upward redistribution led to explosive migration as farmers moved to cities, particularly Casablanca. Simultaneously, the state deprioritized housing in the late 1960s as it invested more in "agriculture, infrastructure, and tourism," allowing for the "autoconstruction" of informal housing as new waves of migrants arrived (Pennell 2001: 329; Abu-Lughod 1980: 257). Brahim el Guabli, who calls this process the "pauperization of the working classes," argues that growing inequality drove Morocco's urban youths to the left of its existing socialist parties, setting the stage for widespread unrest (2020: 150).

6. The guimbri and banjo both come from marginalized groups descended from enslaved sub-Saharans. The Moroccan Gnawa's guimbri (also known as a *sintir* or *hajhuj*), which is foundational to their ritual music, is related to West African bass spike lutes like the *ngoni* or *khalam*. The banjo originated with enslaved Africans in the Caribbean, who constructed a new instrument from their memories of West African spike lutes (Pestcoe and Adams 2018: 4–5).

7. For more on the 1973 Moroccanization law, see Maghraoui 2001b and Gilson-Miller 2013: 184.

8. Like many other performers, Barry began his career in the hip hop arts as a dancer. His dance trio with Amine Snoop, CasaMuslim, may have garnered the emergent genre's earliest media attention when a local journalist organized for them a miniature tour of the region (personal communication, Barry, October 21, 2009).

9. See *Aujourd'hui* staff, "Centre 2000: quel avenir?" *Aujourd'hui*, September 19, 2005, https://aujourdhui.ma/societe/centre-2000-quel-avenir-35536, for information about the dispute between L'ONCF, the national train company, and the commercial center. On a recent visit, Soultana and I heard the 1995 hit "I Got 5 On It" on the radio. "Oh, Da Luniz," she exclaimed, eyes wide, deliberately pronouncing "da" as the band's name was occasionally styled. "When this came on at La Cage, you could not find a place on the dance floor" (personal communication, August 6, 2022).

10. A few examples, such as dance battles in the mid-1990s in Mohammedia, which lies on the train route between Casablanca and Rabat, helped to create both intercity and intracity networks (personal conversation, Soultana, August 5, 2022).

11. *Libération* is the paper of the SUPF.

12. See, e.g., the chorus of Casa Crew's 2006 song "Min Zanka l'Zanka (From Street to Street)" where they sing, "Going from street to street / The police trail us knocking [daqqa daqqa]," implying knocking on doors or perhaps heads.

13. My translations from Es-Sayed 2010.

14. Schuyler is translating several layers of meaning here; presumably he is referencing the line "U mal kasi ḥzin ma bin al-kisan? (And why is my glass the sad one among the glasses?)" (Es-Sayed 2010, my translation).

15. The second half of the song, rarely discussed, continues to address an ambiguous "you" from whom the speaker is running. One could interpret this section in many ways, from a dramatization of addiction or possession to a fear of the era's unchecked and brutal police.

16. El Guabli emphasizes that "other-archives" are often oral and testimonial and that passing them on strengthens community: "*Shahada* (testimony/martyrdom) in Arabic, and in the Moroccan context by extension, is equivalent to being a member of a community of both witnesses and martyrs. . . . Even those who were too young to witness . . . participate in a communal endeavor that is committed to producing other forms of archives that facilitate the writing of taboo histories" (2022: 213).

17. A *zawaya* is a Sufi lodge where members of the brotherhood come to worship.

18. This was dramatically illustrated once when I mentioned the friend with whom I was having coffee to a potential interviewee on the phone. My contact immediately hung up, at which point my friend disclosed their mutual enmity.

19. "Muslim waḥed men chʿab/rap dyali tawra machi ghi lʿab/chamal janoub charq lgharb / jib Lʿaz wla kḥez dayman felqalb." Original from "Lyrics A.K.A Motamarred," Facebook post by Muslim, last edited March 14, 2021, https://www.facebook.com/notes/muslim/lyrics-aka-motamarred/119721359316. "Jib l3az wla k7ez" is Muslim's longtime motto, appearing not only in songs but on T-shirts and as a hashtag. It is perhaps best translated idiomatically as "go big or go home."

20. "Mli bdit kont ʿaref rap machi lʿab/jbart rasi kanmtel chʿab/jbart rasi masʾoul ʿala jil." See "Lyrics A.K.A Motamarred," Facebook post by Muslim, last edited March 14, 2021, https://www.facebook.com/notes/muslim/lyrics-aka-motamarred/119721359316.

21. Remarks in italics here, without quotations, signal that these are paraphrased recollections from my fieldnotes. The young man I spoke to used "underground" in English, though this was a contested term with diverse meanings.

22. Literally, this phrase translates to "it's not me who chose [this]," placing the verb at the end for emphasis.

23. As Hajer (2015) notes, substantial social and economic barriers limit access to traditional, religious, and medical models of mental health care for low-income Moroccans.

24. In this example, the words at the end of the first, second, and fifth lines are adjectives; the third and fourth lines end with verbs with the "us" object attached (*na*).

25. Noting the use of what they call "poetic" or "literary" Derija in hip hop in comparison to Nass el-Ghiwane, Caubet and Miller translate these chorus lines as "what is x without y," leaving aside the noun *qima* altogether (2012: 6).

26. The practice of expressing one's longing for spiritual "reunification" through metaphors of romantic love has a long history that continues to be used ambiguously today.

27. Abraham Serfaty, a leading Moroccan leftist, wrote approvingly in *Souffles* of the Black Panthers' holistic analysis: "The Black Americans have now . . . a scientific method of reflection . . . concretely forged in the historic processes of economic, social, and cultural structuration of American society" (1970: 33, my translation). On the "victim-actors" who rejected monetary compensation alone as sufficient for harms suffered during the Years of Lead, see el Guabli 2020b and 2022.

28. Multiple people also dismissed the conflict as a shameless *copier-coller*, or "cut and paste," of the legendary animosity between the Notorious B.I.G. and Tupac Shakur.

2. A MORAL INSTITUTION:
FORMING AND PERFORMING HIP HOP IN THE 2000s

1. Nadia Bezad, president of an anti-AIDS NGO, explains, "The reality is that [gay Moroccan men] are tolerated but expected to remain invisible" (Alami 2020). Despite the

way I summarize this conversation here, it is important to point out that, for some, placing "the liberty to 'say who one is' . . . at the center of one's identity" is "inherited from European and American LGBT fights" and "recalls that the category of 'homosexual' is situated . . . in the countries called Western" (Gouyon 2018: 111, my translation). I am certainly not suggesting that citizens of non-Western countries cannot or should not identify with the category or with struggles for recognition and equal rights. Instead, I highlight that not all Moroccans understand conforming one's public and private selves to each other as a superior way to live, much less as a right.

2. In addition to describing social acuity, ʿaql can also denote mental ability as an expression of mental health. To this end, Francophone scholars sometimes translate ʿaql as "spirit" (*l'ésprit*) (e.g., Pandolfo 2006).

3. The *Report on Human Development* noted that "90 percent [of respondents] think that the best elected officials must be characterized by *mʿaqul*" (Government of Morocco 2005: 32, my translation).

4. Derija lyrics and annotations at "1956," by Magma (MAR), https://genius.com/Magma-1956-lyrics; my translation.

5. The modernist conflation of "Western" liberal subjectivity with affluence made by the affluent here is not limited to Morocco (Gouyon 2018; Hafez 2013).

6. The earliest recording I can find with "3aqliya" in the title is from the group Tears of Mic, active between 2002 and 2010. According to the website-turned-YouTube-channel DimaRapTV, their song "3aqliya Dirty" was released in 2003. It also appears on my copy of a compilation named *Qamouss Znaqi* from defunct website *Raptiviste.net* and Muslim's Thug Face Productions, which was probably released in 2006.

7. In Derija: "ʿEmerni mantbedel mʿa li wgfo mʿaya nhar lowl" and "ʿEmerni mansa li tbdelo mʿaya wakha mʿarftch ʿalach." See "3a9lia," by Don Bigg, https://genius.com/Don-bigg-3a9lia-lyrics; my translation.

8. "Had lmorceau lgʿa li ʿaqliyathom moskha / Nqder nkon hta ana menhom fhemtini?!" See "3a9lia," by Don Bigg, https://genius.com/Don-bigg-3a9lia-lyrics; my translation.

9. See Salime 2015 for a translation of "al-Khouf."

10. "Mehdi Black Wind - Exclusive Interview 2021, La Base," posted by LaBase, February 8, 2021, YouTube, https://www.youtube.com/watch?v=rvHAGJ398HI; my translation.

11. One woman told me she apprenticed at a recording studio. To my knowledge, to date no Moroccan women have appeared in public as hip hop deejays or produced hip hop tracks professionally in Morocco.

12. "Building a career in rap in Morocco is not easy for a woman, how did you impose yourself on the milieu?" (Aziouzi 2020, my translation).

13. "Maghrebya," by Tigresse Flow, https://genius.com/Tigresse-flow-maghrebya-lyrics; my translation.

14. "Interview 'KRTAS'NSSA' مسلم قطع عليا تيليفون و روابا تعنبو عليا." Posted by TopTivi, January 5, 2018, YouTube, https://www.youtube.com/watch?v=luoYXlzXORY.

15. Miller and Caubet offer a similar sentiment to Khalid Moukdar, a member of the punk band Haoussa: "The revolution must be made in the spirit, and priorities must be established so that we can claim things" (2012: 10, my translation).

16. H-Kayne's "ʿIssawa Style" (2005) might seem like an exception. The ʿIssawa (also ʿAissawa or ʿIsawa) are a Sufi brotherhood based in H-Kayne's home city of Meknes. In the

lyrics, they point out the song's "'Issawa melody" (*naghma*) and rhythm; they also imitate sounds of 'Aissawa *dhikr* (devotional chanting) at the ends of sections. At the same time, they use these as a metaphor for Moroccan identity, explicitly linking moving to 'Aissawa sounds to Meknessi and national belonging rather than identifying themselves as members of the brotherhood.

17. Steph Raggaman is now known as Mustapha Slameur. I refer to him by his former name throughout because it is consistent with the period under discussion.

18. "Bayda Nayda," by Mustapha Slameur, https://genius.com/Mustapha-slameur-bayda -nayda-lyrics; my translation. In the third line, Raggaman (now known as Mustapha Slameur) says "hada style mejdoub," a word that in other contexts would be better rendered as "trance-induced" or "entrancing" (e.g., Caubet 2011: 283).

19. Jil Jilala's song was released days after King Hassan II announced the Green March (Jones 2023: 82–84).

20. See Almeida (2017: 68–72) for more recent responses to the perennial Western Sahara issue.

21. These end-rhymes come from French: "Brancher dak lmic dirou mono wella stéréo / Sm'a laklami yo la fréquence ra maghribiyo / Je représente a khouty fhad style ragga session / Je représente mon bled al Maghrib c'est ma nation / Dakhla m'ak nnaghma f had style vibration." See "Bayda Nayda," by Mustapha Slameur, https://genius.com/Mustapha -slameur-bayda-nayda-lyrics; my translation.

22. Non-Moroccans have conceptualized Morocco via tourism since prior to the French protectorate in 1912; colonists pursued tourism to provide revenue to France (Hillali 2007).

23. The local acts were Under Brother and Sa3er Man.

24. "The participant selected from among the audience members will win a latest-model 'super LG cell phone' as well as the official mascot of the MWC. This free pass permits you to enter according to the order of arrival. Thus, it will be impossible to enter if there are no more seats."

25. In Derija: "Kayna fawda fin mabchiti i wina / F bhar al mawja, Chouf f zham f sfina / Makayn nidam f had zman ghir tchoumirra / A rass idandan o l fawda nayda f les banques." Translated by Youssra Oukaf.

26. "Fin massa'oulin / Fin nass m'aqulin / Manabqawch madloulin / B faqssa m'aloulin." Oukaf translates *m'aqulin* here as "trusted" or "trustworthy," but since the word derives from 'aql, the term includes connotations like "smart," "rational," or "competent."

27. "Kayna lfawda f ramdan (malkom?) / Ana machi men lli kane / Ana moumane billah wlqor'ane / 'alamate ssa'a katbane / Kif chabba kif chobbane / Mchina dakhna wasste tofane / Kayna fawda, w kaane." I translate "kif chabba kif chobbane" more literally than Youssra Oukaf, who glossed this line as "you can't differentiate between men and women" (personal communication, June 2022).

28. For contrasting journalism about emcees' "engagement" from this period, see Ksikes 2006 and al-'Arousi 2007.

29. When I asked him about the musical and social interests of younger musicians, Caprice gently expressed that then-new artists weren't studying hip hop as he had done, just as he asserts in "Kayna Fawda." "I practiced writing and rapping for years," he said, claiming that younger emcees had spent less time on the techniques and history of the genre (August 8, 2010).

30. This is certainly an example of my own complicity with structures of power that aided my research. Like other complicitous relations, intersectional aspects of my identity led others to treat me in this way. While I could have chosen not to go backstage or take pictures from the VIP section in solidarity with those Moroccans who were not granted the same access, that would also have been understood as snubbing the emcees who invited me to the event. Both the emcees and I, however, correctly assumed that others would treat me deferentially once I entered that space.

31. "Fnaire – Intro Yed El Hanna (Yamdah Salem) فناير - مدخل أغنية يد الحنا," posted by Fnaire, January 21, 2016, YouTube, https://www.youtube.com/watch?v=-qNcqEuaYb8.

32. For example, "They found petrol in us and they called it a mistake / The petrol is under the ground, politics is on top of us / We could be wrong, but these are the words that you said / I want only to understand how you have what is mine to enjoy / I want my right to Ceuta and to go until Melilla." See "Fin 7a9na," by L9bi7, https://genius.com/L9bi7-fin-7a9na-lyrics; my translation. For more of the song's lyrics, see Miller and Caubet 2012: 8–9.

33. I hesitated to challenge my interlocutors in part because I wanted to belong. Was it also because I feared losing the privileged "access" I had obtained? My nonaction was influenced by embodied senses of obligation, loyalty, and desire—forms of complicity—that I am socialized to feel but that also structure my work as an academic ethnographer.

34. This logic was familiar to me from frequent advice on how to avoid or cope with public sexual harassment. For those who believe that women and LGBTQIA individuals do not have the same rights to occupy public space as cisgendered, heteronormative men, exercising that control comes as an expression of freedom—the freedom to deny others a central benefit of "real," or holistic, citizenship.

3. THE ETHICS AND AESTHETICS OF COMPETITIONS

1. Bellops passed away unexpectedly in December 2022.

2. Online news site *Ya Biladi* wrote that "a graffiti battle brought together artists from the four corners of the Kingdom in front of a prestigious international jury. Finally it was Ismail Benyamna, alias SAKO, who left victorious, also winning the sum of 22,000 MAD" (La Rédaction 2018, my translation).

3. On transnational markets for Morocco's material and immaterial products, see Cohen and Jaidi 2006; Kapchan 2007; Bono and Hibou 2017; Ciucci 2022.

4. In this way it bears striking resemblance to the way Foucault described ancient Greeks' care of the self (Rabinow and Rose 2003: 153).

5. Hesmondhalgh and Baker write of their UK respondents: "Cultural workers seem torn over the precariousness of their work—bemoaning the mental and emotional states produced, but also resigned to insecurity, and prepared to speak of it as necessary and even desirable" (2010: 13).

6. See chapters 2 and 3 for more discussion of the changing attitudes of the media, the government, and the public after 2003.

7. This conversation took place in English. *Achiri* was a slang term widely used in the Fez-Meknes region. Young men called each other *achiri* as a term of endearment, but it could also be used to describe something cheap or low-class. Red Bull has sponsored dance competitions in Morocco since the mid-2000s.

8. This interview took place in Derija. Here, Khalid said, "Houa ncréeou *industrie* dyal hip hop fil Maghreb."

9. Soultana once canceled a concert after the organizers refused a written contract (personal conversation, Casablanca, March 18, 2010); Don Bigg refused to perform at the 2008 Boulevard festival after his fee shrank in the absence of a written contract (Callen 2009).

10. Though L-Tzack was in his late twenties at this time, as an unmarried man without a steady job, he was understood as a youth. On the liminal status and unstable income of traditional musicians, see Schuyler 1985.

11. Both Bahou (personal conversation, Casablanca, July 2018) and Merhari (Berrada 2015) say they have received 150 to 200 applications in the hip hop category annually since the early 2000s.

12. This information is from Caubet (2016: 251); sponsors in festival program books and media 2004–17; and personal conversations with embassy personnel in 2009, 2010, and 2015.

13. The nonprofit association Maroc Cultures, which runs the Mawazine festival, became a public utility in 2009, allowing for tax-deductible donations. See Kingdom of Morocco, General Secretariat of the Government, "Liste des associations reconnues d'utilité publique," http://www.sgg.gov.ma/eservicesAssociations.aspx. Today, it is "100 percent independent" from government funds (Maroc Cultures 2017: 12). However, during the competition period, it was led by the king's personal secretary, granted royal patronage, and funded by state- and monarch-owned companies (Akalay et al. 2010). Since the king and his family own significant portions of major Moroccan companies, sponsorship from those businesses complicates any separation of state and private funding.

14. See discussion in chapter 2.

15. For example, after extensive national press, Tiraline was chosen by the US Consulate to collaborate with American hip hop musicians The Reminders and DJ Man-O-Wax, all three of whom are Muslim, on their 2010 visit to Morocco. Their song "Tolerance" combines a *guimbri* bass line with punctuation by the *ghuita*, a double-reed instrument associated with the Aissawa Sufi order.

16. This information is from a blog post at https://hakmin-maroc.skyrock.com/2.html.

17. See Tom Pfieffer, "Female Rappers Push Limits in Conservative Morocco," Reuters, May 20, 2009, https://www.reuters.com/article/us-morocco-rappers/female-rappers-push -limits-in-conservative-morocco-idUSTRE54J7FS20090520?edition-redirect; and Sarah Raiss, "MOROCCO: All-Girl Moroccan Rap Bands Break New Ground," Reuters, March 17, 2009, https://reuters.screenocean.com/record/711758.

18. From 2012–14, the competition awarded a single prize across its genre categories. Only the final winner, trap duo Shayfeen, was identified as hip hop.

19. Had they chosen to fully support Tigresse Flow, the Jil Mawazine's intense media presence might have provided an important expectation-setting function, encouraging women artists to pursue musical interests. No other female-led groups or solo female artists reached the finals in any category prior or subsequent to Tigresse Flow's win.

20. The gendered dynamics of Soultana's relative success are explored in chapter 5.

21. Graiouid and Belghazi note the simultaneously political/economic/personal ties that define the Makhzen: "The state has encouraged the establishment of foundations and associations and has provided some of them with substantial resources for the patronage of cultural

events. The most prominent of these . . . include Association Maroc-Cultures (which organizes Mawazine festival in Rabat and is headed by the personal secretary of the monarch), Fondation Esprit de Fès (which organizes the Sacred Music Festival in Fès and is chaired by a prominent banker), Association Essaouira-Mogador (which organizes Gnawa Music Festival and is founded by an advisor to the monarch), and Fondation Festival International du Film de Marrakech (which is headed by the brother of King Mohamed VI)" (2013: 269).

22. For example, cofounder Mohamed Merhari defined "independent" in aesthetic terms: "We have never censured any group nor any musical style, we have never imposed anything. It's a free space" (Despouys 2008: 25).

23. "Ila rasik mlli kunt saghir ygls hna deba, shnou naṣiḥa ʿandik fih? (If your younger self were here right now, what advice would you have for him?)"

24. Originally posted July 23, 2019, on Instagram, on an account that is now closed. https://www.instagram.com/p/BoRdvjPnon4/?igshid=1iqq7fpqk3gmd.

4. EMBODYING THE URBAN POOR

1. "Shuft ḥyati f chariʿa twil fih nas zarbana / Nas ma tʿarf nas ghanwali waḥed minhoum ana." From "3Youn Elhak - Boulevard (Clip officiel)," posted by 3youn, June 29, 2013, YouTube, https://www.youtube.com/watch?v=HqlwEJePqwk. My translation from Derija lyrics provided by ʿAyoun el Ḥak.

2. The term comes from corrugated metal that often serves as building material. See Cohen and Eleb 2002, or Prieprzak 2016, for a review.

3. In recent decades, major Moroccan cities' medinas have housed the working poor until and during their gentrification by Europeans.

4. In Derija: "Klaw flous al-shaʿab wa nta hozi fi ymarsso." *Makhzen* refers to the monarchy and its circle of elites and family members, understood to be the real center of power rather than elected officials.

5. "Bi ism al-shaʿab li fi galbi nkhawihu 3likoum, ya afkar." From "Klab dawla l7a9d feat proof 3askri," posted by Nabil Lakrafi, October 16, 2010, YouTube, https://www.youtube.com/watch?v=EAyZ7R5xmvk.

6. "Arou loubya fil shaʿab bach gʿama y madi snano" and "al-shaʿab makayn, matillsh al-shaʿab." In his English translation, Bigg glossed the latter line as "the people don't do nothing for themselves" (p.c., Don Bigg, Berkeley-Casablanca, 2012).

7. See "Soultana - 35.28," posted by Soultana, August 30, 2017, YouTube, https://www.youtube.com/watch?v=wUP7i9dd4Zs. In Derija: "Baraka mn qelet nefs rah lʿalam kayhder / Skati w skatek khala lmasʿoul ʿal shaʿab ydser / Souti w soutek ḥesbouh ri noqta f akhir ster / mli sout wla kaytbaʿou b dgig zit o sokar." The first phrase acts like a pun; it can translate to "enough of the same thing" or "enough, we're out of breath." However, Soultana translates it as I have here (p.c., August 9, 2019). The final line refers to long-standing subsidies on staple foods.

8. The practice of repurposing traditional expressive forms that Fnaire pioneered is discussed in chapter 2.

9. See "Don Bigg - TJR feat. Ahmed Soultan (Official VIDEO)," posted by Don Bigg, February 13, 2015, YouTube, https://www.youtube.com/watch?v=Ww8YnecpzE4. In the video, Bigg and his son pass a road marker for Fkih Ben Salah, approximately 110 miles southeast of Casablanca.

10. Tashelhit is the most widespread of three Amazight languages. Soultan, from Taroudant in southeastern Morocco, writes lyrics in Tashelhit, Derija, English, and French.

11. "Ara stylo ara lwarqa nqayad lik 7 dlhwayj ghadi nkafrak fihom kola nhar ma ḥaddi ʿayech." Original lyrics from "Don Bigg - TJR feat. Ahmed Soultan (Official VIDEO)," posted by Don Bigg, February 13, 2015, YouTube, https://www.youtube.com /watch?v=Ww8YnecpzE4.

12. "Li kan tmna lik oulad y choufou walidik oh agharass."

13. See "MR CRAZY – KUE PASSA x M-FIX [OFFICIEL CLIP HD] - Mixtape Ya Khasar Ya Tkhasar," posted by Mr Crazy Official, April 11, 2015, YouTube, https://www.you tube.com/watch?v=rG4pw3IcC14. In Derija: "Kanshouf ḥyati dayz gha promo . . . Lqit rasi ana li khayb ḥyati khassha Omo."

14. See also Tendresse, "B.W.B. (Brani Wst Bladi)" (2020), in chapter 1.

15. See "SISIMO – 3id Alfa9r (Starring Said Bey & Fadoua Taleb)," posted by SiSimo, April 11, 2013, YouTube, https://www.youtube.com/watch?v=Gs7Oii6qUFs.

16. See "Lbenj – Anti," posted by Lbenj, March 21, 2018, YouTube, https://www.youtube .com/watch?v=QK7v74Wq46c.

17. The story of Grandwizzard Theodore's discovery is retold, for example, in Katz 2012: 59–60.

18. Grandwizzard Theodore, quoted in Katz 2012: 147.

19. For contemporaneous accounts, see "Terror Blasts Rock Casablanca," BBC, May 17, 2003, http://news.bbc.co.uk/2/hi/africa/3035803.stm; "Moroccans March against Terror," BBC, May 25, 2003, http://news.bbc.co.uk/2/hi/africa/2936918.stm.

20. Pierre Vermeren tartly described the shock of the print-consuming middle and upper classes: "The trauma was immense in a society which the social elite thought was entirely under [their] control" (2004: 108–9, my translation).

21. "Karian" is the Derija version of the French *carrière*, or "quarry." Since the early twentieth century, when Casablanca's first bidonville was built next to Carrière Centrale in what is now part of the neighborhood Hay Mohammedi, the word has connoted informal housing self-built by the very poor (Zaki 2006: note 1).

22. "Complicity" here refers to its legal meaning in the Moroccan penal code.

23. By 2008, Abdellah Tourabi described Karian Toma and similar bidonvilles as "completely abandoned" by the state, yet he insisted that the "sociology of the neighborhood does not suffice to explain the terrorist uprising" (2008: 225, my translation). His position, however, lay outside the foundational assumptions of the public conversation, which were reinforced immediately after the bombings by the actions of the monarchy.

24. In an interview with one of the surviving attackers, *TelQuel* emphasized that his participation was coerced and his beliefs contradictory, closing with the question: "If Rachid Jalil, in the situation where he finds himself [prison], does not understand that it was an inevitable slope to terrorism, who will understand it?" (Benchemsi 2006, my translation).

25. As Koen Bogaert shows, "The problem is presented as one of shepherding its inhabitants toward market integration. . . . Generally, the idea is that once people are good consumers they will eventually become responsible citizens with a 'proper' job and a 'proper' lifestyle (interview with former ADS official, April 16, 2009). . . . [T]he market becomes the norm by which good citizenship is measured" (2011: 725–26).

26. This conversation took place in English.

27. Articles and interviews mention Moroccan and international financial institutions, including La Fondation BNP Paribas and its subsidiary, the BMCI Foundation (Derville 2016); Bank al-Maghrib; and La Caisse Depot de Gestion's foundation (Bouithy 2014).

28. In the original: "Mama / matkhatfish ghay'ajbiksh angoul" and "Mama / Matkhatfish 'arif kasha tguli."

29. In the 2010s, *tcharmil* youths—*mcharmlin*, or those who *tcharmil*—were distinguished by their fashion, haircuts, and embrace of stereotypes about lower-class male violence; they "are perceived as young, delinquent, depressed school drop outs, jobless, marginalised, as well as aggressed by the lifestyle of the rich" (El Maarouf and Belghazi 2018: 293). Moroccan commentators defend *mcharmlin*, who inspired a lasting moral panic among affluent urbanites (Strava 2020), as "distanc[ing themselves] from their sordid reality and everyday life, which is made even unlivable by contempt, exclusion, and rejection, revealing the failure of the country's educational system and limits of its youth policies" (Ghayet 2015, in El Maarouf and Belghazi 2018: 293).

30. My translation from Derija.

31. Mustapha Hamil argues a core insight frames all of the characters' choices in Binebine's novel: "In a way, Yachine and his friends do not need to be convinced to die—not because they are unwilling to do so, but because they do not care one way or the other, an indifference to death which is as tragic as the actual killing" (2011: 557).

32. http://fondationalizaoua.org/wp/en/ali-zaoua-foundation/, last accessed September 24, 2018.

33. My translation from French.

34. In an essay on Binebine's novel, Katarzyna Pieprzak describes his characters as spatially, socially, and psychologically immobilized: "Human being and human meaning remain captive in a representational system that . . . den[ies] . . . any sense of futurity" (2016: 39–41).

35. "Train mcha ou ana ghir kanchouf / Nass katmout ra rabbi kaychouf / Qrtasa ulla ghayklek lḥout / Oulad chaab riski fi bateau lmout." My translation of lyrics from "3YOUN – MR BOULEVARD (music video). Prod by maestro عيون الحق," posted by 3youn, June 10, 2019, https://www.youtube.com/watch?v=bDSG7frB8vE.

36. In the original: "alaaaaaaaaaaaaah 3youn rje3 l'style dialo" and "هدا هوا عيون لي كنعرفو 🥰🥰🥰🥰."

37. In Don Bigg's "LMeryoula" (2020), the lyrics critique the conflation of personal, social, and economic value in direct terms while the video imitates key plot points and camerawork from *Horses of God*, such as an airborne shot panning over the densely packed karian. As of March 2021, the video has over twenty-three million views.

38. As Sara Ahmed notes, "All these forms of fellow-feeling ['compassion, . . . empathy, sympathy and pity'] involve fantasy: one can 'feel for' or 'feel with' others, but this depends on how I 'imagine' the other already feels. So 'feeling with' or 'feeling for' does not mean a suspicion of 'feeling about': *one feels with or for others only insofar as one feels 'about' their feelings in the first place*" (2004: 41n9, italics in original).

5. EXPECTATIONS OF FEMINISM

1. My gratitude and apologies go to James Ferguson for this chapter title.

2. I use "caring labor" to encompass both affective labor—the personal and intersubjective work of generating a certain affect, a disposition toward engagement and receptivity

(e.g., Brian Massumi, Michael Hardt)—and emotional labor, culturally recognized emotion produced "for a wage [that] therefore has *exchange value*" (Hochschild 2012 [1983]: 7, italics in original). Caring labor is in part necessary because individuals recognize "emotion management" as having potential exchange value; that is, they manage both their "publicly observable" (Hochschild 2012 [1983]: 7), enculturated feelings and their affects to make their public and private personae more exchangeable and more attractive to capital. Caring labor requires a disposition that is open to feeling something with others, though not necessarily the same something they feel (Ahmed 2004: 30). Critically, its deployment blurs lines between paid labor and social obligation.

3. *Revolutionary Arab Rap* blog, "Female Rappers," http://revolutionaryarabrap .blogspot.com/p/female-rappers.html; *Revolutionary Arab Rap* blog, "Soultana – Sawt Nssa ('The Voice of Women')," posted February 19, 2012, http://revolutionaryarabraptheindex .blogspot.com/2012/02/soultana-sawt-nssa-voice-of-women.html.

4. Hip hop's association with the Moroccan 2011–12 reform movement was never as strong as in Anglophone coverage of the Tunisian and Egyptian revolutions (e.g., Fernandes 2012; Wright 2011; Westland 2012). Many Moroccan hip hop artists were silent on February 20. Others called for reforms but did not support the campaign's calls for a parliamentary democracy instead of executive monarchy. Still others admitted, in private and on Facebook, to supporting the reformists' goals, but they assured me that the movement's tactics would change nothing. Like many fellow citizens, some artists found the movement's alliance with Islamists unacceptable or frightening. Don Bigg's two songs critiquing the protests, "Mabghitch (I Don't Want It)" and "Fhamtini (Do You Understand Me)," reflected widespread cynicism. Common responses to my inquiries about el-Ḥaqed (Mouad Belghouat, "the enraged") in 2011 were surprise and dismissive comments about his musicianship. While committed to the February 20 movement, he was relatively unknown within Casablanca's hip hop network in 2011 and stated he started rapping in 2007 (el-Ḥaqed 2014).

5. https://www.dapp.dk/en/about/morocco/. This link is now inactive. For more information on work DAPP funds in Morocco today, see https://kvinfo.dk/where-we-work /morocco/?lang=en.

6. https://www.dapp.dk/en/about/partners/.

7. Several organizers have told me they found Soultana through an internet search for female emcees.

8. ECF supports cultural organizations in several European countries. Subtopia promotes arts and cultural production to reframe suburbs like Botkyrka, often understood as concentrating poverty and immigrants outside of Stockholm: "What if we as a municipality could cluster and attract artists and educators, in order to provide cultural, financial and personal growth for passionate individuals in our suburbs[?] . . . We would argue that the most human of all things is culture and relationships so why shouldn't that be at the core of our cities?" (Duregård, Lekberg, and Lindgren 2016).

9. See https://www.botkyrka.se/kommun-och-politik/statistik-och-oppna-data/fakta -om-botkyrka, retrieved November 5, 2024; Statistics Sweden https://www.scb.se/en/, retrieved October 16, 2018. If counting residents born in Sweden with one foreign-born and one Swedish-born parent, the number rises to 67 percent (Statistics Sweden). This does not include those whose parents were born in Sweden but are not ethnically Swedish or considered white.

10. Translation from This Is Alby's Facebook page, https://www.facebook.com/thisisalbyy, posted August 8, 2015.

11. I wrote to Josefin in July 2015 but did not receive a response. Soultana also wrote to Josefin to ask that I be allowed access to the festival's backstage spaces. I used university research funds to travel.

12. "Sawt l-bnat li day'in wast l-bladi / sawt li bghat tgoul, li bghat tgoul / sawt l-g'a li bghau l- hdaya, bab touba meḥloul." More literally, "The voice of she who wants to speak / the voice of everyone who wants a gift, a door to the solution of repentance."

13. Thanks to Ryan Skinner for contextualizing such festivals (personal conversation, October 18, 2018).

14. Sara stressed this was "not normal," writing that "if you are invited for something, everything is payed [sic] for. Like the basics—hotel, meals, transportation" (email, October 10, 2018).

15. After Soultana and Bawss left Sweden, they waited over a month for payment. According to Josefin regulations stipulate that the municipality "can . . . only pay a fee 30 days after an invoice has come in from the artists" (email, August 7, 2018). The bank transfer was addressed to Soultana, not her legal name, causing further delay.

16. Information in the following paragraphs comes from interviews with Hicham Bahou (Casablanca, August 2015 and 2016), Amadou Fall Ba (Dakar, July 2015), and Kane Limam, a.k.a Monza (Casablanca, September 2017) unless otherwise noted.

17. To the best of my knowledge, the Office of African Music Export (BEMA) ran this meeting, which is funded in turn by its West African member nations' ministries of culture, several national and international French organizations, and UNESCO (africul tures.com).

18. In 2015, King Mohamed VI toured West African cities to personally support the maintenance and creation of markets for Moroccan products; the Foundation Mohamed VI for training African *ulemas* (religious scholars) opened in Fez in 2016; and Morocco rejoined the African Union in 2016 (Ministère des Habous 2016; de Saint Périer 2016).

19. The final lines in Wolof translate to: "Women know how to ride the beat better than men / hey fans, yell and say 'Jokko'!" I am grateful to Eben for the translation to French.

20. "Sawt illi fi dar, lli waqtha fi l-trottoir / lli 'aisha fil village u lli katrappi fil Boulevard."

21. To do this with their new lineup, they cut a verse by Eben and added Ami to eight bars of the third verse plus four bars of pre-chorus material.

22. "Nous disons 'non' au violence faite au femmes / Nous disons 'oui' à tout ce quoi qu'elles réclament."

23. See Radio France Internationale, "Jokko Fam, la vitrine d'une expérience réussie d'un projet collectif artistique," September 23, 2017, http://www.rfi.fr/emission/20170924 -jokko-fam-vitrine-une-experience-reussie-projet-collectif-artistique.

24. The Moroccan term *tberguig* describes rumors fueled by malice, jealousy, or pursuit of social capital, regardless of facts, and is used for all genders.

25. Soultana's typical fee has varied little since 2011.

26. See claims by Djur Djura and Zap Mama in Taylor 1997.

27. One might say my writing transforms my experiences into items with use-value and that, by reading, you participate in their transformation into exchange-values. See also Pine 2016.

28. Nettl observes that "comparative musicology entered the academy with the task of providing a corrective to widely held beliefs. It continues sometimes in this function" (2010: 59).

EPILOGUE: THE WORLD THE WAVE MADE, OR THE SINCERITY OF CAPITAL

1. This interview took place in English.

2. Aminoffice was one half of Double A, the duo that put out the first recognized Derija-language hip hop album in 1996.

3. Caprice is referring to J. Cole's "Let Nas Down" (2013).

4. This conversation mixed Derija and English.

5. Derija: "It turns, it turns."

6. Later he clarified, "My musical style don't change. I learn new things, and I can do them, but I'm still doing what I used to do before."

7. *Al-ʿAdl wa al-Tanmia*, or the Justice and Development Party (PJD), is an Islamist party. Throughout the late 2000s, leading members of the PJD criticized the importation of "Western" popular culture into Morocco. In elections in November 2011, held shortly after the peak of the February 20 movement and a referendum on Morocco's constitution, the PJD took nearly one-third of Parliament's seats. As a result, King Mohamed VI appointed the prime minister and most of the ministerial leadership from the PJD.

8. The BMDA is charged with collecting and distributing royalties to registered artists when their recordings are played in Moroccan media. It is notoriously derelict (Almeida 2017: 155). I have met no artist or arts professional who regards the BMDA as functional, and for some, the agency is merely state-legitimized theft (interview with Mohamed Sqalli, 2018; Dizzy Dros on MedinaFM, May 2022). While today Casablanca in particular has more privately owned places to perform, one prominent rehearsal space, and a small network of cultural organizers offering an alternative to postcolonial NGOs like the Institut Français, other aspects of Benchemsi's editorial have changed little, especially for the rest of Morocco (Kamili and Ksikes 2021, for an overview).

9. This interview took place in English.

10. See "Welcome to NAAR," http://naar.fr/welcometonaar/2018.

11. Robin D. G. Kelley has traced the ways that US social scientists' narratives about impoverished Black people pathologized their artistry, sometimes in the name of sympathizing (1997, in Aprahamian 2019). Schloss calls this "cultural . . . [and] class determinism" when applied to narratives about hip hop's origins and significance (2014 [2004]: 27).

12. Despite trying to avoid the classification, NAAR is a good example of Whitmore's analysis of "world music 2.0," in which contemporary independent organizations face the same challenges as the traditional record labels that dominated the first iteration (2020: 208–9).

13. See Ganti 2014: 96 for a concise list of ethnographies that provide more nuanced illustrations of how people yoke ideals of self-entrepreneurship to other discourses in various contexts.

14. Matlon examines men's discourses in particular to theorize *complicit masculinity*, which "explains how articulations from [marginalized men] may perpetuate relations of domination" (2016: 1018, italics in original).

15. For so many Moroccans, as expressed in so many Moroccan hip hop texts and practitioners' actions, migration away from home and into Europe or perhaps North America is the goal. Yet successful migration is not necessarily imagined as permanent departure but as a state of freer circulation, where one accumulates the political means to remain safely anchored in the global north while possessing the financial means to visit one's family and ancestral home in Morocco (Ciucci 2022). This is precisely what the remittance-sending class, *Marocains résidents à l'étranger*, or MREs, does every summer. Flowing in and out of their home like a wave, or a euro, is an ultimate freedom experienced as a birthright by many global north citizens—a freedom in which one does not give up all social ties and obligations, but chooses which to maintain.

16. Rather than locating my use within a particular theory of affect, here I only signify that the expression and reception of the sincerity I invoke is simultaneously embodied and culturally informed. See Desai-Stephens and Reisnour 2020 for an effort to transcend differences between lineages of affect theory.

17. I use "Arab" here because, like many Moroccans, Bigg dis-identified with sub-Saharan Africans at this time. As an example, his song "Ifrikiya" (2009) takes a externalizing, developmentalist perspective on the continent as a place of poverty and helplessness, rather than one of unity or solidarity.

REFERENCES

Abu-Lughod, Lila. 1990. "The Romance of Resistance: Tracing Transformations of Power through Bedouin Women." *American Ethnologist* 17 (1): 41–55.

Ahmed, Sara. 2004. *The Cultural Politics of Emotion*. New York: Routledge.

Aidi, Hisham. 2014. *Rebel Music: Race, Empire, and the New Muslim Youth Culture*. New York: Penguin Random House.

Aidi, Hisham. 2020. "National Identity in the Afro-Arab Periphery: Ethnicity, Indigeneity and (anti)Racism in Morocco." *POMEPS Studies* 40: 64–68.

Akalay, Aicha, Driss Bennani, and Hassan Hamdani. 2011. "Rap Patriotique: Le GI Joe du Flow." *Telquel* 460 (February 12–18).

Akalay, Aicha, Hassan Hamdani, and Mehdi Michbal. 2010. "Mawazine: un miracle royal." *TelQuel* 425 (May 22–28).

Al-'Arousi, Latifa. 2007. "Farq 'al-Rap' al-Maghribi: Aghanyiat 'Thouriya' wa Ta'atir fi al-Shabab" [Moroccan "rap" bands: "Revolutionary" songs and effects on the youths]. *Asharq al-Awsat*, June 11, 2007. http://archive.aawsat.com/details.asp?article=423035&issueno=10422.

Al Jazeera. 2010. ناس الغيوان—الجزء الأول [Nass el-Ghiwane—Part one]. Posted by Al Jazeera Documentary, November 1, 2018. YouTube. https://www.youtube.com/watch?v=DtNDrGdzEKM.

Al-Khayat, Nadir (a.k.a. RedOne). 2012. "Korsa: Avec RedOne." Interview by Younes Lazrak. *Korsa* 2011, episode 20,

Alami, Aida. 2011. "Morocco's Mawazine Festival Stirs Controversy." *The World*, June 4. https://theworld.org/stories/2011-06-04/moroccos-mawazine-festival-stirs-controversy.

Alami, Aida. 2020. "Dozens of Gay Men Are Outed in Morocco as Photos Are Spread Online." *New York Times*, April 26.

Alaoui, Khadija, Mohamed Kadimi, Ayoub Akil, and Nadia Ziane. 2007. "Le rap réinvente la chanson Marocaine." *Libération*, March 19. http://www.bladi.net/rap-marocain.html.

Alim, H. Samy. 2006. *Roc the Mic Right: The Language of Hip Hop Culture*. New York: Routledge.

Allali, Reda. 2006. "Enquête: les nouveaux fascistes." *Tel Quel* 231 (June 29).

Almeida, Cristina Moreno. 2016. "The Politics of *Taqlidi* Rap: Reimagining Moroccanness in the Era of Global Flows." *Journal of North African Studies* 21(1): 116–31. https://doi.org /10.1080/13629387.2015.1084101.

Almeida, Cristina Moreno. 2016. "'Race' and 'Blackness' in Moroccan Rap: Voicing Local Experiences of Marginality." In *American Studies Encounters the Middle East*, edited by Alex Lubin and Marwan M. Kraidy. Chapel Hill: University of North Carolina Press.

Almeida, Cristina Moreno. 2017. *Rap beyond Resistance: Staging Power in Contemporary Morocco*. London: Palgrave Macmillan.

Almeida, Cristina Moreno. 2023. "Moroccan Hip Hop Queens: A (Her)Story of Rap Music in Morocco." In *The Palgrave Handbook of Gender, Media and Communication in the Middle East and North Africa*, edited by L. H. Skalli and N. Eltantawy. London: Palgrave Macmillan.

Alonso, Rogelio, and Marcos García Rey. 2007. "The Evolution of Jihadist Terrorism in Morocco." *Terrorism and Political Violence* 19 (4): 571–92. https://doi.org/10.1080 /09546550701606580.

Agence Nationale de Réglementation des Télécommunications (ANRT). 2006. "Rapport d'activité 2006." Rabat: CLE-Études.

Amine, Khaled. 2001. "Crossing Borders: Al-Halqa Performance in Morocco from the Open Space to the Theatre Building." *The Drama Review* 45 (2): 55–69.

Aouragh, Miriyam. 2017. "L-Makhzan al-'Akbari: Resistance, Remembrance and Remediation in Morocco." *Middle East Critique* 26 (3): 241–63. https://doi.org/10.1080/19436149 .2017.1331516.

Appel, Hannah. 2019. *The Licit Life of Capitalism: US Oil in Equatorial Guinea*. Durham, NC: Duke University Press.

Appert, Catherine. 2017. "Engendering Musical Ethnography." *Ethnomusicology* 61 (3): 446–67. https://doi.org/10.5406/ethnomusicology.61.3.0446.

Appert, Catherine. 2018. *In Hip Hop Time: Music, Memory, and Social Change in Urban Senegal*. Oxford: Oxford University Press.

Aprahamian, Serouj. 2019. "Hip-Hop, Gangs, and the Criminalization of African American Culture: A Critical Appraisal of *Yes Yes Y'all*." *Journal of Black Studies* 50 (3): 298–315.

Arendt, Hannah. 1990 [1963]. *On Revolution*. London: Penguin Group.

Asad, Talal. 2009 [1986]. "The Idea of an Anthropology of Islam." *Qui Parle* 17 (2): 1–30.

Asen, Joshua, and Jennifer Needleman, dirs. 2007. *I Love Hip-Hop in Morocco*. New York and Los Angeles: Rizz Productions.

Atia, Mona. 2019. "Refusing a 'City without Slums': Moroccan Slum Dwellers' Nonmovements and the Art of Presence." *Cities* 125 (2022). https://doi.org/10.1016/j.cities.2019.02.014.

Aubel, François. 2013. "Nabil Ayouch: 'Je remonte aux sources de la violence.'" *Le Figaro*, February 19. https://www.lefigaro.fr/cinema/2013/02/19/03002–20130219ARTFIG00455 -nabil-ayouch-je-remonte-aux-sources-de-la-violence.php

Austin, Joe A. 2016. "From the City Walls to 'Clean Trains': Graffiti in New York City, 1969–1990." In *Routledge Handbook of Graffiti and Street Art*, edited by Jeffery Ian Ross. New York: Routledge.

Aydoun, Ahmed. 2014 [1995]. *Les Musiques du Maroc*. Casablanca: Editions Eddif.

Aziouzi, Kenza. 2020. "Tendresse: 'Certaines femmes ont laissé une empreinte, Je me suis dit: pourquoi pas moi?'" *L'Opinion*, September 20. https://www.lopinion.ma/Tendresse-Certaines-femmes-ont-laisse-une-empreinte-je-me-suis-dit-pourquoi-pas-moi_a6675.html.

Baird, Saxon. 2011. "Tigresse Flow: Soultana." *Afropop Worldwide*, May 24, 2011. https://afropop.org/articles/tigresse-flow-soultana.

Bargach, Jamila. 1999. "Liberatory, Nationalising and Moralising by Ellipsis: Reading and Listening to Lhussein Slaoui's Song 'Lmirikan.'" *Journal of North African Studies* 4 (4): 61–88. https://doi.org/10.1080/13629389908718380.

Barthel, P. A., and S. Planel. 2010. "Tanger-Med and Casa-Marina, Prestige Projects in Morocco: New Capitalist Frameworks and Local Context." Built Environment 36 (2): 48–63. http://dx.doi.org/10.2148/benv.36.2.176.

Bartolucci, Valentina. 2010. "Analysing Elite Discourse on Terrorism and its Implications: The Case of Morocco." *Critical Studies on Terrorism* 3 (1): 119–35. https://doi.org/10.1080/17539151003594269.

Becker, Gary S. 1993. *A Treatise on the Family: Enlarged Edition*. Cambridge, MA: Harvard University Press.

Behar, Ruth, and Deborah A. Gordon, eds. 1995. *Women Writing Culture*. Berkeley: University of California Press.

Belghazi, Taieb. 2006. "Festivalization of Urban Space in Morocco." *Critique: Critical Middle Eastern Studies* 15 (1): 97–107. https://doi.org/10.1080/10669920500515168.

Belhaj, Imane. 2008. "Female Rappers Win Morocco's First National Hip-Hop Competition." *Magharebia*, May 7, 2008. https://web.archive.org/web/20080512231821/http://www.magharebia.com:80/cocoon/awi/xhtml1/en_GB/features/awi/features/2008/05/07/feature-02.

Belyazid, Fatima, and Abdelrrahim Mettour, dirs. 2007. *Casanayda!* Casablanca: Sigma Technologies.

Ben Srhir, Khalid. 2005. *Britain and Morocco during the Embassy of John Drummond Hay, 1845–1886*. London: Routledge Curzon.

Benchemsi, Ahmed R., et al. 2004. "Les jeunes ouvrent leur gueule: les pionniers du parler-vrai." *Telquel* 130 (June 5–11). http:// www.telquel-online.com/130/couverture_130_1.shtml.

Benchemsi, Ahmed R. 2006. "Mémoires d'un kamikaze." *TelQuel* 228 (July 3–9). https://web.archive.org/web/20060702221019/http://www.telquel-online.com/228/couverture_228_1.shtml.

Benchemsi, Ahmed R. 2008. "Coup de pouce royal." *TelQuel* 326 (May 30–June 6). http://www.telquel-online.com/326/edito_326.shtml.

Bencherki, Fatmi Zahra. 2019. *Des histoires et des hommes: wa drari*. Casablanca: 2M Media and Ali'N Productions.

Benjelloun, Tahar. 2010. "Mémoire heureuse." In *Omar Es-Sayed raconte Nass el-Ghiwane*, edited by Es-Sayed et al. Casablanca: Senso Unico Éditions and Éditions du Sirocco.

Bennani, Driss. 2004. "Rétrospective : il était une fois la presse." *TelQuel* 130 (June 5–11). https://web.archive.org/web/20111211154230/http://www.telquel-online.com/130/sujet2.shtml.

Bennani-Chraïbi, Mounia. 2011. "Jeux de miroir de la 'politisation': les acteurs associatifs de quartier à Casablanca." *Critique Internationale* 50 (1): 55–71. https://doi.org/10.3917/crii.050.0055.

Bennani-Chraïbi, Mounia, and Mohamed Jeghllaly. 2012. "La dynamique protestataire du Mouvement du 20 février à Casablanca." *Revue francaise des sciences politiques* 62 (5): 867–94.

Bensalmia, Chadwane. 2004. "Portrait: Vigon, le petit ange noir." *Telquel* 111 (January 24–30).

Bergh, Sylvia. 2012. "'Inclusive' Neoliberalism, Local Governance Reforms and the Redeployment of State Power: The Case of the National Initiative for Human Development (INDH) in Morocco." *Mediterranean Politics* 17 (3): 410–26. https://doi.org/10.1080/13629395.2012.725304.

Berrada, Rania. 2015. "L'histoire du rap marocain vue par Momo, cofondateur de L'Boulevard." *Huffington Post Maghreb*, May 17, 2015. https://www.huffpostmaghreb.com/2015/05/17/rap-momo-lboulevard_n_7292872.html.

Bihi, Brahim. 2009. "Boucler la boucle!" *L'Kounache* (6): 18.

Binkley, Sam. 2011. "Psychological Life as Enterprise: Social Practice and the Government of Neoliberal Interiority." *History of the Human Sciences* 24 (3): 83–102. https://doi.org/10.1177/0952695111412877.

Bogaert, Koenraad. 2011. "The Problem of Slums: Shifting Methods of Neoliberal Urban Government in Morocco." *Development and Change* 42 (3): 709–31. https://doi.org/10.1111/j.1467-7660.2011.01706.x.

Bogaert, Koenraad. 2012. "New State Space Formation in Morocco: The Example of the Bouregreg Valley." *Urban Studies* 49 (2): 255–70. https://doi.org/10.1177/0042098011400770.

Bono, Irene, and Beatrice Hibou. 2017. "Development as a Battlefield." Translated by Andrew Brown. *International Development Policy* 8: 3–36. https://doi.org/10.4000/poldev.2301.

Bono, Irene, et al. 2015. *L'Etat d'injustice au Maghreb. Maroc et Tunisie.* Paris: Karthala.

Bouanani, Ahmed. 1966. "Introduction à la poésie populaire Marocaine." *Souffles* 3 (3): 3–9.

Bouaziz, Mostefa. 1999. "Mouvements Sociaux et Mouvement National au Maroc: de la Liaison Organique à l'Amorce du Désengagement." In *Émeutes et Mouvements Sociaux au Maghreb: Perspective Comparée*, edited by Didier Le Saout and Marguerite Rollinde. Paris: Karthala.

Boughrine, Jihane. 2014. "Génération Mawazine, génération à talent." *Les Inspirations Eco*, January 21. https://www.maghress.com/fr/lesechos/117311.

Bouithy, Alain. 2010. "C'est parti pour le 5ème concours Génération Mawazine: Les jeunes musiciens sur la ligne de départ." *Libération*, February 16.

Bouithy, Alain. 2014. "Sophia Akhmisse, directrice de la Fondation Ali Zaoua: 'l'une de nos missions c'est la formation et l'initiation des jeunes aux métiers des arts et de la scène.'" *Libération*, December 3. https://www.libe.ma/%E2%80%8BSophia-Akhmisse-directrice-de-la-Fondation-Ali-Zaoua_a56620.html.

Boum, Aomar. 2012a. "Festivalizing Dissent in Morocco." *Middle East Report* (Summer): 22–25.

Boum, Aomar. 2012b. "Moroccan Rappers and Political Descent in the Age of the 'Arab Spring.'" *IPRIS* [Portuguese Institute of International Relations and Security] *Maghreb Bulletin* 13: 4–7.

Bourquia, Rahma, Mohammed El Ayadi, Mokhtar El Harras, and Hassan Rachik. 2000. *Les jeunes et les valeurs religieuses*. Casablanca: Eddif-Codesria.

Bradley, Regina. 2012. "Contextualizing Hip Hop Sonic Cool Pose in Late Twentieth- and Twenty-First-Century Rap Music." *Current Musicology* 93: 55–70. https://doi.org/10.7916/cm.v0i93.5220.

Brown, Danielle. 2020. "An Open Letter on Racism in Music Studies." *My People Tell Stories* blog, June 12. https://www.mypeopletellstories.com/blog/open-letter.

Brown, Kenneth L. 1976. *People of Salé: Tradition and Change in a Moroccan City*. Manchester: Manchester University Press.

Brown, Wendy. 2003. "Neoliberalism and the End of Liberal Democracy." *Theory and Event* 7 (1). https://dx.doi.org/10.1353/tae.2003.0020.

Brown, Wendy. 2015. *Undoing the Demos: Neoliberalism's Stealth Revolution*. New York: Zone Books.

Butler, Judith. 2020. *The Force of Nonviolence: An Ethico-Political Bind*. London: Verso.

Burton, Justin. 2017. *Posthuman Rap*. London: Oxford University Press.

Callen, Jeffrey. 2006. *French Fries in the Tagine: Re-Imagining Moroccan Popular Music*. PhD Diss., University of California, Los Angeles.

Callen, Jeffrey. 2009. "Don Bigg Works the Room: Moroccan Hip Hop Hits the Big Time." Afropop Worldwide. http://www.afropop.org/multi/feature/ID/863/Moroccan_hip_hop_comes_of_age.

Carey, Matthew. 2012. "'The Rules' in Morocco? Pragmatic Approaches to Flirtation and Lying." *HAU: Journal of Ethnographic Theory* 2 (2): 188–204. https://doi.org/10.14318/hau2.2.011.

Catusse, Myriam. 2008. *Le temps des entrepreneurs: politique et transformations du capitalisme au Maroc*. Paris: Maisonneuve et Larose.

Catusse, Myriam. 2009. "Morocco's Political Economy: Ambiguous Privatization and the Emerging Social Question." In *The Arab State and Neo-liberal Globalization: The Restructuring of State Power in the Middle East*, edited by Laura Guazzone and Daniela Pioppi. London: Garnet Publishing (UK) Ltd.

Caubet, Dominique. 1999. "Entretien avec Omar Sayed (Nass el-Ghiwane): 'Ed-Darija Dyal-na, Fi-ha el-'aṭriya!'" [Interview with Omar Sayed (Nass el-Ghiwane): "Our Derija, it has a perfume!"] *Estudios de dialectología noretaficana y andalusí* 4: 121–30.

Caubet, Dominique. 2011. "Nayda ou les enfants des Ghiwane" [Nayda or the children of the Ghiwane). In *Omar Sayed raconte Nass El Ghiwane*. Casablanca: Senso Unico Éditions and Éditions du Sirocco.

Caubet, Dominique. 2016. "DIY in Morocco from the Mid 90s to 2015: Back to the Roots?" In *Keep It Simple, Make It Fast!: An Approach to Underground Music Scenes*, edited by Paula Guerra and Tânia Moreira, vol. 2. Porto: Faculdade de Letras Universidade do Porto.

Cavatorta, Francesco. 2007. "More than Repression: The Significance of Divide et Impera in the Middle East and North Africa–The Case of Morocco." *Journal of Contemporary African Studies* 25 (2): 188–203. https://doi.org/10.1080/02589000701396223.

Cavatorta, Francesco. 2013. "Introduction: Civil Society under Authoritarian Constraints." In *Civil Society Activism under Authoritarian Rule: A Comparative Perspective*, edited by Francesco Cavatorta. New York: Routledge.

Cavatorta, Francesco. 2020. "Beyond Quietism: Party Institutionalisation, Salafism, and the Economy." *Politics and Religion* 13: 796–817. https://doi.org/10.1017/S1755048320000292.

Cestor, Élisabeth. 2008. "L'irruption du rap au Maroc: entretien d'Élisabeth Cestor avec Hicham Abkari." Africultures. http://www.africultures.com/php/index.php?nav=article&no=8120.

Chabaa, Qods. 2006. "Mawazine: des rythmes et des prix." *Aujourd'hui le Maroc*, March 28. https://www.maghress.com/fr/aujourdhui/45008.

Chabaa, Qods. 2007. "Mawazine laisse les jeunes s'exprimer." *Aujourd'hui le Maroc*, March 22. https://www.maghress.com/fr/aujourdhui/53253

Chang, Jeff. 2005. *Can't Stop Won't Stop: A History of the Hip-Hop Generation.* New York: St. Martin's Press.

Chari, Anita. 2020. "Reification and the Ready-Made Artist: Towards a Sensate Critique of Neoliberalism." *Social Dynamics* 46 (1): 10–21. https://doi.org/10.1080/02533952.2020.1732715.

Charon, Aurélie. 2017. "Les bonnes pistes aux etoiles de Sidi Moumen." *Libération*, November 16. https://next.liberation.fr/cinema/2017/11/16/les-bonnes-pistes-aux-etoiles-de-sidi-moumen_1610577.

Chauffour, Jean-Pierre. 2018. *Morocco 2040: Emerging by Investing in Intangible Capital.* Washington, DC: World Bank. https://openknowledge.worldbank.org/handle/10986/28442.

Cheng, William. 2017. "Staging Overcoming: Narratives of Disability and Meritocracy in Reality Singing Competitions." *Journal of the Society for American Music* 11 (2): 184–214. https://doi.org/10.1017/S1752196317000062.

Cheng, William. 2018. "Black Noise, White Ears: Resilience, Rap, and the Killing of Jordan Davis." *Current Musicology* 102 (Spring 2018): 115–89. https://doi.org/10.7916/cm.v0i102.5367.

Ciucci, Alessandra. 2022. *The Voice of the Rural: Music, Poetry, and Masculinity among Migrant Moroccan Men in Umbria.* Chicago: University of Chicago Press.

Cohen, Jean-Louis, and Monique Eleb. 2002. *Casablanca: Colonial Myth and Architectural Ventures.* New York: Monacelli Press.

Cohen, Shana. 2017. "Analyzing Moroccan 'Youth' in Historical Context: Rethinking the Significance of Social Entrepreneurship." *Middle East–Topics and Arguments* 9: 45–59. https://doi.org/10.17192/meta.2017.9.7584.

Cohen, Shana, and Larabi Jaidi. 2006. *Morocco: Globalization and Its Consequences.* London: Routledge.

Crapanzano, Vincent. 1983. *Tuhami: Portrait of a Moroccan.* Chicago: University of Chicago Press.

Crawford, David, Bart Deseyn, and Abdelkrim Bamouh. 2014. *Nostalgia for the Present: Ethnography and Photography in a Berber Village.* Leiden: Leiden University Press.

Crawford, David, and Rachel Newcomb. 2013. *Encountering Morocco: Fieldwork and Cultural Understanding.* Bloomington: Indiana University Press.

Crétois, Jules. 2018. "Musique: quand le rap Marocain passe à la rap." *Jeune Afrique*, November 29. https://www.jeuneafrique.com/mag/670721/culture/musique-quand-le-rap-marocain-passe-a-la-trap/.

Daadaoui, Mohamed. 2011. *Moroccan Monarchy and the Islamist Challenge: Maintaining Makhzen Power.* London: Palgrave Macmillan.

Dades, Hamid. 1999. "Le premier tremplin musical." *Le Matin*.

Derville, Claire. 2016. "À Sidi Moumen, au Maroc, la danse et la musique pour combattre le fanatisme." *France24*, February 4. https://www.france24.com/fr/20160402-etoiles-sidi -moumen-maroc-art-culture-combattre-integrisme-Nabil-Ayouch.

Desai-Stephens, Anaar, and Nicole Reisnour. 2020. "Musical Feelings and Affective Politics." *Culture, Theory and Critique* 61 (2–3): 99–111. https://doi.org/10.1080/14735784.20 21.1878468.

Despouys, Marion. 2008. "Boulevard, Ma Liberté, Mon Expression . . ." *Exit Magazine* 59 (June): 24–31.

Dialmy, Abdessamad. 2005. "Le terrorisme Islamiste au Maroc." *Social Compass* 52 (1): 67–82.

DJ Key [Douache, Khalid]. 2004. "La Route du Rap: Les Origines du Hip Hop de New York au Maroc." *Le Kounache du Boulevard des Jeunes Musiciens* (May 2004): 12.

Docherty, Thomas. 2016. *Complicity: Criticism between Collaboration and Commitment*. London: Rowman and Littlefield International.

Donzelot, Jacques. 2008. "Michel Foucault and Liberal Intelligence." *Economy and Society* 37 (1): 115–34. https://doi.org/10.1080/03085140701760908.

Doublier, Sara. 2017. "Jokko Fam, la vitrine d'une expérience réussie d'un projet collectif artistique." Radio France International. https://www.rfi.fr/fr/emission/20170924-jokko -fam-vitrine-une-experience-reussie-projet-collectif-artistique.

Duregård, Ludvig. 2016. "This Is Alby: A Documentary." *Connected Action for the Commons*. http://politicalcritique.org/connected-action/2016/this-is-alby-a-documentary/.

Duregård, Ludvig, Karin Lekberg, and Anders Lindgren. 2016. "Connected Action for the Commons: Meet the Hubs: Sweden." http://politicalcritique.org/connected-action/meet -the-hubs/#sweden.

Dwyer, Kevin, and Faqir Muhammad. 1982. *Moroccan Dialogues: Anthropology in Question*. Baltimore, MD: Johns Hopkins University Press.

Dwyer, Kevin. 2013. "Afterword: Anthropologists among Moroccans." In *Encountering Morocco: Fieldwork and Cultural Understanding*, edited by David Crawford and Rachel Newcomb. Bloomington: Indiana University Press.

EAC-L'Boulvart. 2008. *L'Kounache* [The notebook]. Casablanca.

EAC-L'Boulvart. 2009. "Modeles d'un génération." Press release, September 2009.

EAC-L'Boulvart. 2017. "17eme édition du Festival L'Boulevard." Press release, September 26.

Eickelman, Dale. 1976. *Moroccan Islam: Tradition and Society in a Pilgrimage Center*. Austin: University of Texas Press.

El Hamel, Chouki. 2013. *Black Morocco: a History of Slavery, Race, and Islam*. London: Cambridge University Press.

El Guabli, Brahim. 2020a. "Reading for Theory in the Moroccan Marxist-Leninist Testimonial Literature." *African Identities* 18 (1–2): 145–61. https://doi.org/10.1080/14725843.2020 .1773243.

El Guabli, Brahim. 2020b. "The Absent Perpetrators: Morocco's Failed Accountability, Tazmamart Literature and the Survivors' Testinomy for their Jailers (1973–1991)." *Violence: An International Journal* 1 (1): 80–101. https://doi.org/10.1177/2633002420904672.

El Guabli, Brahim. 2022. "Rethinking Archives, Rewriting History: Other-Archives and the Interdisciplinary Approaches to Moroccan History of the 'Years of Lead.'" *History in Africa* 49: 207–34. https://doi.org/10.1017/hia.2022.6.

El Hachimi, Mohamed. 2020. "Power Outside the Institutions: Debating the Metamorphosis of Non-state Actors in North Africa." *Journal of North African Studies* 25 (6): 896–917. https://doi.org/10.1080/13629387.2019.1644921.

El Maarouf, Moulay Driss. 2014. "Nomadictates: Staging Roots and Routes in the Essaouira Gnawa Festival." *Globalizations* 11 (2): 255–71. https://doi.org/10.1080/14747731.2013.814445.

El Maarouf, Moulay Driss, and Taeib Belghazi. 2018. "The Urban and Virtual Rhetoric of *Tcharmil*: Display, Violence and Resistance." *Journal of North African Studies* 23 (1–2): 292–310. https://doi.org/10.1080/13629387.2017.1364630.

El-Issawi, Fatima. 2016. "Moroccan National Media: Between Change and Status Quo." London: London School of Economics Middle East Centre Report.

El-Zein, Rayya S. 2016. *Performing el Rap el ʿArabi 2005–2015: Feeling Politics amid Neoliberal Incursions in Ramallah, Amman, and Beirut.* Unpublished PhD Diss., City University of New York.

Elyachar, Julia. 2005. *Markets of Dispossession: NGOs, Economic Development, and the State in Cairo.* Durham, NC: Duke University Press.

Emperador, Montserrat Badimon. 2007. "Diplômes chômeurs au Maroc: dynamiques de pérennisation d'une action collective plurielle." *L'Année du Maghreb* 3: 279–311. https://doi.org/10.4000/anneemaghreb.376

Es-Sayed, ʿOmar. 2010. *Klam el-Ghiwane* [Words of Ghiwane]. Casablanca: Maṭbʿa al-Njaḥ al-Jadid [New Success Press].

Ewoodzie, Joseph C., Jr. 2017. *Break Beats in the Bronx: Rediscovering Hip Hop's Early Years.* Chapel Hill: University of North Carolina Press.

Fabian, Johannes. 2014 [1983]. *Time and the Other: How Anthropology Makes its Object.* New York: Columbia University Press.

Feher, Michel. 2009. "Self-Appreciation; or, The Aspirations of Human Capital." Translated by Ivan Ascher. *Public Culture* 21 (1): 21–41. https://doi.org/10.1215/08992363-2008-019.

Feld, Steven. 2000. "A Sweet Lullaby for World Music." *Public Culture* 12 (1): 145–71.

Feld, Steven, and Annette Kirkegaard. 2010. "Entangled Complicities in the Prehistory of 'World Music': Poul Rovsing Olsen and Jean Jenkins Encounter Brian Eno and David Byrne in the Bush of Ghosts." *Popular Musicology Online.* http://www.popular-musicology -online.com/issues/04/feld.html.

Ferguson, James. 1999. *Expectations of Modernity: Myths and Meanings of Urban Life on the Zambian Copperbelt.* Berkeley: University of California Press.

Fernandes, Sujatha. 2012. "The Mixtape of the Revolution." *New York Times,* January 29, 2012. https://www.nytimes.com/2012/01/30/opinion/the-mixtape-of-the-revolution.html.

Fernández Parrilla, Gonzalo, and Helio Islán Fernández. 2009. "La leyenda Nass el Ghiwane." *Al-Andalus Maghreb* (16): 149–61.

Fields, Karen E., and Barbara J. Fields. 2012. *Racecraft: The Soul of Inequality in American Life.* New York: Verso.

Fondation Ali Zaoua. n.d. Press booklet. Casablanca, Morocco.

Foucault, Michel. 1983. "Afterword: The Subject and Power." In *Michel Foucault: Beyond Structuralism and Hermeneutics,* edited by Hubert L. Dreyfus and Paul Rabinow, 2nd ed. Chicago: University of Chicago Press.

Foucault, Michel. 1988. *Technologies of the Self: A Seminar with Michel Foucault.* Edited by Luther H. Martin, Huck Gutman, and Patrick H. Hutton. Amherst: University of Massachusetts Press.

Foucault, Michel. 2008. *The Birth of Biopolitics: Lectures at the Collège du France, 1978–1979*. Translated by Graham Burchell. New York: Palgrave Macmillan.

Fredericks, Rosalind. 2014. "'The Old Man Is Dead': Hip Hop and the Arts of Citizenship of Senegalese Youth." *Antipode* 46 (1): 130–48. https://doi.org/10.1111/anti.12036.

French Institute: Alliance Française. 2011. "World Nomads Morocco [festival program]." New York: FI:AF.

Fricke, J., and C. Ahearn. 2002. *Yes Yes Y'all: The Experience Music Project Oral History of Hip-Hop's First Decade*. Cambridge, MA: Da Capo Press.

Frith, Simon. 2000. "The Discourse of World Music." In *Western Music and Its Others: Difference, Representation, and Appropriation in Music*, edited by Georgina Born and Desmond Hesmondhalgh. Berkeley: University of California Press.

Ganti, Tejaswini. 2014. "Neoliberalism." *Annual Review of Anthropology* 43 (2014): 89–104. https://doi.org/10.1146/annurev-anthro-092412-155528.

Gershon, Ilana. 2011. "Neoliberal Agency." *Current Anthropology* 52 (4): 537–55. https://doi.org/10.1086/660866.

Ghayet, Ahmed. 2008. "Post-Scriptum: Musique!" *Aujourd'hui le Maroc*, June 2. https://www.maghress.com/fr/aujourdhui/62102.

Gill, Denise. 2020. "On Theory, Citational Practices and Personal Accountability in the Study of Music and Affect." *Culture, Theory and Critique* 61 (2–3): 338–57. https://doi.org/10.1080/14735784.2020.1893486.

Gilmore, Ruth Wilson. 1998. "Globalization and US Prison Growth: From Military Keynesianism to Post-Keynesian Militarism." *Race and Class* 40 (2–3): 171–87. https://doi.org/10.1177/030639689904000212.

Gilroy, Paul. 1993. *The Black Atlantic: Modernity and Double Consciousness*. Cambridge, MA: Harvard University Press.

Gilson-Miller, Susan. 2013. *A History of Modern Morocco*. Cambridge: Cambridge University Press.

Gosa, Travis. 2015. "The Fifth Element: Knowledge." In *The Cambridge Companion to Hip Hop*, edited by Justin A. Williams. Cambridge: Cambridge University Press.

Gouyon, Marien. 2018. "La sincérité des sentiments et des mots. Les logiques essentialisantes d'une économie morale occidentale des homosexualités masculines au Maroc." *L'année du Maghreb* 18: 111–26. https://doi.org/10.4000/anneemaghreb.3616.

Government of Morocco. 2005. *Rapport général: 50 ans de développement humain et perspectives 2025. Rapport commandité par SM le Roi Mohammed VI à l'occasion de la célébration du cinquantenaire de l'indépendance du Maroc.*

Graeber, David. 2001. *Toward an Anthropological Theory of Value: The False Coin of Our Own Dreams*. New York: Palgrave.

Graiouid, Said. 2010. "The Particular and the Transnational in Moroccan Youth Music: Hip Hop Music and its Reception among Moroccan Youth." Talk given at Qalam wa Lawh Center for Arabic Study, Rabat, Morocco, April 24.

Graiouid, Said. 2021. "The Intellectual as *Zaṭāṭ*: The Public Sphere, the State, and the Field of Contentious Politics in Morocco." *Journal of North African Studies* 26 (6): 1221–45. https://doi.org/10.1080/13629387.2020.1768853.

Graiouid, Said, and Taieb Belghazi. 2013. "Cultural Production and Cultural Patronage in Morocco: The State, the Islamists, and the Field of Culture." *Journal of African Cultural Studies* 25 (3): 261–74. https://doi.org/10.1080/13696815.2013.822795.

Gramsci, Antonio. 1992. *Prison Notebooks: Volume 1*. Edited by Joseph A. Buttigieg. Translated by Joseph A. Buttigieg and Antonio Callari. New York: Columbia University Press.

Greene, Douglas. 2008. "Moroccan Royal Family Holding ONA Fires CEO." Reprinted as "US Embassy Cables: Moroccan Sacking Exposes King's Business Role." *The Guardian*, December 6, 2010. https://www.theguardian.com/world/us-embassy-cables-documents/151131.

Grue, Jan. 2016. "The Problem with Inspiration Porn: A Tentative Definition and a Provisional Critique." *Disability and Society* 31 (6): 838–49. https://psycnet.apa.org/doi/10.1080/09687599.2016.1205473.

Guessous, Nadia. 2011. *Genealogies of Feminism: Leftist Feminist Subjectivity in the Wake of the Islamic Revival in Contemporary Morocco*. Unpublished PhD Diss., Columbia University.

Guilbault, Jocelyne. 1993. "On Redefining the 'Local' through World Music." *World of Music* 35 (2): 33–47.

Guilbault, Jocelyne. 1997. "Interpreting World Music: A Challenge in Theory and Practice." *Popular Music* 16 (1): 31–44. https://doi.org/10.1017/S0261143000000684.

Haddad, Lahcen. 2001. *Le résiduel et l'émergent: le devenir des structures sociales traditionnelles (le cas de la tribu hors et dans le ville)*. Rabat: Publications de la Faculté des Lettres.

Haddad, Lahcen. 2009. "Women Singers and Representations of *Nashat* in Popular Culture." *Langues et Litteratures* 19: 197–205.

Haeri, Niloofar. 2017a. "The Sincere Subject: Mediation and Interiority among a Group of Muslim Women in Iran." *HAU: Journal of Ethnographic Theory* 7 (1). https://doi.org/10.14318/hau7.1.014.

Hafez, Sherine. 2013. "Will the Rational Religious Subject Please Stand Up? Muslim Subjects and the Analytics of Religion." In *Anthropology of the Middle East and North Africa: Into the New Millennium*, edited by Sherine Hafez and Susan Slyomovics. Indianapolis: Indiana University Press.

Hajer, Charlotte. 2015. "The Economy of Mental Health: Inequalities in Access to Care in Morocco." *Jadaliyya*. https://www.jadaliyya.com/Details/31935.

Hamil, Mustapha. 2010. "Plotting Terrorism: Mahi Binebine's Les Etoiles de Sidi Moumen." *International Journal of Francophone Studies* 14 (4): 549–69. https://doi.org/10.1386/ijfs.14.4.549_7.

Hammoudi, Abdellah. 1997. *Master and Disciple: The Cultural Foundations of Moroccan Authoritarianism*. Chicago: University of Chicago Press.

Hammoudi, Abdellah, and John Borneman. 2009. *Being There: The Fieldwork Encounter and the Making of Truth*. Berkeley and Los Angeles: University of California Press.

Harit, Fouad. 2013a. "Maroc: Vers une loi contre le racisme envers les Noirs?" Afrik.com, July 22, 2013. http://www.afrik.com/maroc-vers-une-loi-contre-le-racisme-envers-les-noirs

Harit, Fouad. 2013b. "Maroc: Mohammed VI veut régulariser les sans-papiers." Afrik.com, September 11, 2013. http://www.afrik.com/maroc-mohammed-vi-veut-regulariser-les-sans-papiers

Harmach, Amine. 2008. "Concours Génération Mawazine: les groupes 'Tigresse Flow,' 'Sakadoya' et 'Taghrast' primés." *Aujourd'hui le Maroc*, May 26. https://aujourdhui.ma/culture/concours-generation-mawazine-les-groupes-tigresse-flow-sakadoya-et-taghrast-primes-56940.

Harmach, Amine. 2009a. "On est resté SDF pendant quatre ans." *Aujourd'hui le Maroc*, March 24. https://www.maghress.com/fr/aujourdhui/67840.

Harmach, Amine. 2009b. "Un don royal de 2 millions DH sauve L'Boulevard." *Aujourd'hui le Maroc*, June 18. https://www.maghress.com/fr/aujourdhui/69694.

Harrison, Anthony Kwame. 2006. "'Cheaper than a CD, Plus We Really Mean It': Bay Area Underground Hip Hop Tapes as Subcultural Artefacts." *Popular Music* 25 (2): 283–301. https://doi.org/10.1017/S0261143006000833.

Harrison, Anthony Kwame. 2009. *Hip Hop Underground: The Integrity and Ethics of Racial Identification*. Philadelphia, PA: Temple University Press.

Harvey, David. 2005. *A Brief History of Neoliberalism*. Oxford: Oxford University Press.

Heckman, Alma. 2021. *The Sultan's Communists: Moroccan Jews and the Politics of Belonging*. Stanford, CA: Stanford University Press.

Hesmondhalgh, Desmond, and Sarah Baker. 2010. "'A Very Complicated Version of Freedom': Conditions and Experiences of Creative Labour in Three Cultural Industries." *Poetics* 38: 4–20. https://doi.org/10.1016/j.poetic.2009.10.001.

Hibou, Beatrice. 2015. *The Bureaucratization of the World in the Neoliberal Era: An International and Comparative Perspective*. New York: Palgrave Macmillan.

Hibou, Beatrice, and Irene Bono, eds. 2016. *Le gouvernement du social au Maroc*. Paris: Karthala.

Hilgers, Mathieu. 2011. "The Three Anthropological Approaches to Neoliberalism." *International Social Science Journal* 61: 351–64. https://doi.org/10.1111/j.1468-2451.2011.01 776.x.

Hilgers, Mathieu. 2013. "Embodying Neoliberalism: Thoughts and Responses to Critics." *Social Anthropology* 21(1): 75–89. http://dx.doi.org/10.1111/1469-8676.12010.

Hillali, Mimoun. 2007. *La politique du tourisme au Maroc: diagnostic, bilan et critique*. Paris: L'Harmattan.

Hochschild, Arlie Russell. 2012 [1983]. *The Managed Heart: Commercialization of Human Feeling*. 3rd edition. Berkeley: University of California Press.

Holt, K. C. 2020. "Emcee Ethnographies: A Brief Sketch of U.S. Hip-Hop Ethnography." *Current Musicology* (105). https://doi.org/10.7916/cm.v0i105.5400.

Hutcheon, Emily, and Bonnie Lashewicz. 2014. "Theorizing Resilience: Critiquing and Unbounding a Marginalizing Concept." *Disability and Society* 29 (9): 1383–97. https://doi.org/10.1080/09687599.2014.934954.

Jackson, John L. 2005. *Real Black: Adventures in Racial Sincerity*. Chicago: University of Chicago Press.

Jackson, John L. 2010. "On Ethnographic Sincerity." *Current Anthropology* 51 (Supplement 2): S279-S287. https://doi.org/10.1086/653129.

Jadraoui, Siham. 2009. "Génération Mawazine est de retour." *Aujourd'hui le Maroc*, March 18. https://www.maghress.com/fr/aujourdhui/67734.

James, Robin. 2015. *Resilience and Melancholy: Pop Music, Feminism, Neoliberalism*. New York: Zero Books.

Jeffers, Mary. 2012. "Hip Hop, Soccer, and Women's Voices." *Take Five Blog*, March 8. https://blogs.gwu.edu/ipdgcsmartpower/2012/03/08/hip-hop-soccer-and-womens-voices/.

Jones, Benjamin Miller. 2023. "Nass el Ghiwane: Radical Aesthetics in Moroccan Popular Music." Unpublished master's thesis, Georgetown University, Washington, DC.

Joseph, Jonathan. 2013. "Resilience as Embedded Neoliberalism: A Governmentality Approach." *Resilience: International Policies, Practices and Discourses* 1 (1): 38–52. https://doi.org/10.1080/21693293.2013.765741.

Joseph, Karine, and Ileana Marchesani, eds. 2010. *'Omar Sayed raconte Nass el-Ghiwane*. Milan and Paris: Senso Unico Éditions and Éditions du Sirocco.

Kabel, Ahmed. 2021. "The Neoliberal Linguistic Consensus: Neoliberal Multilingualism and Linguistic Governmentality in Morocco." *Journal of North African Studies* 28 (4): 788–814. https://doi.org/10.1080/13629387.2021.1932481.

Kamili, Sabrina, Mehdi Azdem, and Driss Ksikes. 2021. "Industries Culturelles et Créatives Maroc: Musique, Édition, Arts de la Scène." Casablanca: K&Co.

Kapchan, Deborah. 1996. *Gender on the Market: Moroccan Women and the Revoicing of Tradition*. Philadelphia: University of Pennsylvania Press.

Kapchan, Deborah. 2007. *Traveling Spirit Masters: Moroccan Gnawa Trance and Music in the Global Marketplace*. Middletown, CT: Wesleyan University Press.

Kapchan, Deborah. 2008. "The Promise of Sonic Translation: Performing the Festive Sacred in Morocco." *American Anthropologist* 110 (4): 467–83. https://doi.org/10.1111/j.1548-1433.2008.00079.x.

Kapchan, Deborah. 2009. "Learning to Listen: The Sound of Sufism in France." *World of Music* 51 (2): 65–89. http://dx.doi.org/10.2307/41699883.

Karl, Brian. 2016. "The Coming of Americans: Moroccan Popular Music, Modernity, and Mimetic Encounters." *Journal of North African Studies* 19 (3): 358–75. http://dx.doi.org/10.1080/13629387.2014.884365.

Katz, Mark. 2012. *Groove Music: The Art and Culture of the Hip Hop DJ*. New York: Oxford University Press.

Katz, Mark. 2020. *Build: The Power of Hip Hop Diplomacy in a Divided World*. New York: Oxford University Press.

Keane, Webb. 2002. "Sincerity, 'Modernity,' and the Protestants." *Cultural Anthropology* 17 (1): 65–92. https://doi.org/10.1525/can.2002.17.1.65.

Khabeer, Su'ad Abdul. 2016. *Muslim Cool: Race, Religion, and Hip Hop in the United States*. New York: New York University Press.

Khalil, Andrea. 2012. "The Political Crowd: Theorizing Popular Revolt in North Africa." *Contemporary Islam* 6: 45–65. https://doi.org/10.1007/s11562-011-0182-7.

Kheshti, Roshanak. 2015. *Modernity's Ear: Listening to Race and Gender in World Music*. New York: New York University Press.

Kim, Tammy E., and Michael Veal. 2016. *Punk Ethnography: Artists and Scholars Listen to Sublime Frequencies*. Middletown, CT: Wesleyan University Press.

Kiwan, Nadia. 2014. "Moroccan Multiplicities: Performing Transnationalism and Alternative Nationalism in the Contemporary Urban Music Scene." *Cahiers d'Études Africaines* 54 (216): 975–97. https://doi.org/10.4000/ETUDESAFRICAINES.17905.

Kohstall, Florian. 2015. "From Reform to Resistance: Universities and Student Mobilisation in Egypt and Morocco before and after the Arab Uprisings." *British Journal of Middle Eastern Studies* 42 (1): 59–73. http://dx.doi.org/10.1080/13530194.2015.973183.

Konbini. 2018. "Avec Shayfeen, Toto et Madd, têtes d'affiche du rap Marocain." Posted by Konbini, November 8. YouTube. https://www.youtube.com/watch?v=GV4uRa_BvZM.

Kreitmeyr, Nadine. 2019. "Neoliberal Co-Optation and Authoritarian Renewal: Social Entrepreneurship Networks in Jordan and Morocco." *Globalizations* 16 (3): 289–303. https://doi.org/10.1080/14747731.2018.1502492.

KVINFO. 2014. "Moroccan Rap Is the Voice of the People." *KVINFO.dk*, May 2. http://kvinfo.dk/moroccan-rap-is-the-voice-of-the-people/?lang=en.

Kydd, Jonathan, and Sophie Thoyer. 1992. "Structural Adjustment and Moroccan Agriculture: An Assessment of the Reforms in the Sugar and Cereal Sectors." OECD Development Centre Working Paper No. 70.

La Rédaction, the editors. 2018. "Casablanca: cloture en beauté du festival Sbagha Bagha." *Ya Biladi*, July 7. https://www.yabiladi.com/articles/details/66815/casablanca-cloture-beaute-festival-sbagha.html.

La Vie Éco, editors. 2008. "Future gare de Casa-port: les travaux commencent." *La Vie Éco*, May 16. https://www.lavieeco.com/en-direct/future-gare-de-casa-port-les-travaux-commencent-8579/.

Laidlaw, James. 2014. *The Subject of Virtue: An Anthropology of Ethics and Freedom.* Cambridge: Cambridge University Press.

Lambek, Michael. 2008. "Value and Virtue." *Anthropological Theory* 8 (2): 133–57. https://doi.org/10.1177/1463499608090788.

Le Matin. 2009. "Musique. Casa Crew révèle 'Kayna Fawda.'" *LeMatin.com*, January 12. https://lematin.ma/journal/2009/Musique_Casa-Crew-revele-Kayna-Fawda/105528.html.

Libération. 2010. "Première étape du Concours Génération Mawazine: coup d'envoi des compétitions à Meknès." *Libération*, March 18.

Livermon, Xavier. 2020. *Kwaito Bodies: Remastering Space and Subjectivity in Post-Apartheid South Africa.* Durham, NC: Duke University Press.

Loudiy, Fadoua. 2014. *Transitional Justice and Human Rights in Morocco: Negotiating the Years of Lead.* New York: Taylor and Francis.

Maghraoui, Abdeslam. 2001a. "Political Authority in Crisis: Mohammed VI's Morocco." *Middle East Report* 218 (Spring): 12–17.

Maghraoui, Abdeslam. 2001b. "Monarchy and Political Reform in Morocco." *Journal of Democracy* 12(1): 73–86. https://doi.org/10.1353/jod.2001.0010.

Maghraoui, Abdeslam. 2002. "Democratization in the Arab World? Depoliticization in Morocco." *Journal of Democracy* 13 (4): 24–32. https://doi.org/10.1353/jod.2002.0070.

Maghrebia. 2007. "Interview avec le rapper Marocain Bigg." *Maghrebia*. http://magharebia.com/fr/articles/awi/features/2007/05/30/feature-02?change_locale=true.

Magidow, Melanie. 2016. "Trending Classic: The Cultural Register of Moroccan *Malhun* Poetry." *Journal of North African Studies* 21 (2): 310–34. https://doi.org/10.1080/13629387.2016.1130943.

Mahmood, Saba. 2001. "Rehearsed Spontaneity and the Conventionality of Ritual: Disciplines of 'Salāt.'" *American Ethnologist* 28 (4): 827–53.

Mahmood, Saba. 2005. *The Politics of Piety: The Islamic Revival and the Feminist Subject.* Princeton, NJ: Princeton University Press.

Mamdani, Mahmood. 2004. *Good Muslim, Bad Muslim: America, the Cold War and the Roots of Terror.* New York: Doubleday.

Marcus, George E. 1997. "The Uses of Complicity in the Changing Mise-en-Scène of Anthropological Fieldwork." *Representations* 59: 85–108.

Maroc Cultures. 2017. *Festival Mawazine rythmes du monde.* Press book. Rabat: Maroc Cultures Association.

Matlon, Jordanna. 2016. "Racial Capitalism and the Crisis of Black Masculinity." *American Sociological Review* 81 (5): 1014–38. https://doi.org/10.1177/0003122416658294.

Mavelli, Luca. 2019. "Resilience beyond Neoliberalism? Mystique of Complexity, Financial Crises, and the Reproduction of Neoliberal Life." *Resilience: International Policies, Practices and Discourses* 7 (3): 224–39. https://doi.org/10.1080/21693293.2019.1605661.

McClanahan, Annie. 2019. "Serious Crises: Rethinking the Neoliberal Subject." *boundary 2* 46 (1): 103–32. https://doi.org/10.1215/01903659-7271363.

McNay, Lois. 2009. "Self as Enterprise: Dilemmas of Control and Resistance in Foucault's *The Birth of Biopolitics.*" *Theory, Culture and Society* 26 (6): 55–77. https://doi.org/10.1177/0263276409347697.

Meintjes, Louise. 2004. *Sound of Africa! Making Music Zulu in a South African Studio.* Durham, NC: Duke University Press.

Meintjes, Louise. 2017. *Dust of the Zulu: Ngoma Aesthetics after Apartheid.* Durham, NC: Duke University Press.

Melamed, Jodi. 2015. "Racial Capitalism." *Critical Ethnic Studies* 1 (1): 76–85. https://doi.org/10.5749/jcritethnstud.1.1.0076.

Mellema, Gregory. 2016. *Complicity and Moral Accountability.* Notre Dame, IN: Notre Dame Press.

Miller, Catherine, and Dominique Caubet. 2012. "Langue et textes: des Ghiwanes à la nouvelle scène avant et après le 20 Fèvrier." https://shs.hal.science/halshs-00682688.

Miller, Catherine. 2017. "Contemporary Dārija Writings in Morocco: Ideology and Practices." In *The Politics of Written Language in the Arab World: Writing Change*, edited by Jacob Høigilt and Gunvor Mejdell. London: Brill.

Mirowski, Philip, and Dieter Plehwe, eds. 2015. *The Road from Mont Pèlerin: The Making of the Neoliberal Thought Collective.* Cambridge, MA: Harvard University Press.

Morcom, Anna. 2020. "Music, Exchange, and the Production of Value: A Case Study of Hindustani Music." In *The Oxford Handbook of Economic Ethnomusicology*, edited by Anna Morcom and Timothy Taylor. New York: Oxford University Press.

Morgan, Marcyliena H. 2009. *The Real Hiphop: Battling for Knowledge, Power, and Respect in the LA Underground.* Durham, NC: Duke University Press.

Moten, Fred. 2003. *In the Break: The Aesthetics of the Black Radical Tradition.* Minneapolis: University of Minnesota Press.

Muehlebach, Andrea. 2012. *The Moral Neoliberal: Welfare and Citizenship in Italy.* Chicago: University of Chicago Press.

Muhanna, Elias. 2003. "Folk the Casbah: A Conversation with Omar Sayyed, Leader of Nass el-Ghiwane." *Transition* 94: 132–49.

Mundy, Jacob. 2006. "Neutrality or Complicity? The United States and the 1975 Moroccan Takeover of the Spanish Sahara." *Journal of North African Studies* 11 (3): 275–306. https://doi.org/10.1080/13629380600803001.

NAAR. 2018. "Manifesto." http://naar.fr/about/.

Narotzky, Susana, and Niko Besnier. 2014. "Crisis, Value, and Hope: Rethinking the Economy: An Introduction to Supplement 9." *Current Anthropology* 55 (Supplement 9): S4–S16. https://doi.org/10.1086/676327.

Nielsen, Erik, et al. 2015. "*Amici Curiae* Brief of Erik Nielson, Charis S. Kubrin, Travis L. Gosa, Michael Render (aka 'Killer Mike') and Other Scholars and Artists in Support of Petitioner [Taylor Bell]." Washington, DC.

Nielsen, Erik, and Andrea Dennis. 2019. *Rap on Trial: Race, Lyrics, and Guilt in America.* New York: The New Press.

Neocleous, Mark. 2013. "Resisting Resilience." *Radical Philosophy* 178: 2–7.

Nettl, Bruno. 2010. "A Tradition of Self-Critique." In *Nettl's Elephant: On the History of Ethnomusicology.* Chicago: University of Illinois Press.

Nickell, Chris. 2020. *Masculinities under Pressure in Beirut's Independent Music Scenes.* Unpublished PhD Diss., New York University.

Nooshin, Laudan. 2005. "Subversion and Counter-Subversion: Power, Control and Meaning in the New Iranian Pop Music." In *Music, Power and Politics*, edited by A. J. Randall. London: Routledge.

Nsouli, Saleh M., et al. 1995. *Resilience and Growth through Sustained Adjustment: The Moroccan Experience.* Washington, DC: International Monetary Fund.

Nuti, Alasia. 2019. *Injustice and the Reproduction of History: Structural Inequalities, Gender and Redress.* Cambridge: Cambridge University Press.

Ong, Aihwa. 2006. *Neoliberalism as Exception: Mutations in Citizenship and Sovereignty.* Durham, NC: Duke University Press.

Oukaf, Youssra. 2012. "MC Soultana on Respect." *World Hip Hop Market.* http://worldhi phopmarket.com/mc-soultana-on-respect-a-word-that-new-moroccan-female-mcs - are-searching-for/4440.

Pandolfo, Stefania. 2006. "Bghit n'anni hnaya (Je veux chanter ici): voix et témoignage en marge d'une rencontre psychiatrique." *Arabica* 53 (2): 232–79.

Park, Thomas K., and Aomar Boum. 2005. *Historical Dictionary of Morocco.* 2nd edition. Lanham, MD: Scarecrow Press.

Pennell, C. R. 2000. *Morocco since 1830: A History.* New York: New York University Press.

Pennell, C. R. 2001. "The Geography of Piracy: Northern Morocco in the Mid-Nineteenth Century." In *Bandits at Sea: A Pirates Reader*, edited by C. R. Pennell. New York: NYU Press.

Péristiany, Jean G., ed. 1966. *Honour and Shame: The Values of Mediterranean Society.* Chicago: University of Chicago Press.

Perry, Marc D. 2008. "Global Black Self-Fashionings: Hip Hop as Diasporic Space." *Identities* 15 (6): 635–64. https://doi.org/10.1080/10702890802470660.

Perry, Marc D. 2016. *Negro Soy Yo: Hip Hop and Raced Citizenship in Neoliberal Cuba.* Durham, NC: Duke University Press.

Pestcoe, Shlomo, and Greg C. Adams. 2018. "Banjo Roots Research: Changing Perspectives on the Banjo's African American Origins and West African Heritage." In *Banjo Roots and Branches*, edited by Robert B. Winans. Urbana: University of Illinois Press.

Pfeifer, Karen. 1999. "How Tunisia, Morocco, Jordan and Even Egypt Became IMF 'Success Stories' in the 1990s." *Middle East Report* (210): 23–27.

Piekut, Benjamin. 2014. "Actor-Networks in Music History: Clarifications and Critiques." *Twentieth-Century Music* 11 (2): 191–215. http://dx.doi.org/10.1017/S147857221400005X.

Pieprzak, Katarzyna. 2016. "Zones of Perceptual Enclosure: The Aesthetics of Immobility in Casablanca's Literary Bidonvilles." *Research in African Literatures* 47 (3): 32–49. http:// dx.doi.org/10.2979/reseafrilite.47.3.03.

Pine, Jason. 2016. "Last Chance Incorporated." *Cultural Anthropology* 31 (2): 297–318.

Porter, Geoffrey. 2001. "From Madrasa to Maison d'Hôte: Historic Preservation in Mohammed VI's Morocco." *Middle East Report* 218 (Spring): 34–37.

Powers, Paul. 2004. "Interiors, Intentions, and the 'Spirituality' of Islamic Ritual Practice." *Journal of the American Academy of Religion* 71 (2): 425–59. https://doi.org/10.1093/jaarel/lfho36.

Quinn, Eithne. 2005. *Nuthin' But a "G" Thang: the Culture and Commerce of Gangsta Rap*. New York: Columbia University Press.

Rabinow, Paul. 1997 [2007]. *Reflections on Fieldwork in Morocco*. Berkeley: University of California Press.

Rabinow, Paul, and Nicholas Rose, eds. 2003. *The Essential Foucault*. New York: The New Press.

Raiss, Sarah. 2009. "Morocco: All-Girl Moroccan Rap Bands Break New Ground." Reuters, March 17. https://reuters.screenocean.com/record/711758.

Ramírez, J. Jesse. 2021. "Keeping It Unreal: Rap, Racecraft, and MF Doom." *Humanities* 10: 5. https://doi.org/10.3390/h10010005.

Read, Jason. 2009. "A Genealogy of Homo-Economicus: Neoliberalism and the Production of Subjectivity." *Foucault Studies* 6: 25–36. http://dx.doi.org/10.22439/fs.v0i0.2465.

Reed, Trevor, et al. 2023. "Listen, Watch Your Step." Charles Seeger Lecture (Keynote) at Society for Ethnomusicology Annual Meeting. Ottawa, Canada.

Regier, Terry, and Muhammad Ali Khalidi. 2009. "The 'Arab Street': Tracking a Political Metaphor." *Middle East Journal* 63 (1): 11–29. http://dx.doi.org/10.3751/63.1.11.

Rhannan, Maha. 2019. "Casablanca Jungle: Music and Positive Youth Development in Morocco." Unpublished master's thesis, University of Amsterdam.

Rinker, Courtney. 2020. "Problematizing Neoliberalism and Development: Creating Citizens (and Future Citizens) through Reproduction and Childrearing in Morocco." *Hespéris-Tamuda* 55 (4): 151–72.

Robinson, Dylan. 2020. *Hungry Listening: Resonant Theory for Indigenous Sound Studies*. Minneapolis: University of Minnesota Press.

Rogers, Amanda E. 2012. "Warding off Terrorism and Revolution: Moroccan Religious Pluralism, National Identity and the Politics of Visual Culture." *Journal of North African Studies* 17 (3): 455–74. https://doi.org/10.1080/13629387.2012.657882.

Rollefson, J. Griffith. 2017. *Flip the Script: European Hip Hop and the Politics of Postcoloniality*. Chicago: University of Chicago Press.

Rose, Tricia. 1994. *Black Noise: Rap Music and Black Culture in Contemporary America*. Middletown, CT: Wesleyan University Press.

Rosen, Lawrence. 1984. *Bargaining for Reality: The Construction of Social Relations in a Moroccan Community*. Chicago: University of Chicago Press.

Rudnyckyj, Daromir. 2010. *Spiritual Economies: Islam, Globalization, and the Afterlife of Development*. Ithaca, NY: Cornell University Press.

Rynell, Julia, and Subtopia. 2016. "This is Alby 2015 – English." Posted by Subtopia Botkyrka April 21, 2016, YouTube. https://www.youtube.com/watch?v=OIlxaQkPj_w.

Saadi, Meryem. 2012. "Portrait. Rap Psychédélique." *TelQuel* 510 (February 23–30). https://telquel.ma/2012/02/23/portrait-rap-psychedelique_1225.

Sabry, Tarik. 2010. *Cultural Encounters in the Arab World: On Media, the Modern and the Everyday*. London: I. B. Tauris.

Sadiq, Abdelhaï. 2014. *Nass el-Ghiwane: 40 ans de chanson protestataire Marocaine*. Marrakesh: Self-published.

Saghi, Omar. 2016. *Comprendre la monarchie Marocaine*. Casablanca: La Croisée des Chemins.

Salime, Zakia. 2015. "'I Vote, I Sing': The Rise of Aesthetic Citizenship in Morocco." *International Journal of Middle East Studies* 47: 36–139. https://doi.org/10.1017/S0020 743814001494.

Salime, Zakia. 2022. "Soundtracks of Citizenship: Social and Political Genealogies of Moroccan Hip Hop." *Journal of North African Studies* 29 (1): 131–52. https://doi.org /10.1080/13629387.2022.2089125.

Salois, Kendra. 2012. "Jihad against Jihad against Jihad." *The New Inquiry* 1 (9).

Salois, Kendra. 2013. *The Networked Self: Hip Hop Musicking and Muslim Identities in Neoliberal Morocco*. Unpublished PhD Diss., University of California, Berkeley.

Salois, Kendra. 2014. "Make Some Noise, Drari: Embodied Listening and Counterpublic Formations in Moroccan Hip Hop." *Anthropological Quarterly* 87 (4): 1017–48. http:// dx.doi.org/10.1353/anq.2014.0054.

Salois, Kendra. 2018. "The 'Schizophrenic Nation': Ethics of Critique in Morocco's Post-Arab Spring Popular Music." *Journal of World Popular Music* 5 (1): 88–107. https://doi .org/10.1558/jwpm.36675.

Samie, Amale. 2001. "Les adorateurs de Larsen." *Maroc Hebdo International* 454 (March 2–8).

Samie, Amale. 2004. "Culture: Être underground ou ne pas être." *TelQuel* 127 (May 15–21). http://www.telquel-online.com/archives/127/sujet6.shtml.

Samie, Amale. 2018 [2004]. "L'histoire du Marock." In *L'kounache dial tonton: les chroniques d'Amale Samie pour Boulevard*. Casablanca: EAC-L'Boulvart.

Sanders, Mark. 2002. *Complicities: The Intellectual and Apartheid*. Durham, NC: Duke University Press.

Scharff, Christina. 2016. "The Psychic Life of Neoliberalism: Mapping the Contours of Entrepreneurial Subjectivity." *Theory, Culture and Society* 33 (6): 107–22. https://doi .org/10.1177/0263276415590164.

Schloss, Joseph G. 2004. *Making Beats: The Art of Sample-Based Hip Hop*. Middletown, CT: Wesleyan University Press.

Schloss, Joseph G. 2009. *Foundation: B-Boys, B-Girls and Hip Hop Culture in New York*. London: Oxford University Press.

Schmoll, Katharina. 2021. "Listening as a Citizenship Practice Post-Arab Spring: Mediated Civic Listening as a Struggle, Duty and Joy in Urban Morocco." *Media, Culture and Society* 43 (1): 84–100. https://doi.org/10.1177/0163443720939455.

Schroeter, Daniel. 1988. *Merchants of Essaouira: Urban Society and Imperialism in Southwestern Morocco, 1844–1886*. Cambridge: Cambridge University Press.

Schuyler, Philip D. 1984. "Berber Professional Musicians in Performance." In *Performance Practice: Ethnomusicological Perspectives*, edited by Gerard Béhague. Westport, CT: Greenwood Press.

Schuyler, Philip D. 1993. "A Folk Revival in Morocco." In *Everyday Life in the Muslim Middle East*, edited by Donna Lee Bowen and Evelyn Early, 1st ed., 287–93. Bloomington: Indiana University Press.

Scott, David. 2004. *Conscripts of Modernity: The Tragedy of Colonial Enlightenment*. Durham, NC: Duke University Press.

Sefrioui, Kenza. 2014. *La revue Souffles 1966–1973: espoirs de révolution culturelle au Maroc.* Casablanca: Éditions du Sirocco.

Seilstad, Brian, and Mehdi Essiffi. 2015. "Hip Hop Culture in a Small Moroccan City." *Journal of Hip Hop Studies* 2 (1): 1–34. https://doi.org/10.34718/6G9D-HV05.

Seligman, Adam B., Robert P. Weller, Michael J. Puett, and Bennett Simon. 2008. *Ritual and Its Consequences: An Essay on the Limits of Sincerity.* Oxford: Oxford University Press.

Serfaty, Abraham. 1970. "Salut aux Afro-Americans." *Souffles* 16–17 (1969–70): 32–34.

Shank, Barry. 2014. *The Political Force of Musical Beauty.* Durham, NC: Duke University Press.

Sharma, Nitasha Tamar. 2010. *Hip Hop Desis: South Asian Americans, Blackness, and a Global Race Consciousness.* Durham, NC: Duke University Press.

Shipley, Jesse Weaver. 2013. *Living the Hiplife: Celebrity and Entrepreneurship in Ghanaian Popular Music.* Durham, NC: Duke University Press.

Silver, Christopher. 2020. "The Sounds of Nationalism: Music, Moroccanism, and the Making of Samy Elmaghribi." *International Journal of Middle East Studies* 52: 23–47. https://doi.org/10.1017/S0020743819000941.

Simonian, Jacques. 2018. "Êtes-vous prêts pour la trap Marocaine?" *LesInrockuptibles,* February 23. https://www.lesinrocks.com/musique/etes-vous-prets-pour-la-trap-maro caine-135844–23–02–2018/.

Simour, LHoussain. 2016. *Larbi Batma, Nass el-Ghiwane and Postcolonial Music in Morocco.* Jefferson, NC: McFarland and Company.

Skeggs, Beverly. 2004. "Exchange Value and Affect: Bourdieu and the Self." In *Feminism after Bourdieu,* edited by L. Adkins and B. Skeggs. Oxford: Blackwell.

Skeggs, Beverly. 2014. "Values beyond Value? Is Anything beyond the Logic of Capital?" *British Journal of Sociology* 65 (1): 1–20. https://doi.org/10.1111/1468-4446.12072.

Skinner, Ryan Thomas. 2019. "Walking, Talking, Remembering: n Afro-Swedish Critique of Being-in-the-World." *African and Black Diaspora: An International Journal* 12 (1): 1–19. https://doi.org/10.1080/17528631.2018.1467747.

Slimani, Leila. 2012. "Maroc: rappeurs et sans reproches." *Jeune Afrique,* January 3. https://www.jeuneafrique.com/143179/politique/maroc-rappeurs-et-sans-reproches/.

Slobodian, Quinn. 2018. *Globalists: The End of Empire and the Birth of Neoliberalism.* Cambridge, MA: Harvard University Press.

Slyomovics, Susan. 2001. "A Truth Commission for Morocco." *Middle East Report* 218: 18–21.

Slyomovics, Susan. 2005. *The Performance of Human Rights in Morocco.* Philadelphia: University of Pennsylvania Press.

Smith, Troy L. 2010. "Interview with Buddy Esquire." In *Break Beats in the Bronx: Rediscovering Hip Hop's Early Years,* edited by Joseph C. Ewoodzie, Joseph C. Chapel Hill: University of North Carolina Press.

Sonay, Ali. 2017. "Radio and Political Change: Listening in Contemporary Morocco." *Journal of North African Studies* 22 (3): 411–34. https://doi.org/10.1080/13629387.2017.1307903.

Spence, Lester. 2011. *Stare in the Darkness: The Limits of Hip-Hop and Black Politics.* Minneapolis: University of Minnesota Press.

Sqalli, Mohamed, with Nicolas Griyeb. 2017. "What If We Let It up to Arab Artists to Be the Ones to Tell Their (Hi)story?" Translated by Meriem Bennani. *Medium.* https://medium.com/@mohamedsqalli/what-if-we-let-it-up-to-arab-artists-to-be-the-ones -to-tell-their-hi-story-ca8a65fd8712.

Stanyek, Jason, and Benjamin Piekut. 2010. "Deadness: Technologies of the Intermundane." *TDR: The Drama Review* 54 (1): 14–38. http://dx.doi.org/10.2307/40650520.

Stein, Rebecca Luna. 1998. "National Itineraries, Itinerant Nations: Israeli Tourism and Palestinian Cultural Production." *Social Text* 56: 91–124.

Strava, Cristiana. 2018. "A Tramway Called Atonement: Genealogies of Infrastructure and Emerging Political Imaginaries in Contemporary Casablanca." *Middle East-Topics and Arguments* 10: 22–29.

Strava, Cristiana. 2020. "Dissenting Poses: Marginal Youth, Viral Aesthetics, and Affective Politics in Neoliberal Morocco." *Focaal—Journal of Global and Historical Anthropology* (2020): 1–18. http://dx.doi.org/10.3167/fcl.2020.072005.

Struch, Rebecca. 2022. "Confronting Coloniality's Unpayable Debts." *Performance Research* 27 (5): 74–84. https://doi.org/10.1080/13528165.2022.2160905.

Stuckey, Mary. 2013. "Soultana: 'The Voice of Women' Raps in Morocco." *The World*, August 15. https://theworld.org/stories/2013/08/15/soultana-voice-women-raps-morocco

Swearingen, Will D. 1988. *Moroccan Mirages: Agrarian Dreams and Deceptions, 1912–1986.* London: I. B. Tauris and Co.

Taylor, Timothy. 1997. *Global Pop: World Music, World Markets.* New York: Routledge.

Taylor, Timothy. 2014. "Thirty Years of World Music." *Journal of World Popular Music* 1 (2): 192–200. https://doi.org/10.1558/jwpm.v1i2.26062.

Teitelbaum, Benjamin. 2019. "Collaborating with the Radical Right: Scholar-Informant Solidarity and the Case for an Immoral Anthropology." *Current Anthropology* 60 (3): 414–35. https://doi.org/10.1086/703199.

Thornton, Sarah. 1995. *Club Cultures: Music, Media and Subcultural Capital.* Cambridge: Polity.

Titon, Jeff Todd, and Svanibor Pettan. 2016. "An Introduction to Applied Ethnomusicology." In *The Oxford Handbook of Applied Ethnomusicology*, edited by Jeff Todd Titon and Svanibor Pettan. New York: Oxford University Press.

Tolan-Szkilnik, Paraska. 2023. *Maghreb Noir: The Militant Artists of North Africa and the Struggle for a Pan-African, Postcolonial Future.* Stanford, CA: Stanford University Press.

Tourabi, Abdellah. 2008. "Les attentats du 16 mai 2003 à Casablanca et l'émergence du salafisme jihadist." In *Qu'est-ce que le salafisme?*, edited by Bernard Rougier. Paris: Presses Universitaires de France.

Trilling, Lionel. 1972. *Sincerity and Authenticity.* Boston, MA: Harvard University Press.

Tsing, Anna. 2005. *Friction: An Ethnography of Global Connection.* Princeton, NJ: Princeton University Press.

Tuck, Eve, and K. Wayne Yang. 2012. "Decolonization Is Not a Metaphor." *Decolonization: Indigeneity, Education and Society* 1 (1): 1–40.

Van de Peer, Stefanie. 2017. *Negotiating Dissidence: The Pioneering Women of Arab Documentary.* Edinburgh: Edinburgh University Press.

Vermeren, Pierre. 2004. "Dans le nouveau Maroc, le palais seul face aux Islamistes?" *Esprit* 308 (10): 103–14.

Vermeren, Pierre. 2009. *Le Maroc de Mohammed VI: la transition inachevée.* Paris: Éditions La Découverte.

Visweswaran, Kamala. 1997. "Histories of Feminist Ethnography." *Annual Review of Anthropology* 26: 591–621. https://doi.org/10.1146/annurev.anthro.26.1.591.

Wa Ngũgĩ, Mukoma. 2021. "White Privilege in African Studies: When You Are Done, Please Call Us." *Brittle Paper*. https://brittlepaper.com/2021/01/white-privilege-in-african -studies-when-you-are-done-please-call-us/.

Wacquant, Loïc. 2008. *Urban Outcasts: A Comparative Sociology of Advanced Marginality*. Cambridge: Polity Press.

Wacquant, Loïc. 2012. "Three Steps to a Historical Anthropology of Actually Existing Neoliberalism." *Social Anthropology* 20: 166–79. https://doi.org/10.1111/j.1469-8676.2011 .00189.x.

Walker, Jeremy, and Melinda Cooper. 2011. "Genealogies of Resilience: From Systems Ecology to the Political Economy of Crisis Adaptation." *Security Dialogue* 42 (2): 143–60. http://dx.doi.org/10.1177/0967010611399616.

Waterbury, John. 1970. *The Commander of the Faithful: The Moroccan Political Elite— A Study in Segmented Politics*. New York: Columbia University Press.

Watkins, S. Craig. 2004 [1998]. "Black Youth and the Ironies of Capitalism." Reprinted in *That's the Joint!: The Hip Hop Studies Reader*, edited by Marc Anthony Neal and Murray Forman. New York: Routledge.

Waugh, Earle H. 2005. *Memory, Music, and Religion: Morocco's Mystical Chanters*. Columbia: University of South Carolina Press.

Wells, Maia Morgan. 2016. "Graffiti, Street Art and the Evolution of the Art Market." In *Routledge Handbook of Graffiti and Street Art*, edited by Jeffery Ian Ross. New York: Routledge.

Westland, Naomi. 2012. "Rappers Provide Anthems Rising over Arab Spring." *USA TODAY*, May 22, 2012.

Whitmore, Aleysia. 2013. "'Cuban Music Is African Music': Productive Frictions in the World Music Industry." *MUSICultures* 40 (1): 121–44. https://journals.lib.unb.ca/index .php/MC/article/view/21132.

Whitmore, Aleysia. 2016. "The Art of Representing the Other: Industry Personnel in the World Music Industry." *Ethnomusicology* 60 (2): 329–55. http://dx.doi.org/10.5406 /ethnomusicology.60.2.0329.

Whitmore, Aleysia. 2020. *World Music and the Black Atlantic: Producing and Consuming African-Cuban Musics on World Music Stages*. London: Oxford University Press.

Widman, Ella. 2015. "How to Celebrate Multiculturalism: This Is Alby ft. Urban Voices Festival." *Stocktown*. http://stocktown.com/how-to-celebrate-multiculturalism-this-is -alby-ft-urban-voices-festival/.

Wolf, Eric R. 2010 [1982]. *Europe and the People without History*. Berkeley and Los Angeles: University of California Press.

Wong, Deborah. 2014. "Sound, Silence, Music: Power." *Ethnomusicology* 58 (2): 347–53.

Wright, Robin. 2011. "Hip Hop and the Arab Spring." *Soundcheck*, October 14, 2011. https:// www.wnycstudios.org/podcasts/soundcheck/segments/164643-rock-casbah

Wyrtzen, Jonathan. 2015. *Making Morocco: Colonial Intervention and the Politics of Identity*. Ithaca, NY: Cornell University Press.

Zaid, Bouziane. 2017. "The Authoritarian Trap in State/Media Structures in Morocco's Political Transition." *Journal of North African Studies* 22 (3): 340–60. https://doi.org/10 .1080/13629387.2017.1307910.

Zaki, Lamia. 2006. "L'action publique au Bidonville : l'état entre gestion par le manque, 'éradication' des kariens et accompagnement social des habitants." *L'Année du Maghreb* 2: 303–20. https://doi.org/10.4000/anneemaghreb.128.

Zaki, Lamia. 2007. "Après le Bidonville. Les relogés de Lahjajma (Casablanca): entre déni et nostalgie." In *L'enseignement supérieur dans la mondialisation libérale: une comparaison libérale (Maghreb, Afrique, Canada, France)*, edited by Sylvie Mazzella. Institut de Recherche sur le Maghreb Contemporain.

Zanfanga, Christina. 2017. *Holy Hip Hop in the City of Angels*. Berkeley: University of California Press.

Zerhouni, Saloua. 2004. "Morocco: Reconciling Community and Change." In *Arab Elites: Negotiating the Politics of Change*, edited by Volker Perthes. Boulder, CO: Lynne Rienner Publishers.

Zemni, Sami, and Koenraad Bogaert. 2011. "Urban Renewal and Social Development in Morocco in an Age of Neoliberal Government." *Review of African Political Economy* 38 (1): 403–17. https://doi.org/10.1080/03056244.2011.603180.

Ziemer, Gesa. 2017. *Complicity: New Perspectives on Collectivity*. Bielefeld, Germany: Transcript.

Zine, Reda. 2006. "Vue globale sur l'interet mediatique pour la scene Marocaine." *L'Kounache del Boulvard* (3): 32–33.

Ziraoui, Youssef. 2007. "Bigg: 'J'ai plus d'impact que l'USFP.'" *TelQuel* (October). Reprinted at http://www.bladi.net/bigg-usfp.html.

Zola, Emile. 1996. *The Dreyfus Affair: 'J'Accuse' and Other Writings*. Edited by Alain Pagès. Translated by Eleanor Levieux. New Haven, CT: Yale University Press.

Zoulef, Boudjemaa, and Mohamed Dernouny. 1980. "Naissance d'un chant protestataire: le groupe Marocaine Nass el Ghiwane." *Peuples Mediterranéens* 12: 3–31.